"I enjoy reading Phil Moore's books. He writes about Jesus and the Christian life with perception, wisdom and wit."
– Nicky Gumbel – Vicar, HTB London

"In taking us straight to the heart of the text, Phil Moore has served us magnificently. We so need to get into the Scriptures and let the Scriptures get into us. The fact that Phil writes so relevantly and with such submission to biblical revelation means that we are genuinely helped to be shaped by the Bible's teaching."
– Terry Virgo

"Fresh. Solid. Simple. Really
– R. T. Kendal

"Phil makes the deep truths of Scripture ali
to grow in your understanding of each book of the Bible, then buy these books and let them change your life!"
– P. J. Smyth – GodFirst Church, Johannesburg, South Africa

"Most commentaries are dull. These are alive.
Most commentaries are for scholars. These are for **you**!"
– Canon Michael Green

"These notes are amazingly good. Phil's insights are striking, original, and fresh, going straight to the heart of the text and the reader! Substantial yet succinct, they bristle with amazing insights and life applications, compelling us to read more. Bible reading will become enriched and informed with such a scintillating guide. Teachers and preachers will find nuggets of pure gold here!"
– Greg Haslam, Westminster Chapel, London, UK

"A strong combination of faithful scholarship, clear explanation and deep insight make these an invaluable tool. I can't recommend them highly enough."
– Gavin Calver – Director of Mission, Evangelical Alliance

"The Bible is living and dangerous. The ones who teach it best are those who bear that in mind – and let the author do the talking. Phil has written these studies with a sharp mind and a combination of creative application and reverence."
– Joel Virgo – Leader of Newday Youth Festival

"Phil Moore's new commentaries are outstanding: biblical and passionate, clear and well-illustrated, simple and profound. God's Word comes to life as you read them, and the wonder of God shines through every page."

– **Andrew Wilson**, Author of Incomparable and If God Then What?

"Want to understand the Bible better? Don't have the time or energy to read complicated commentaries? The book you have in your hand could be the answer. Allow Phil Moore to explain and then apply God's message to your life. Think of this book as the Bible's message distilled for everyone."

– **Adrian Warnock**, Christian blogger

"Phil Moore presents Scripture in a dynamic, accessible and relevant way. The bite-size chunks – set in context and grounded in contemporary life – really make the Word become flesh and dwell among us."

– **Dr David Landrum**, The Bible Society

"Through a relevant, very readable, up-to-date storying approach, Phil Moore sets the big picture, relates God's Word to today and gives us fresh insights to increase our vision, deepen our worship, know our identity and fire our imagination. Highly recommended!"

– **Geoff Knott**, former CEO of Wycliffe Bible Translators UK

"What an exciting project Phil has embarked upon! These accessible and insightful books will ignite the hearts of believers, inspire the minds of preachers and help shape a new generation of men and women who are seeking to learn from God's Word."

– **David Stroud**, Leader of ChristChurch London and author of Planting Churches, Changing Communities

For more information about the Straight to the Heart series, please go to **www.philmoorebooks.com**.

You can also receive daily messages from Phil Moore on Twitter by following **@PhilMooreLondon**.

STRAIGHT TO
THE HEART OF

The Minor Prophets

60 BITE-SIZED INSIGHTS

Phil Moore

MONARCH
BOOKS

Oxford, UK & Grand Rapids, Michigan, USA

Text copyright © 2017 by Phil Moore
This edition copyright © 2017 Lion Hudson.

The right of Phil Moore to be identified as the author of this work has been asserted by him in accordance with the Copyright, Designs and Patents Act 1988.

All rights reserved. No part of this publication may be reproduced or transmitted in any form or by any means, electronic or mechanical, including photocopy, recording, or any information storage and retrieval system, without permission in writing from the publisher.

Published by Monarch Books
an imprint of
Lion Hudson IP Ltd
Wilkinson House, Jordan Hill Road,
Oxford OX2 8DR, England
Email: monarch@lionhudson.com
www.lionhudson.com/monarch

ISBN 978 0 85721 837 7
e-ISBN 978 0 85721 838 4

First edition 2017

Acknowledgments

Scripture quotations taken from the *Holy Bible, New International Version* Anglicised. Copyright © 1979, 1984, 2011 Biblica, formerly International Bible Society. Used by permission of Hodder & Stoughton Ltd, an Hachette UK company. All rights reserved. "NIV" is a registered trademark of Biblica. UK trademark number 1448790. Both 1984 and 2011 versions are quoted in this commentary.

p. 56, extract from *Preaching and Preachers* © 1971, Martyn Lloyd-Jones. Used by permission of Zondervan.

p. 63, extract from *The Knowledge of the Holy* © 1961, A. W. Tozer. Used by permission of BiblioTech Press.

p. 67, extract from *Lectures on Revival* © 1988, Charles Finney. Used by permission of Revival Press. RevivalPress.net

pp. 100–101 extract taken from *Just As I Am* by Billy Graham. Copyright © 1997. Used by permission of Zondervan and HarperCollins. www.zondervan.com

p. 148, extract from *Disappearing Church* © 2016, Mark Sayers. Used by permission of Moody Publishers.

p. 248, extract from *Disappointment with God* © 1988, Philip Yancey. Used by permission of Zondervan.

p. 265, extract from *Civilization: The Six Killer Apps of Western Power* © 2011, Niall Ferguson. Used by permission of Penguin Random House.

A catalogue record for this book is available from the British Library.

This book is for Greg Haslam, who taught me how to prophesy judgment and revival in our own day.

CONTENTS

PART THREE: JUDAH

PART FOUR: A BETTER ISRAEL

About the "*Straight to the Heart*" Series

On his eightieth birthday, Sir Winston Churchill dismissed the compliment that he was the "lion" who had defeated Nazi Germany in World War Two. He told the Houses of Parliament that *"It was a nation and race dwelling all around the globe that had the lion's heart. I had the luck to be called upon to give the roar."*

I hope that God speaks to you very powerfully through the "roar" of the books in the *Straight to the Heart* series. I hope they help you to understand the books of the Bible and the message which the Holy Spirit inspired their authors to write. I hope that they help you to hear God's voice challenging you, and that they provide you with a springboard for further journeys into each book of Scripture for yourself.

But when you hear my "roar", I want you to know that it comes from the heart of a much bigger "lion" than me. I have been shaped by a whole host of great Christian thinkers and preachers from around the world, and I want to give due credit to at least some of them here:

Terry Virgo, Dave Holden, Guy Miller, John Hosier, Adrian Holloway, Greg Haslam, Lex Loizides and all those who lead the Newfrontiers family of churches; friends and encouragers, such as Stef Liston, Joel Virgo, Stuart Gibbs, Scott Taylor, Nick Sharp, Nick Derbridge, Phil Whittall, and Kevin and Sarah Aires; Tony Collins, Margaret Milton, Jenny Muscat, Jessica Scott and Simon Cox at Monarch books; Malcolm Kayes and all the elders of The

Coign Church, Woking; my fellow elders and church members here at Everyday Church in London; my great friend Andrew Wilson – without your friendship, encouragement and example, this series would never have happened.

I would like to thank my parents, my brother Jonathan and my in-laws, Clive and Sue Jackson. Dad – your example birthed in my heart the passion which brought this series into being. I didn't listen to all you said when I was a child, but I couldn't ignore the way you got up at five o'clock every morning to pray, read the Bible and worship, because of your radical love for God and for his Word. I'd like to thank my children – Isaac, Noah, Esther and Ethan – for keeping me sane when publishing deadlines were looming. But most of all, I'm grateful to my incredible wife, Ruth – my friend, encourager, corrector and helper.

You all have the lion's heart, and you have all developed the lion's heart in me. I count it an enormous privilege to be the one who was chosen to sound the lion's roar.

So welcome to the *Straight to the Heart* series. My prayer is that you will let this roar grip your own heart too – for the glory of the great Lion of the Tribe of Judah, the Lord Jesus Christ!

Introduction: Blessing or Curse – You Decide

Surely the Sovereign Lord does nothing without
revealing his plan to his servants the prophets.

(Amos 3:7)

As Abraham Lincoln looked out over the graves of countless soldiers who had died in the Battle of Gettysburg, he knew what he needed to do. He invoked the past to explain the present and to call a nation to lay hold of the future. He cleared his throat and began:

> *Four score and seven years ago, our fathers brought forth on this continent a new nation, conceived in liberty and dedicated to the proposition that all men are created equal. Now we are engaged in a great civil war, testing whether that nation, or any nation so conceived and so dedicated, can long endure... Here we highly resolve that these dead shall not have died in vain – that this nation, under God, shall have a new birth of freedom – and that government of the people, by the people, for the people, shall not perish from the earth.*[1]

A lot of people struggle to understand the message of the Minor Prophets. I find it helps to view them in the same way as Abraham Lincoln on his podium at Gettysburg. These twelve prophets called the twelve tribes of Israel to look backwards to

---

[1] Lincoln gave this Gettysburg Address by the civil-war battlefield on 19th November 1863.

the past in order to understand their present and to prepare for the future. They put the world in its proper context to call a nation back to God. We still need their message in our own day.

The twelve Minor Prophets address many of their words to *sinners*. A lot of the chapters that we are going to study together do not make for pleasant reading. They take the Hebrew nation back to its founding fathers and to the covenant that the Lord made with them at Mount Sinai after he delivered them from slavery in Egypt. They remind us that the Law of Moses ended with an urgent choice in Deuteronomy 28. If the people of Israel obeyed the Lord's commands, they would reap great blessing as a nation, so that the whole world would see the benefits of friendship with the Lord. But if they disobeyed the Lord's commands, they would endure heavy curses in order to make it clear to the world that the Lord was displeased with their behaviour, and that he was nothing like the sinful hypocrites who claimed falsely to follow him. The prophets take us back to Deuteronomy 28 and issue a stark ultimatum: *Blessing or curse – you decide.*

That's why it really matters when Christians dismiss these twelve books as too obscure for them to read and study. We still need the message of the Minor Prophets, because God doesn't change as time goes by. He still offers the same choice to his people. If the Church follows him wholeheartedly, he promises to bless it with fruitfulness and rapid advance across the world. If the Church chases idols, cutting a dirty deal with the culture around it, he promises to thwart it on every side, so we need to let these twelve books challenge our own sin and compromise. Alec Motyer points out that, *"In their own day the prophets were headline makers and pacesetters in the national news, so if we find their ways tedious, unclear, less than exciting the fault does not lie with them."*[2]

The twelve Minor Prophets also address many of their words to the *self-absorbed*. They frequently speak into a context

---

[2] Alec Motyer in *A Scenic Route Through the Old Testament* (1994).

of prosperity, not despair. They warn complacent people that their disregard for God has brought their nation to the precipice of judgment. They have mistaken God's loving patience for lack of resolve. Unless they look back to God's words in the past and grasp that they are running out of time to restore God to a proper place in their lives, they are about to reap a terrible future. The prophets therefore issue the same stark ultimatum to the self-absorbed: *Blessing or curse – you decide.*

But it isn't all bleak. The twelve Minor Prophets also speak very tenderly to the *sorrowful*. These chapters are full of comfort for anybody who grieves over their sin. The Lord repeats over and over again that his true desire is to forgive people and to bless them as he promised in the Law of Moses. The fact that he sends prophets to call people back to him is proof that he does not want to have to judge them, so as we study these twelve books together we are going to discover God's great tenderness towards the people he has made. It is because he longs for us to embrace his plan to bless us that he keeps repeating through the prophets: *Blessing or curse – you decide.*

The twelve Minor Prophets tell us that God is able to be merciful towards us, even when we sin, because he is about to come into the world to be our *Saviour*. The New Testament quotes from these twelve books at least thirty times because they speak about what would happen when Jesus came into the world to save God's disobedient people. He would live the perfect life that we have failed to live, earning all the blessings promised in Deuteronomy 28, yet he would choose to bear the judgment that we deserve for our sin, embracing all the curses spoken over us in Deuteronomy 28. *"Christ redeemed us from the curse of the law by becoming a curse for us,"* the apostle Paul explains in Galatians 3:13. The Minor Prophets are therefore Gospel preachers: *Blessing or curse – you decide.*

As a result of these four big themes, the message of the Minor Prophets remains vital for us today. Whenever we are sinful and self-absorbed, we need to heed their warning that we are displeasing God and are about to reap disaster from his hand. Whenever we feel sorrow for our sin, we need to heed their words of comfort that God longs to forgive us and restore us through his Saviour. These twelve men are not called *minor* prophets because their message is less important than that of Isaiah, Jeremiah, Ezekiel and Daniel, but simply because their books are shorter.[3] Their words are just as inspired by God and just as essential to the development of a proper understanding of God and of ourselves.

In Part 1 of this commentary we will study **Amos and Hosea**, the two prophets sent by God to confront the northern kingdom of **Israel**. In Part 2, we will study **Jonah and Nahum**, two prophets who were sent to offer the same choice between a blessing and a curse to the pagan superpower **Assyria**. In Part 3, we will study **Joel, Micah, Zephaniah, Habakkuk and Obadiah**, five prophets who addressed the southern kingdom of **Judah**. In Part 4, we will study **Haggai, Zechariah and Malachi**, three prophets inspired by God after the destruction of Jerusalem and the return from Babylon to speak glorious promises about his plans to found **a better Israel**.

So get ready to hear God speak to you as you read these twelve short books of prophecy. Get ready to make your own response to the Lord. The arrival of Jesus to be our Saviour has not rendered the message of the Minor Prophets irrelevant today. It has amplified the urgent choice that they offer us. God still warns us: *Blessing or curse – you decide.*

---

[3] Lamentations is also listed among the Major Prophets because it was written by Jeremiah.

Part One:

Israel

Sucker Punch
(Amos 1:1–2:16)

The words of Amos, one of the shepherds of Tekoa –
the vision he saw concerning Israel.

(Amos 1:1)

When Amos started prophesying, the Israelites were pleased. There was no way that such a man would ever dare to speak bad news against them. For a start, he was a common shepherd who had been forced to supplement the meagre income from his flock by tending sycamore-fig trees. Poor people knew their place in ancient Israel, so a prophet like Amos could be expected to kowtow to his betters.[1]

16

Even more importantly, Amos was a foreigner. The twelve tribes of Israel had split into two competing kingdoms after the death of King Solomon. The southern kingdom of Judah prided itself on the fact that it was home to God's Temple and was still ruled by the dynasty of David. The ten tribes that had broken away to form the northern kingdom of Israel boasted that they were more progressive. They chose their own kings and their own priests and their own way of worshipping the Lord at their great shrines in Bethel and in Dan. There was no love lost between Israel and Judah. The two kingdoms were often at war. Since Amos came from Tekoa, eleven miles south of Jerusalem, that made him a foreign guest to the northern kingdom. I remember sharing the Gospel with a man in his home and being

---

[1] We know little about Amos other than what he tells us in his book, but in 7:14–15 he uses his poor background to assert his authority to prophesy, since it means that God alone appointed him to such a role.

warned by him angrily, *"May I remind you whose house you are in?"* Amos must have lived under that threat all the time.[2]

Besides, it seemed obvious to the Israelites that God was exceedingly pleased with them. They had never had it so good. Amos started prophesying in around 760 BC, while King Jeroboam II was presiding over a golden age for Israel.[3] The Assyrian Empire had greatly weakened the old enemy Aram. King Jeroboam had seized this as an opportunity to extend his borders and to pioneer trade links that turned Israel into one of the best economies in the region. When Amos opens his mouth to prophesy, the Israelites therefore expect that he will say the Lord is pleased with them and is about to set a day to judge their pagan neighbours so that they can expand their borders even further. They hope that he will tell them that the "Day of the Lord" is drawing near.[4]

The Israelites are delighted when Amos begins by prophesying judgment. He likens the Lord to one of the lions that used to attack his sheep, but with a roar that echoes right across the nations.[5] They love it when he prophesies in 1:3–5 that the Day of the Lord is coming to the Arameans because of the brutal manner in which King Hazael and his son Ben-

---

[2] Although both kingdoms spoke the Hebrew language and shared a common history, Amos was very much a cross-cultural missionary. In 7:12, he is told angrily to *"Get out!... Go back to the land of Judah!"*

[3] The Minor Prophets are not listed in the Bible in chronological order. We can date the book of Amos from 1:1. The earthquake of 758 BC was so severe that it is still mentioned over 200 years later in Zechariah 14:5.

[4] See 2 Kings 14:23–28. Amos will address their self-delusion about the "Day of the Lord" in 5:18–20.

[5] Jerusalem was built on *Mount Zion*. The Lord wanted to be Israel's shepherd (Genesis 49:24; Psalm 23:1; Psalm 80:1), but since they rejected this he would become a lion bent on slaughtering them. *Mount Carmel* was in Israel and was so well watered by the rainclouds that blew in from the sea that its name meant *Fertile Garden*. God had disciplined sinful Israel at Carmel in the past through lack of rain (1 Kings 18:16–46).

Hadad annexed Israel's territory east of the River Jordan.[6] God will destroy the Aramean capital Damascus and send their few survivors into captivity in Assyria.[7]

The Israelites are even more delighted when Amos prophesies in 1:6–8 that God is also going to judge the Philistines so thoroughly that there will be no survivors. It was about time that he punished the cities of Gaza, Ashdod, Ashkelon and Ekron for raiding and abducting entire Israelite communities in order to conduct a slave trade with Edom.[8]

As far as the Israelites are concerned, what Amos says gets even better when he prophesies in 1:9–10 that the Lord will also destroy the port city of Tyre for its role in this slave trade with Edom.[9] They are delighted when he turns on the Edomites themselves in 1:11–12 and promises to punish them for forgetting that the Israelites are their brothers – descended from Jacob, the twin of their own ancestor Esau – by destroying their fortress cities of Teman and Bozrah.

The Israelites can hardly contain their excitement when Amos prophesies in 1:13–15 and 2:1–3 that the Day of the Lord will also extend to the Ammonite and Moabite descendants of Lot and his daughters. The Ammonite capital city Rabbah will be destroyed to avenge the brutal way in which its people tried to annex the Israelite territory east of the River Jordan. The Moabite stronghold of Kerioth will be destroyed for the nasty way in which it defiled the corpse of the king of Edom in a superstitious

---

[6] 2 Kings 10:32–33. The prophet Elisha had wept as he warned Hazael not to be so brutal in 2 Kings 8:7–15.

[7] *Aven* means *Wickedness* and *Beth Eden* means *House of Delight*. The Lord has seen the best and worst of Aram. They had originally come from *Kir* (9:7), so he would take them back there in 732 BC (2 Kings 16:9).

[8] This slave trade is mentioned in 2 Chronicles 28:17–18. The Lord also promises in Isaiah 14:28–32 and Zephaniah 2:4–7 to wipe out any Philistine survivors. He would do this through the Babylonians in 586 BC.

[9] King Nebuchadnezzar of Babylon burned Tyre in 573 BC at the end of a brutal 13-year-long siege.

attempt to ruin his afterlife.[10] The Israelites can hardly believe their ears when they hear what Amos has to say. They knew that God was pleased with them, but not this pleased!

Their smiles turn to laughter when Amos prophesies against his own nation of Judah in 2:4–5. The Israelites hated their southern relatives, with their snooty insistence that their ruler was God's true king and that their Temple was God's true place of worship. To hear the news that the Lord considered the people of Judah to be Law-breakers and idolaters was music to their northern ears. If the Lord was about to destroy Judah because of its sin, it meant happy harvest time for expansionist Israel.

Amos has been building up to this moment. He wanted to get the Israelites smiling and laughing, nodding that God's judgment was entirely deserved, in order to land a sudden sucker punch in their own midriff. Having spoken the same curse over seven nations – *"For three sins... even for four, I will not relent"* – he now repeats the curse an eighth time to deal a heavy body blow to the northern kingdom of Israel! He has reserved the last, and by far the longest, oracle of judgment for them. *"For three sins of Israel, even for four, I will not relent."*

The Israelites are winded. It takes them a moment to catch their breath. Having nodded at the rightness of God's judgment towards Aram, Philistia, Tyre, Edom, Ammon, Moab and Judah, they cannot argue that it is unfair when God's judgment is directed towards them too. Suddenly their smiling faces turn to anger.

Amos may be a poor shepherd. He may be a foreigner. But he hasn't come to tell the Israelites what they want to hear. He has come to land a sucker punch on them. God has seen their sin and he is issuing them a final ultimatum: *Blessing or curse – you decide.*

---

[10] See Genesis 19:30–38. Since the Hebrew word for *king* is very similar to the name of the Ammonite god *Molech*, 1:15 is also God's declaration of war against an idol worshipped through ritual child sacrifice.

The Right Lines
(Amos 2:4–16)

You made the Nazirites drink wine and commanded the prophets not to prophesy.

(Amos 2:12)

Looking back, it is hard to believe that anybody ever thought it was a good idea. Laurence Olivier was a brilliant actor, but he was white. He was clearly not the right man to play the part of Othello in William Shakespeare's play about the Moor of Venice. Even back in 1965, the movie-makers ought to have thought twice before asking him to black up and to take the leading role. With so many great parts for white actors in the movie, you can't help feeling that the casting director gave Olivier the wrong lines to say.

However ridiculous we may find it watching Laurence Olivier deliver his lines as a black man, Christians can be even more ridiculous when it comes to sharing the Word of God with unbelievers. I have lost count of the number of times I have heard well-meaning Christians take words that were spoken by the Old Testament prophets to the nation of Israel and apply them directly to what is happening in their own nation today. In the same way, I have long since ceased to be surprised when Christians try to convert unbelievers by accusing them of breaking God's commands. But Amos says that when we do this we are delivering the wrong lines. He wants to teach us the right lines through the very different way in which Amos addresses the pagan nations and the nation of Israel. He wants to show us how to challenge people in an appropriate way.

When Amos confronts the pagan nations in his first six oracles, he informs them that the God of Israel is Lord of the whole earth and that they therefore owe him their allegiance. He warns them that the Lord oversaw the rise of their nation and that he will oversee its destruction.[1] He doesn't shy away from telling these six pagan nations that God is calling them to repentance. Each oracle begins with *"This is what the Lord says."*

But note that Amos does not address these pagan nations as if they have received the same amount of revelation as Israel. Never once does he accuse them of breaking the Law of Moses or of disobeying the words of Scripture. He recognizes that they are unbelievers and that God will therefore not judge them as if they were believers. He focuses instead on the limited amount of revelation that they have received. He accuses them of contravening their own natural sense of right and wrong – of being inhumane (Aram), of enslaving their neighbours (Philistia), of breaking peace treaties (Tyre),[2] of killing their kinsmen (Edom), of killing unborn babies (Ammon) and of inflicting cruel and unusual punishments on their foes (Moab).[3] The New Testament explains that God will not judge people for having broken commands of which they were unaware, but for having done what even their own sinful consciences shouted out to them was wrong.[4]

So don't take Old Testament words of prophecy to the nation of Israel and apply them unthinkingly to your own nation. You do not live in a theocracy, where church and state are the same thing.

---

[1] See also Amos 9:5–7. Amos refers to God as *"the Sovereign Lord"* 19 times in 9 chapters.

[2] Tyre had a long-standing peace treaty with Israel, which went back to the time of David and Solomon (1 Kings 5:1 and 12) and which had recently been renewed through a royal marriage (1 Kings 16:30–31).

[3] The Moabites believed that by destroying a corpse they could do more than just kill a person. They could spite the person even further by robbing them of any blessing in the afterlife.

[4] Romans 2:12–15. This explains the statements in Matthew 11:21–24, Luke 12:47–48 and Acts 17:30.

The words that the prophets speak to Israel and Judah are more applicable to your church today, while your state is more like one of the pagan nations. In the same way, when you share the Gospel with unbelievers don't accuse them of disobeying Bible verses that they have never read. Convince them instead that they have failed to live up even to the lesser standards of their own consciences and that Jesus says to them in Luke 19:22, *"I will judge you by your own words, you wicked servant!"*

Note the way that Amos adjusts his lines when he addresses the people of Judah in 2:4–5. What would have been the wrong thing to say to out-and-out unbelievers becomes the right thing to say to people who claim to follow God. The Lord accuses the people of Judah of rejecting his Law and of failing to obey the commands of Scripture. He accuses them of betraying him as their true God by running after false religion that Scripture tells them very clearly is a total pack of lies.[5] This is the right way to go about convicting believers of sin, which is why Stephen quotes from God's warning to Israel in Amos 5:25–27 and applies it directly to members of the Jewish Sanhedrin in Acts 7:42–43. God's people have greater revelation of him, which means greater responsibility. Use God's Word to convict believers that their sin makes them even guiltier than the pagans.

When we compare the first six oracles to the pagan nations and the seventh oracle to Judah, we see how utterly devastating the eighth and final oracle to Israel truly is. Although the ten northern tribes were there at Mount Sinai when the Law of Moses was given, God treats them now as a semi-pagan nation. Instead of accusing them of Law-breaking, like Judah, he recognizes that their consciences have long since forgotten the Scriptures. He confronts their social injustice, taking bribes to convict the innocent and enslaving debtors who owe no more than the price of a pair of sandals (2:6–7). He confronts their sexual depravity

---

[5] Amos uses the Hebrew word *kāzāb* in 2:4 to dismiss these idols literally as *lies*.

and drunkenness (2:7–8), and their shocking ingratitude for his help in the past (2:9–10).[6] The fact that he doesn't even bother to mention the Law is the most damning judgment of all. It means he knows that they care little for his Word.

The Lord knows that whenever anybody in the northern kingdom starts to take him seriously, their fellow Israelites slap them down. If someone takes the same Nazirite vow as the prophet Samuel, abstaining from alcohol in order to devote themselves to prayer, they are regarded as a zealot and angrily forced to drink wine.[7] If someone starts to prophesy by the power of the Holy Spirit, they are viewed as a dangerous radical and commanded to keep their words to themselves. The Israelites are happy to receive Elisha's promise that their generation will be prosperous (2 Kings 13:17–19) or Jonah's prophecy that God will help them to restore their ancient borders (2 Kings 14:25), but they refuse to accept any prophecy that calls them to repentance. Therefore Amos warns them that their nation is about to be destroyed.[8]

God has called us to speak out just as courageously as Amos in our own generation. That's why we need to echo the prophet's wisdom and speak the right lines to the right people. When confronting out-and-out unbelievers, we must not make assumptions that they revere the Scriptures in the same way that we do. When challenging pretend believers, we must not act as if they are truly committed to the Word of God. We need to learn to confront people's natural sense of right and wrong. We need to speak the right lines to the right people in order to convict different people of their sin in different ways.

---

[6] These things are forbidden in Exodus 22:26–27, in Leviticus 18:15 and 20:12, and in Deuteronomy 24:12–17. However, Amos does not quote from those verses. He appeals instead to natural revelation.

[7] Numbers 6:1–21; Judges 13:5; 1 Samuel 1:11; Luke 1:15; Acts 18:18.

[8] Churches can be just as guilty of this today. Church leaders and congregations often sideline and silence people who believe and preach God's Word as foolish firebrands or as rabble-rousing radicals.

Three Good Reasons
(Amos 3:1–5:17)

Hear this word… Hear this word… Hear this word.

(Amos 3:1; 4:1; 5:1)

The Israelites had been floored by the prophet's sucker punch, but it didn't take them very long to catch their breath and to tell Amos that they didn't believe a word he said. How could God be displeased with them, when the borders of their kingdom were larger than ever and when it was enjoying an unprecedented period of prosperity?

Amos refuses to back-pedal. His name is Hebrew for *Burden-Bearer*, and he has no intention of heading back home to Judah until he has fully discharged what God has laid on him to say.[1] He therefore backs up his message of judgment with three good reasons for the Israelites to accept that their nation is teetering on the brink of destruction. Each of the three reasons begins with the same threat: *"Hear this word."*

In 3:1–15, Amos gives them his first good reason: the Israelites have rejected God's covenant with them. The Lord chose the twelve tribes of Israel and delivered them from slavery in Egypt in order to display his glory to the world. He brought them to Mount Sinai and warned them that he had a Plan "A" and a Plan "B" for doing so. His preferred option was to bless them in their obedience as an advertisement for the pagan nations to throw away their idols and to worship the God of Israel too. If the Israelites obeyed him, he would grant them

---

[1] Amos says in 3:8 that he feels he has no choice but to prophesy. See Jeremiah 4:19, and Isaiah 42:14 and 62:1.

such great harvests that the pagans would jettison their fertility idols, and such great battlefield victories that their neighbours would sue for peace and ask to join them at their Temple. Plan "B" would only be enacted if the Israelites were disobedient. He would strike them with such severe judgment that the nations around them would take him seriously, even if they did not. It was a simple choice that the Lord had given them: *Blessing or curse – you decide.*[2]

So Amos tells the Israelites to take a good look at their nation. The fact that God has chosen them to be his holy nation only makes their sinfulness worse. Their special status in God's purposes demands that he judge them for their sin. *"Hear this word, people of Israel... You only have I chosen of all the families of the earth; therefore I will punish you for all your sins."* How can God not enact his Plan "B"? Deep down they know that he does nothing without revealing his plan to his prophets, so they dare not ignore Amos when he warns them in 1:2 that the God of Israel is roaring over their nation like a lion.[3] If they refuse to believe the prophet's words of warning, they will become the lion's prey.

Amos calls the pagan nations to act as witnesses against Israel. Even the Egyptians and the Philistines of Ashdod can tell that God is displeased with their worship of a golden calf at Bethel.[4] Even they can see that God will judge them for decorating their second homes with ivory while the poor people starve. Only the Israelites fail to see this, having so neglected Scripture that *"they do not know how to do right"*.[5] Amos therefore warns

---

[2] Leviticus 26; Deuteronomy 28. Romans 2:9–11 also emphasizes that when God chooses people it makes them liable either for greater blessing or for greater judgment. They get to decide.

[3] Amos 3:7 serves as a summary for all the Minor Prophets. God has revealed his plans to these men.

[4] See 1 Kings 12:26–33. Amos contrasts their lifeless idol with *the Sovereign Lord God Almighty* (3:13).

[5] When it comes to serving God, ignorance is never bliss. Neglect of the Bible always spells disaster. That's why effective evangelism and discipleship always involve educating people in the Scriptures. See Hosea 4:6.

that the Lord is about to destroy them, with few survivors. He is not fooling around.[6]

In 4:1–13, Amos gives the Israelites a second good reason to believe that God's judgment is coming: it has already started. They are not as prosperous as they pretend.[7] The Lord has already started to judge them for their self-indulgence and self-righteous religion.[8] When they tried to secure good harvests by having sex with shrine prostitutes at the temples of the Canaanite fertility gods, God made their fields so barren that they lacked enough bread to fill their bellies.[9] When they refused to repent, he held back the rain so that they lacked even basic drinking water, let alone water for their fields. When they still failed to repent, he devastated their vineyards and orchards with blight, mildew and locusts. When they still refused to repent, he made their soldiers die in battle and in plagues that ravaged their army camps, then allowed raiders to burn their cities, like Sodom and Gomorrah.[10] These five waves of judgment are clear proof that Amos is talking sense and that Israel is already experiencing God's Plan "B".[11]

---

[6] Snatching only a leg bone or a severed ear from the mouth of a lion speaks of near-complete destruction. It also speaks of God's intense love for Israel. He is willing to take unreasonable risks to save his flock.

[7] Since there is nobody greater than the Lord for him to swear by, he swears by his own holiness in 4:2. See also 6:8; 8:7 and Hebrews 6:13–18.

[8] The fields of Bashan, east of the River Jordan, were so lush that they were full of fat cows that did nothing all day but consume grass (Deuteronomy 32:14; Psalm 22:12). The cows were controlled using nose-rings, like the hooks that the Assyrians put through the noses of their enslaved prisoners of war.

[9] In Hebrew the Lord says literally in 4:6, *"I gave you cleanness of teeth."* The Israelites had gone hungry so often that they barely needed to own a toothbrush!

[10] Genesis 19. This image of *a burning stick snatched from the fire* is echoed by Zechariah 3:2 and Jude 23.

[11] Amos loves to use powerful repetition in his prophecies. His three good reasons all start with *"Hear this word"* (3:1; 4:1; 5:1), and his five judgments all end with *"yet you have not returned to me, declares the Lord"*.

Unless they repent now, he has only one thing left to say to them: *"Prepare to meet your God."*[12]

In 5:1–17, Amos gives a third good reason to believe that God's judgment is coming: their injustice towards one another betrays their hatred of the Lord. There is a reason why their once-unstoppable armies have of late been decimated on the battlefield.[13] The Lord detests their perverted religion at Bethel and at their other high places, as well as the injustice that their false view of God spawns.[14] It is commonplace in Israel to see judges taking bribes and the rich harshly taxing the poor. How can they therefore imagine that the Lord could ever be pleased with them? Three times Amos has called them to *"Hear this word"*, so now he calls them three times to face up to their sin: *"Seek the Lord and live."*[15] The third time, he promises them that this will bring them back to God's Plan "A". *"Then the Lord God Almighty will be with you, just as you say he is."*[16]

So take a good look at your own life. In what ways might you be as self-deluded about your own sin as the people of Israel? In what ways might God be fighting for your attention? Tell him that you are listening and that you want his Plan "A", not his Plan "B".

---

[12] They have ignored God for so long that he actually commands them in 4:4 to keep on sinning, like Judas Iscariot in John 13:27. Since they offered their sacrifices and their tithes in disobedience, their religion could not atone for their sin. It was merely adding to it! See Leviticus 6:17; 7:12 and 17:8–9, and 1 Samuel 15:22.

[13] They saw their nation as a mighty fighting machine, but the Lord says it is like a dead young girl (5:1–3).

[14] They had originally erected a golden calf at Bethel to avoid having to worship in the southern kingdom of Judah (1 Kings 12:26–33). However, now they are worshipping idols at Beersheba in the far south of Judah!

[15] God uses puns in 5:5 to grab the Israelites' attention. *Gilgal* sounds like the Hebrew for *surely go into exile*. The word for *nothing* is *'āven*, as in the other name for Bethel – *Beth Aven*. See Hosea 5:8 and 10:5.

[16] In the midst of these three reasons for judgment, the Lord reminds Israel three times in 5:14–16 that he is the Lord God Almighty. The ruler of the universe will be either their Judge or their Saviour (5:8–9). They have to decide.

Three Curses
(Amos 5:18–6:14)

Woe to you who long for the day of the Lord!... That day will be darkness, not light.

(Amos 5:18)

Amos can tell that the Israelites still don't believe him. He therefore reaches for a different weapon in the prophet's arsenal. Having given them three good reasons to believe him, each one starting with *"Hear this word"*, he now proclaims three curses over them if they refuse to believe. Amos is upping the ante here: *Blessing or curse – you decide.*

Amos speaks the first of his curses in 5:18–27. It begins with the word *"Woe!"* and it curses Israel for their smug and self-righteous religion. They fool themselves that their religious assemblies and their sacrifices have obliged God to help them, but this is an insult to his holiness and his majesty. The Creator does not need anything from his creatures, so their loud worship services are failed currency when it comes to paying off their sin. When they pray for the "Day of the Lord" to come swiftly, they have no idea what they are asking for. That day will not just bring judgment on the pagan nations, offering a bright new dawn for further Israelite expansion. It will also spell terrible judgment upon Israel. It will be like fleeing from a lion onto the claws of a bear, or like fleeing from a man and treading on a cobra.[1] Amos curses their empty religion. *"Will not the day of*

---

[1] These are ancient Hebrew equivalents of our saying in English: *Out of the frying pan and into the fire.*

the Lord be darkness, not light – pitch-dark, without a ray of brightness?"

The Israelites were very religious. They had built high places where they could worship the Lord outside all of their major cities. They gathered frequently for worship festivals and to offer sacrifices on their altars. In short, they appeared to be devout in every way. But they were ignorant of the Scriptures. They didn't know that God had already spelled out for them the kind of worship that he wanted. They were to worship at the Temple in Jerusalem, where the fire that burned on the altar had fallen from heaven as a sign that our salvation can only come from God's initiative, never from our own.[2] They were to worship on the days that God stipulated instead of inventing feast days of their own. They were to submit to the leaders that God appointed instead of choosing leaders of their own.[3] They were to back up what they sang in their worship songs by living for God the whole week long instead of being as fickle as a dried-up Middle Eastern stream.

We ought to find these verses very challenging. It's not just that we live in a self-promoting generation, where anyone can become a church leader or demand that churches pander to their preferred worship style. It's that these verses are strongly echoed in the New Testament, where Paul tells one church that *"I have no praise for you, for your meetings do more harm than good."* Martin Luther King pointed out in his *"I have a dream"* speech that our worship services are still repugnant to God unless we back up what we sing on Sunday through our actions all week long. He declared, *"No, no, we are not satisfied, and*

---

[2] Leviticus 6:8–13; 9:24–10:2; 17:8–9; 1 Chronicles 21:26; 2 Chronicles 7:1. If forgetting this turned Israel's worship into *noise*, it is ridiculous for us to imagine that non-Christian religions can save anyone.

[3] Numbers 3:10; 18:7; 1 Kings 12:31–33; 13:33; 2 Kings 17:32.

we will not be satisfied until justice rolls down like waters and righteousness like a mighty stream."[4]

Martin Luther King was not the only famous orator to quote from these verses. Stephen quotes from 5:25–27 while standing before the Jewish Sanhedrin in Acts 7, in order to accuse them of the same idolatry as the Israelites who worshipped a golden calf at the foot of Mount Sinai.[5] Whenever our worship services become man-made performances, we can be certain that God's judgment is never far away.[6]

Amos speaks the second of his curses in 6:1–7. It also begins with the word *"Woe!"* and it curses Israel for complacently refusing to heed his words. They are so convinced that the hilltop location of their fortified capital, Samaria, is unassailable that they are more concerned with fine foods, fine wine, fine music, fine furniture and fine fragrances than they are with finding forgiveness. Their minor victories over fortified cities such as Kalneh, Hamath and Gath have blinded them to the fact that their nation is about to be destroyed.[7] Amos indicates that complacency is part of Judah's problem too by referring to *Zion* and to *two kingdoms*, but his reference to *Joseph* makes it clear that the ten northern tribes will reap disaster before the southern ones.[8] He therefore ends this second curse with a second promise of imminent exile unless they listen to him.[9]

---

[4] 1 Corinthians 11:17. Dr King spoke these words from Amos in his speech on 28th August 1963.

[5] The Hebrew word for *king* is similar to the name of the idol *Molech*. The ambiguity is deliberate, because the king had led Israel astray into sacrificing their children to Molech (1 Kings 11:33; 2 Kings 17:17).

[6] Israel saw their enemy as the Aramean capital Damascus, but God says a far worse enemy lies beyond.

[7] I find this challenging. To what extent have our minor advances blinded us to the church's massive decline?

[8] Judah had conquered Gath (2 Chronicles 26:6) and Israel had conquered Hamath (2 Kings 14:25).

[9] Note the warning in 6:3. Acting as if God's judgment will never come does not put it off. It brings it nearer.

Amos speaks the third of his curses in 6:8–14. Although this time he does not begin with the word *"Woe!"*, this is in many ways the worst of the three, cursing Israel for its pride. Instead of attributing their military victories and their economic prosperity to the fact that the Lord took pity on their weakness and prophesied in 2 Kings 14:25 that he would graciously help them, they have attributed it all to themselves! The Lord points out that, without him, they could no more have won these victories than they could have ridden horses up a cliff edge or planted crops in the sea. He warns them that their puny victories so far are small fry compared to the terrible battle that is heading their way.[10] Because they have forgotten that he is *"the Sovereign Lord"*, he will bring upon them such a devastating exile that they will learn to fear the very utterance of his name.[11]

All of this makes sober reading, and even more so when we turn to the New Testament. If we expected God to have mellowed over the centuries, we are wrong. Jesus speaks four similar woes over us in Luke 6:24–26 if we become as complacent as the Israelites about responding to his call upon our lives. Jesus speaks six woes over us in Luke 11:42–52 if we become as smug and self-righteous as the Israelites in our worship. Jesus speaks seven woes over us in Matthew 23:1–39 if we adopt the same proud attitude towards the Lord that made the Israelites reject Amos and, centuries later, their Messiah.

So read these verses slowly, as a mirror for your soul. Can you spot any traces in your own heart of Israel's pride in their religion, in their possessions and in the strength of their hands? Repent swiftly and wholeheartedly of your sin. *Blessing or curse – you decide.*

---

[10] Although *Karnaim* means *Horns* and therefore *Strength* in Hebrew, *Lo Debar* means *Nothing*. Lebo Hamath and the Arabah, representing the far north and south of Israel, were the very places named in 2 Kings 14:25!

[11] 6:8 is one of 19 times that Amos refers to God as *"the Sovereign Lord"* in just 9 chapters. Amos was proved correct in his prediction in 6:9 that far fewer people would survive the exile from Israel than from Judah.

The Kind of Person God Can Use (Amos 7:1–17)

I cried out, "Sovereign Lord, forgive! How can Jacob survive? He is so small!" So the Lord relented.

(Amos 7:2–3)

Cross-cultural ministry is difficult. I never realized just how hard it is until I spent a year working as a cross-cultural missionary myself. It therefore seems odd that the Lord sent Jonah, a prophet from the northern kingdom, to speak his words to the Assyrian Empire and at the same time sent Amos from the southern kingdom to speak his words to Israel.

Perhaps the Lord just likes cross-cultural mission. After all, he instigates quite a lot of it in the New Testament. If you are personally engaged in cross-cultural evangelism, you ought to find this encouraging. Nothing rids us of pride faster than ineptitude in a foreign language and confusion over unfamiliar customs. Cross-cultural mission is one of the ways that God rids his workers of the pride that brought his judgment upon Israel.

But there was probably more to it than that when the Lord called Amos to leave his sheep in the fields of Tekoa and travel as a foreign missionary to Israel. It appears that he had very few people in the northern kingdom that he could have used instead of him. Amos had remarkable character and, unlike Jonah, he wouldn't run away when the going got tough. These verses show us the kind of person that God delights to use.

First, we see that Amos *was a good listener*. He receives three visions in just nine verses: a swarm of locusts devastating Israel, a fire devouring Israel and the Lord holding up a plumb line to a wonky wall that represents Israel.[1] As Amos sees these three pictures, he also grasps immediately what they mean. It may sound obvious, but if we want God to use our lives, we need to make listening to him our number-one priority. For me, that has meant at times getting rid of my television and disabling my car stereo to free my world from background noise. It has meant saying "no" to many legitimate things so that I can tuck myself away with just a Bible and a notepad. It has meant dealing radically with the unforgiveness, pride and overbusyness that makes me lose my signal.

Second, we see that Amos *loved what God loves and hated what God hates*. It is easy to tell from his words how much he hated Israel's sin, but in these verses we discover just how much he loved the Israelites themselves. Many people would have been overjoyed to hear that God was about to vindicate them, but Amos isn't out to score points. He is out to save souls. He reacts to his visions of judgment with great love and pity towards the people of Israel.[2] The nineteenth-century evangelist D. L. Moody was convinced that such love for sinners is the forgotten key to our saving many souls:

> *If we are co-workers with God, there is one thing we must possess, and that is love. A man may be a very successful lawyer and have no love for his clients, and yet get on very well. A man may be a very successful physician and have no love for his patients, and yet be a very good physician... But no man can be a co-worker with God without love... We cannot work for God without love. It is the only tree that can produce fruit on this sin-cursed earth... I believe God cannot use many of His servants,*

---

[1] The Lord refers to *"my people Israel"* for the first time in the book of Amos in 7:8, and he will do so four more times before the book ends. His message of judgment is about to give way to a message of hope.

[2] In neither of his two prayers does Amos appeal to Israel's virtue, but only to their pitiful weakness.

because they are full of irritability and impatience... If they have not love, they cannot work for God... The work of the Holy Ghost is to impart love.[3]

Third, we see that Amos *was a man of prayer*. He does not receive his visions passively. He sees them as part of a two-way conversation with God. He is so devastated by his vision of locusts that he cries out in prayer for God to forgive Israel. The Hebrew word *nāham* in 7:3 can be translated as *"The Lord changed his mind."* When Amos sees a second vision of fire devouring Israel, he prays once again and the same Hebrew word informs us in 7:6 that *"The Lord changed his mind."*[4] One of the great themes of the book of Amos is that the Lord is unstoppable in his judgment. He is called *"the Sovereign Lord"* six times in the first six verses of this chapter alone. Nevertheless, God has endued the prayers of his people with such power that they can bring changes to his plans. The Lord longs to shape history with anyone who is willing to partner with him in prayer.

Fourth, we see that Amos *was confident of his authority*. Sooner or later, preachers of God's Word will run into opposition, so this quality is indispensable. When one of the corrupt priests of Bethel tries to persuade King Jeroboam to arrest Amos for inciting revolution, he stands firm. When the priest insults him as a foreigner and orders him to go back to the southern kingdom where he came from, he does not flinch in his reply. He says that it was not his own idea to put on the prophet's mantle. His authority stems from the fact that it was entirely God's idea. He has been sent by the Lord.[5]

---

[3] D. L. Moody in his book *Secret Power* (1881).

[4] We also see this in Exodus 32:14; Jeremiah 18:8 and Jonah 3:9–10. God often reveals his plans so that we can "change his mind" through our prayers, partnering with him to bring about his perfect plan.

[5] Amaziah dismisses Amos as an unqualified seer (*hōzeh*) rather than a graduate of the official school of prophets (*nābî'*) that had been established by Elijah and Elisha. See 1 Kings 20:35, and 2 Kings 2:3; 6:1 and 9:1.

Fifth and finally, we therefore see that Amos *was a man of great courage*. Prophets had been lynched for saying less than he had – that the royal dynasty would be wiped out and the northern kingdom taken into exile – yet he refuses to shrink from his duty.[6] He responds to the priest's threats by prophesying that he will die in exile, his wife will be reduced to prostitution and his children will die in the slaughter that is coming.

This is the kind of person God delights to use, so how much does it describe you? How good are you at stopping and listening? How much do you allow the Spirit of God to stir your heart with love and fervent prayer? How confident and courageous are you in the face of opposition? A. W. Tozer encourages us that this is what our world needs:

> *The curious crowd that gathered to watch him work soon branded him as extreme, fanatical, negative. And in a sense they were right. He was single-minded, severe, fearless, and these were the qualities the circumstances demanded. He shocked some, frightened others, and alienated not a few, but he knew who had called him and what he was sent to do... To such men as this the church owes a debt too heavy to pay. The curious thing is that she seldom tries to pay him while he lives, but the next generation builds his sepulchre and writes his biography... Such a man as this is not an easy companion... for he cannot turn off the burden of the Holy Ghost as one would turn off a faucet. He insists on being a Christian all the time, everywhere.*[7]

---

[6] Amaziah is misquoting Amos in 7:11. He predicted the assassination of Jeroboam's son (2 Kings 15:8–12).

[7] Tozer says this in his foreword to Leonard Ravenhill's book *Why Revival Tarries* (1959).

Darkest Before the Dawn
(Amos 8:1–9:10)

Many, many bodies – flung everywhere! Silence!

(Amos 8:3)

They say that the night is always darkest before the dawn. In the book of Amos, that is definitely true. Having been rudely interrupted by the priest of Bethel after receiving three visions of judgment against Israel, the prophet now turns back to the matter in hand and receives two visions more. These visions are even darker than the ones he saw in chapter 7, but they pave the way for a bright new dawn at the end of chapter 9.

In 8:1–14, Amos sees a vision of a basket of fruit. Like the locusts, the fire and the poorly built wall, it represents God's impending judgment upon Israel. Amos used to supplement his income as a shepherd by tending sycamore-fig trees, so he spots straightaway that the fruit in the basket is ripe for eating. That's the essence of the vision. God declares that *"The time is ripe for my people Israel; I will spare them no longer."*

This declaration prompts the Lord to make a list of the sins that he has tolerated for far too long throughout the land of Israel. In 8:4, he begins with the way in which the rich ruling classes abuse their power by trampling on the poor instead of helping them.[1] In 8:5–6, he adds that they insult him by wishing away their Sabbaths and religious festivals so that they can get back to worshipping their real god – making money.[2] He catalogues the

---

[1] 8:4 can compete with 5:24 as a one-verse summary of the book of Amos. Worship without justice is a lie.

[2] Let's not judge them. Many Christians today treat Sunday as if it were a workday.

different ways in which they swindle one another: their inflated prices, their falsifying of the weights on their scales, their short-changing of customers by short-filling bags and mixing chaff in with the wheat, and their luring of people into debt in order to enslave them. Since their ancestor Jacob's name means *Deceiver*, the Lord refers to himself, not as the Pride of Israel, but as the Pride of Jacob. His dark words of judgment are staccato: *"Many, many bodies – flung everywhere! Silence!"*

Next, the Lord turns his attention in 8:9–14 to the sins of the religious leaders of Israel. He has hinted from the very start of the book of Amos that one of the biggest sins of Israel is that of worshipping idols at their high places instead of worshipping the Lord at his Temple in Jerusalem. The book began with his roaring like a lion from Mount Zion, as a reminder that their neglect of his Temple had not made it any less his home.[3] Now he tells them that he does not live at Bethel or at Dan, where their rulers have erected golden calves to worship through man-made festivals, led by man-made priests who burn their sacrifices using man-made fire.[4] He has heard them swearing by the names of these false gods instead of by his name, so he will judge their idols as *"the sin of Samaria"*.

The Lord declares that the time is ripe for the shrines at Bethel and Dan to be destroyed. He promises to turn the sky dark at noonday – presumably through the dark clouds of smoke that will go up from their cities when they are sacked by the Assyrians. Their religious festivals will become funerals. Their worship songs will become dirges. Even their well-dressed priests and their long-haired shrine prostitutes will wear sackcloth and shave their heads in grief at what has happened

---

[3] The Lord refers to their shrine at Bethel as a *temple* in 8:3, but only so that he can prophesy its doom.

[4] 1 Kings 12:26–33 says that the Israelites had originally built these shrines at Bethel and Dan to avoid needing to travel south to worship in Judah. By the time of Amos, they were so deeply entrenched in their idolatry that they happily travelled to a shrine at Beersheba, in the far south of Judah (5:5; 8:14).

to their nation. The people of Israel will weep like parents at the funeral of their only child – with utter dark despair.

All of this is terrible, but the Lord considers his final act of judgment to be worst of all. Instead of striking the handful of Israelite survivors with a famine of food and water, he promises to strike them with a famine of his Word. You can tell how much you grasp the power of Bible study and of Bible preaching from whether or not you feel horrified when the Lord describes survivors staggering from the Mediterranean Sea to the Dead Sea in search of any prophet or preacher.[5] After Israel's exile, this came horribly true. While the prophets Daniel and Ezekiel spoke hope to the survivors of Judah in Babylon, there were no such voices among the survivors of the northern kingdom. To be saved people needed to turn their backs on Bethel and return south to the Temple in Jerusalem.

In 9:1–10, Amos sees his fifth and final vision. It is of the Lord standing by the bronze altar where blood sacrifices were offered at the Temple in Jerusalem. Since the Israelites have refused to come there to lay hold of his mercy through its prophetic picture of the future death and resurrection of the Messiah, God makes it the scene for an announcement of his judgment. They have chosen his curse instead of his blessing, so he will fix his eyes on them until they have all been destroyed.[6] Those who flee from the Assyrians will not be safe in their hiding places, and those who surrender to the Assyrians will not be safe in exile. Just as the River Nile bursts its banks and floods the whole land of Egypt, the Lord's judgment will not subside until it covers the whole of their land. There is no talk here of any survivors, but take heart. The night is always darkest just before the dawn.[7]

---

[5] As we will see later, in Jonah 3:4–5, the faithful preaching of God's Word is powerful to transform a nation.

[6] Amos 9:2–4 is a horrible parody of the promise of blessing that David gives us in Psalm 139:7–12.

[7] In 5:8–9, the Lord interrupted his words of judgment to reveal himself as the God who controls the sun and stars and rainclouds. Now he breaks off again

Even as he speaks his most hurtful curse so far over Israel in 9:7, the dawn of the Lord's salvation begins to pierce the darkness. He ends his words of judgment as he began them in chapters 1 and 2, by telling the northern kingdom of Israel that they are no better than the pagan nations. Sure, he brought their ancestors up out of Egypt and into the Promised Land, but he also brought the ancestors of the Philistines over the sea from Crete and the ancestors of the Arameans from a city in Assyria.[8] They are fooling themselves if they think that their ethnicity has made them whiter than white and that *"Disaster will not overtake or meet us"* – because they are black as Ethiopia to him.[9] Their sinful kingdom is right at the top of his to-do list of destruction on the Day of the Lord.

Even as God says this, his light breaks through the darkness. *"'I will not totally destroy the descendants of Jacob,' declares the Lord."* The Lord promises to use the destruction of the northern kingdom at the hands of the Assyrians as a sieve to remove every sinner from their nation so that a pure and obedient remnant of survivors can find their way home. These final two visions from the prophet Amos are dark – there is no doubt about that – but they also signal a change in the book's tone, from confrontation to comfort.

I'm sure that, like me, you have found Amos pretty bleak so far. We have had to look at some terrible verses of judgment together, but it has been worth all the darkness. In the book's final few verses, we are about to discover the Lord's bright new dawn for Israel.

---

in 9:5–6 with a similar interruption. The message of God's judgment makes no sense to people unless it also describes the greatness of the God that our sin offends.

[8] *Caphtor* was an ancient name for Crete, which is why historians sometimes refer to the ancestors of the Philistines as the Sea People. The Lord promised in 1:3–5 to return the Arameans to their former home in *Kir*.

[9] The Lord is not condoning their racial prejudice towards the black inhabitants of Cush in Africa. He is simply using a vivid metaphor that he knows even the least educated Israelite will understand.

The Rebuild
(Amos 9:11–15)

*I will restore David's fallen shelter – I will repair its
broken walls and restore its ruins – and will rebuild it
as it used to be.*

I have been involved in a lot of building projects in my time. I
am currently living in the fourth house I have owned, and every
single one has been a fixer-upper. I have also overseen two major
renovation projects for decrepit church buildings in London. I
find ripping out the old to make way for the new painful. It takes
a lot of vision to keep going.

When we arrive at the end of the book of Amos, we discover
that the Lord has that kind of vision by the boatload. He takes no
pleasure in tearing down the sinful northern kingdom of Israel,
but in these final five verses he explains why he is so unflinching
in his judgment. His eyes are fixed on the rebuild he has planned.
Because he has the wisdom not to stay his hand too early, he is
able to declare:

> *In that day, "I will restore David's fallen shelter – I will
> repair its broken walls and restore its ruins – and will
> rebuild it as it used to be, so that they may possess the
> remnant of Edom and all the nations that bear my name,"
> declares the Lord, who will do these things.*

If we are to get as excited about this promise as the Lord expects
us to be, we are going to need a little bit of explanation. King

David did four things at the start of his reign over Israel. He captured the city of Jerusalem from the pagans, he brought the Ark of the Covenant into his new capital, he built a Tabernacle to house it on Mount Zion and he called people from every nation to come and worship the Lord with him there. Amos is therefore prophesying several things to the Israelite survivors in these final five verses.

Amos is telling them that the Lord will reunite them with the southern tribe of Judah. He will not bring them back to their idols at Bethel and Dan. That's part of what their exile was for. He will bring them back to where his presence dwells on Mount Zion and back under the godly rule of the dynasty of David. He will ensure that David's heir – normally referred to as the Messiah – will not only include them in the new congregation that he is forming on Mount Zion, but will also include many out-and-out foreigners. He will fulfil all of David's greatest hopes in 1 Chronicles 16 at the dedication of his Tabernacle: *"Ascribe to the Lord, all you families of nations, ascribe to the Lord glory and strength. Ascribe to the Lord the glory due to his name; bring an offering and come before him... Cry out, 'Save us, God our Saviour; gather us and deliver us from the nations.'"*

Now fast-forward 800 years from the time that Amos prophesied. James, the leader of the church in Jerusalem, quotes from the book of Amos in Acts 15:13–21.[1] The apostles and elders have gathered in order to sense God's will together on what to do with the large numbers of non-Jews who have responded to the Gospel and who have been baptized in water and in the Holy Spirit. Suddenly James gets up and addresses the assembly. Can they not see that this is all part of the rebuild

---

[1] The other time that Amos is quoted is in Acts 7:42–43. The early Christians believed that the book of Amos could help them to understand the ups and downs of Church history. So should we.

of Israel that the Lord promised through Amos that he was going to perform?[2]

James argues that the prophet Amos was not talking about a Tabernacle made from acacia wood and scarlet yarn and ram skins dyed red. All those things were prophetic pictures of the cross of Jesus Christ. Nor was Amos talking about a literal Mount Zion. He was describing a true and better Tabernacle that Jesus is building by turning everyone who believes in him into living stones.[3] The Lord judged the ten northern tribes of Israel and sent them into exile in order to rid their land of idols and reunite them with the tribe of Judah. He brought their survivors back to obedience so that the nations would look in on the arrival of their Messiah and be drawn into the blessings of his Plan "A" rather than driven away by the curses of his Plan "B". None of the judgments in the book of Amos were therefore meaningless. They were all necessary to the rebuild.

The first eight and a half chapters of Amos are like a doctor diagnosing an illness and prescribing his remedy. The final half chapter is like the end of that painful course of treatment, when the patient is given a clean bill of health and sent home free from pain. Amos reassures the Israelites that God knows what he is doing, even as he judges them. They have left the path of blessing, and he will do what it takes to bring them home. Together with the people of Judah and the converts from the pagan nations around them, they will celebrate the salvation of God, revealed in Jesus the Messiah, when he comes.

That's the period of history in which we are now living. James saw the start of it when Greeks and Syrians were saved, but we now live at a time when God is saving people from

---

[2] James follows the Septuagint translation of 9:12, which treats *Edom* as shorthand for the *Gentiles* in general.

[3] 1 Corinthians 3:16–17; 2 Corinthians 6:16; Ephesians 2:21–22; 1 Peter 2:5; Hebrews 12:22–24. We can tell from Amos 9:15 that the primary fulfilment of this prophecy was never meant to be the return of Israel's survivors from Assyria, since they were uprooted from their land again in 70 AD.

every nation of the world. We must not forget this whenever newspaper headlines seek to discourage us by telling us that the Church is in unstoppable decline. That may be true if we repeat the foolish sins of the northern kingdom of Israel – if we sing one thing to God when we gather together and then live a lie from Sunday to Sunday; if we forget that the way we treat the poorest person around us reveals how much we truly love the Lord;[4] if we take our beliefs and our sexual ethics from the non-Christian culture around us; if we are proud and complacent when God speaks to us about his holiness and judgment – but if we repent of these sins, such newspaper headlines are not a true description of our situation at all![5]

If we repent of the sins of Israel, we can step into the realization that these are the days in which Jesus is building a better Tabernacle on a better Mount Zion, and in which he is harvesting believers from every nation. We can step into the revival promises that he now gives to us: *"The reaper will be overtaken by the ploughman and the planter by the one treading grapes."*[6] We can live in the good of his promise to rebuild our ruined churches through us and to open up new nations to the Gospel.

Amos prophesied these words for us: *"I will restore David's fallen shelter."* Jesus echoed them when he gave us a similar promise in Matthew 16:18. *"I will build my church, and the gates of hell will not overcome it!"* The long chapters of judgment in the book of Amos were therefore worth it. They were his ground-clearing operation; now the rebuild has begun.

---

[4] Proverbs 14:31; 17:5; Matthew 25:31–46.

[5] Of course churches can fall into the trap we are warned against in 9:7, thinking that God is bound to bless them simply because they are churches. Amos 1:1–9:10 warns that God will shut down such churches (Revelation 2:5), yet Amos 9:11–15 promises that God will bless any church that repents and follows him.

[6] In other words, our harvest will be so great that we will still be reaping when the sowing season starts again!

Crazy Love (Hosea 1:1–11)

The word of the Lord that came to Hosea son of Beeri... during the reign of Jeroboam son of Joash king of Israel.

(Hosea 1:1)

Hosea and Amos were on the same team. They are the only Minor Prophets who ministered principally to the northern kingdom of Israel. Their opening verses suggest that they were also contemporaries, but that's where the common ground ends. What really strikes us as we begin the book of Hosea is how different the two prophets were.

Amos was a cross-cultural missionary, who had travelled to Israel from the southern kingdom of Judah. Hosea had been born and bred in the northern kingdom of Israel, so he prophesied as a local man.[1] Amos was a common shepherd, but Hosea appears to have been a sophisticated city-dweller. Amos spoke about a vague and distant enemy somewhere *"beyond Damascus"*, but Hosea names it nine times as Assyria.[2] Amos delivered all of his prophecies in just two years, whereas Hosea prophesied for forty years or more.[3] He prophesied to Israel from within the northern kingdom until 753 BC, before fleeing south from the anarchy of civil war to carry on prophesying to

---

[1] We know nothing about Hosea beyond what we read in his book, but he demonstrates too much local knowledge about the geography and customs of Israel to have been a foreigner.

[2] Amos 5:27. Hosea 5:13; 7:11; 8:9–10; 9:3; 10:6; 11:5, 11; 12:1; 14:3.

[3] Amos 1:1. Hosea 1:1 lists only one king of Israel, who reigned until 753 BC. It lists four kings of Judah, the last of whom began his reign in 715 BC. After Jeroboam, five different dynasties ruled Israel in its final 31 years.

Israel from the safety of Judah. He kept his focus on the northern kingdom, but as a result of this relocation he mentions Judah far more often than Amos.[4]

Bigger than all of these other differences, however, is the change of tone. Although both men prophesied to Israel at the same time, the Lord gave Amos a message about his terrible judgment and Hosea a message about his crazy love. As a result, Amos is tough while Hosea is tender. Amos accuses, whereas Hosea appeals. Amos warns, but Hosea woos. Amos emphasizes God's purity, while Hosea emphasizes God's pity. These aren't conflicting messages. We need them both if we are to understand God's character fully.

In the first chapter of Hosea, we discover how costly it was for the prophet to complete the picture for us. He was a single man in search of a wife, and one day the Lord instructed him to go and marry a woman who was well-known for her promiscuity.[5] Gomer means *Complete*, and everybody knew she was on track to get through all the men in the city, but the Lord reassured Hosea that their marriage would become a prophetic picture of his unreasonable love towards unfaithful Israel. At first, Hosea must have thought that he had misheard God and was going crazy. He was ready for a prophet's platform but not for a prophet's pain. Nevertheless, he embraced his prophetic calling by marrying the town trollop. His family and friends must have been appalled.

When Hosea and Gomer have a baby together, everyone is looking to see if it is really his. This gives him a chance to prophesy to his nation. The boy's name is Jezreel, because the Lord is about to judge the ruling dynasty of Israel for its sin towards the

---

[4] Hosea's flight south was the start of the famine of God's Word that the Lord had prophesied in Amos 8:11–14. See Hosea 1:7, 11; 4:15; 5:5, 10, 12–14; 6:4, 11; 8:14; 10:11; 11:12; 12:2.

[5] The Hebrew word *zānāh* can either mean *to sleep around* or *to work as a prostitute*. It is therefore possible that Gomer was a prostitute in the city, although the Hebrew text of 3:1 says that she slept with *friends*.

southern dynasty of David. When Jehu seized the throne, the Lord commanded him to wipe out the wicked dynasty of Ahab, but he went further by massacring forty-two princes from the royal house of Judah outside the city of Jezreel. Since in Hebrew the city's name means *God Will Scatter*, Hosea is able to prophesy that the Lord will not only destroy the dynasty of Jehu for its sin. He will also defeat and scatter Israel in battle at Jezreel.[6]

When Hosea and Gomer have two more children, the neighbours quickly spot that neither of the babies looks very much like him. Hosea adds fuel to the rumour that they are the fruit of his wife's affairs by naming them Lo-Ruhamah and Lo-Ammi, which is Hebrew for *Not Loved* and *Not My People*. As the sniggering crowds gather around him, Hosea seizes it as an opportunity to prophesy again to the northern kingdom. He uses his children's names to warn that the Lord now considers Israel to be like one of the foreign nations. He will bless the southern kingdom of Judah by rescuing it from the hands of the Assyrian invader, but he will not show any such love and forgiveness towards Israel.[7] They have behaved like an adulterous wife towards him, so they are about to be destroyed.

The crowds are not surprised that a few years of putting up with Gomer has turned Hosea into a prophet of gloom, just like Amos. After all, hadn't they warned him not to marry her? But Hosea hasn't finished. While he has their attention, he suddenly prophesies hope for survivors of the northern kingdom after their exile. He picks up where Amos left off at the end of his book, proclaiming that the Lord will reunite the twelve tribes of Israel under a single Messiah in a new, united kingdom. Although he will scatter them like seed, he will do so in order to reap a

---

[6] Jehu's actions in 2 Kings 9:1–10:14 had paved the way for Jezebel's daughter Athaliah to usurp the throne of Judah. His dynasty was wiped out six months after Jeroboam died. See 2 Kings 15:8–12; Amos 7:9.

[7] God doesn't just love us. He is love (1 John 4:8, 16). Yet if we treat him with disdain and disobedience, we step outside his love and mercy and choose to dwell under his judgment instead.

marvellous harvest. He will bring them back from exile and will multiply their numbers beyond measure. Best of all, he will teach them once again how to live as *"children of the living God"*.[8]

The crowds are taken completely by surprise. They had been bracing themselves to hear more words of judgment, like the ones they heard from Amos. The last thing that they had expected was to hear about God's crazy love for the northern kingdom, in spite of its sin. As Hosea puts his arm around his adulterous wife and takes her home with the two babies that she conceived through her promiscuity, the people of Israel start to readjust their understanding of God. He isn't just the one who hates their sin and who threatens to punish them. He is also the one who loves sinners and who forgives them.[9]

The apostle Paul drew great hope from the book of Hosea every time he was tempted to despair over the way in which the Jewish nation had rejected Jesus. He accepts that the Lord has to judge his sinful people in order to prevent them from projecting a wrong impression of his character to the world, but he quotes from 1:10 in Romans 9:26 in order to celebrate the fact that this is only half the story. God will ensure that mercy triumphs over judgment by saving many sinful people from Israel, and many sinful foreigners besides.[10] He will create a glorious, united Church out of people from every nation of the world. The God who hates sin also loves sinners with undying, crazy love.

If you found the book of Amos hard going, take a moment now to worship. Praise the Lord that he judges sin, but don't stop there. Thank him also that he is merciful to sinners in the same way that Hosea was merciful to Gomer. Marvel at his amazing grace.

---

[8] Note the way in which the promise in 1:10 echoes God's promise to Abraham in Genesis 22:17.

[9] Hosea's name means *Salvation* in Hebrew. It was the original name of Joshua (Numbers 13:8, 16).

[10] When 1 Peter 2:10 refers back to this verse, it also emphasizes that God saves sinful non-Israelites too.

The Big "A" (Hosea 2:1–3:5)

"Go, show your love to your wife again, though she is loved by another man and is an adulteress. Love her as the Lord loves the Israelites."

(Hosea 3:1)

In the classic novel *The Scarlet Letter*, Hester Prynne is punished by the Puritans of seventeenth-century America for her adultery. She is forced to stitch a big "A" to the front of her dress to mark her out as a sinful woman and she is shackled to a pillory in the town square so that all her neighbours will witness her guilt and shame. When the crowd see her wearing the scarlet letter "A", they hurl so many insults at her that *"the unhappy woman grew pale, and trembled"*. But the pillory is just the start of her punishment. She is condemned *"then and thereafter, for the remainder of her natural life to wear a mark of shame upon her bosom"*.[1] For Hester Prynne's community, the big "A" was unforgivable.

The prophet Hosea is caught up in his own version of *The Scarlet Letter*. His marriage to Gomer has turned into a living nightmare. By the start of chapter 2, enough years have passed for him to be able to teach his children how to address one another and their mother, who is no longer at home. She has left him and moved in with one of her rich lovers, led astray by presents and promises of pleasure. His marriage is effectively over.

On one level, the words Hosea speaks in 2:1–13 are his own personal response to Gomer's sin against him. He informs

---

[1] Nathaniel Hawthorne published *The Scarlet Letter* in 1850.

his children that their mother is no longer his wife. He does not want to be the husband of a woman who strips off and lies on her back for anyone.[2] He does not want to stay at home and raise children that he knows are not his own. He has decided to throw Gomer out of the family home, depriving her of the clothes and possessions that she has left there, in the hope that blocking her out will force her to take stock of her ways.[3] If not, he will put her in the pillory so that everyone can see her sin. He will turn her into spoiled goods that nobody wants to sleep with.

On another level, these are also the words that the Lord speaks to unfaithful Israel. His immediate reaction is to treat her in the same way that the Puritan communities of early America treated women like Hester Prynne. He pins a big "A" on the shirt-fronts of all the people of the northern kingdom. Their adultery is spiritual – the Lord makes that clear in 2:8 by naming one of her lovers as the Canaanite fertility god Baal – but it is every bit as serious as the sexual favours that Hosea's wife is dispensing freely across the city. The Lord had sent prosperity to Jeroboam's kingdom, blessing Israel with all of the grain, wine, wool, linen, silver and gold that they could possibly need, but they offered those things as sacrifices in the temple of their idol.[4] Since Baal was said to reward his worshippers with great harvests by sending rain upon the earth, the Lord promises to punish the people of Israel through a drought so severe that

---

[2] Hosea uses shocking language in the second half of 2:2 to help us feel the full horror of Gomer's adultery.

[3] An Israelite husband supplied his wife with her clothing (Exodus 21:10; Ezekiel 16:10–14). In Hosea's culture, therefore, these verses would have been understood as a statement of intent to divorce Gomer.

[4] Hosea reminds us in 2:7–8 that false gods always promise to make us happy, but that in reality they can only plunder us of the good gifts the Lord has given us. Contrast Exodus 12:35–36 with 32:1–4.

many of them will die of thirst.[5] He will turn adulterous Israel into a shocking parable for the whole world to see.[6]

But the big "A" in these two chapters is not adultery. It is *afterwards*. The Lord is not like Hester Prynne's implacable accusers. By rights, there should be no afterwards at all, yet in 2:14–23 he speaks tender words of forgiveness to unfaithful Israel. He promises to woo her back after she goes into exile (the Hebrew word *pāthāh* in 2:14 means *to seduce* or *to entice*) and to bring her back to the Promised Land. He will not treat her like sinful Achan, who was destroyed without pity in the Valley of Achor in Joshua 7.[7] He will open up a door of hope for her so that she can return to the message of salvation that she threw on the scrapheap alongside the covenant that he made with her. Since the name of the false god Baal means *master* in Hebrew, the Lord promises to be such a loving husband to the people of Israel that they will be ashamed to use their old idol's name any more. Gone will be the days of drought, replaced by rain. Gone will be the days of fruitless scattering, replaced by harvest. Gone will be the days when a prophet needs to name his children *Not Loved* and *Not My People*, for the Lord will again be known as the God of Israel.[8] Gone will be the days of feeling far from God, replaced by intimate love.[9]

In 3:1–5, the Lord commands Hosea to do something very painful. He is to show the same love and forgiveness towards

---

[5] This would be poetic justice. It was how he had judged Baal-worshipping Israel before, in 1 Kings 17–18.

[6] Hosea 2:11 echoes Amos 5:21–27. The Hebrew word for *stop* here is *shābath*, so the Lord is using a play on words. He is promising to sabbath all their Sabbaths.

[7] God wants the reference to Achan to jog our memories that he saved the prostitute Rahab in Joshua 6:23–25.

[8] The references to *Jezreel*, meaning *God Will Scatter Seed*, and to *Lo-Ruhamah* and *Lo-Ammi* in 2:22–23 are meant to constitute a glorious reversal of Israel's destruction, as described in 1:4–9.

[9] The Hebrew word *yāda'* in 2:20 is the same word that is used for Adam *knowing* Eve in Genesis 4:1 and 25.

Gomer that the Lord has described towards Israel. By the time Hosea finds her, she is no longer at her lover's house. She has sunk even lower and has now become a prostitute for money. He has to pay a large sum of money to her pimp to bring her home. He does so without hesitation, but when they get home he informs her that their marriage is going to be sexless for a season. He wants to prophesy to the nation of Israel that, unless they repent, they will have to spend a season in captivity before they can receive the Lord's promise of forgiveness and restoration.[10]

This is not somebody else's story. It is yours and mine. All of us are guilty of spiritual adultery. None of us has worshipped God as we ought. We have all been led astray by idols, but we have all been promised this way back. This is the big "A" that the apostle Paul celebrates in his letters – that the Lord has given us an *afterwards*, in spite of our sin. He quotes from 2:23 in Romans 9:25 to help us celebrate with him that God extends his mercy, not just to Israel, but also to sinners from every single nation of the world.

Perhaps you feel far from God right now. Perhaps nine chapters of judgment in the book of Amos have made you wonder whether you will ever find your way back to him.[11] Do not despise the Lord's discipline and the way that he is punishing you. He is romancing you, leading you into the desert so that you have nothing to rely on instead of him.

This is what happened to me. I was Gomer, and God found me. He opened up a doorway of hope for me and he has done the same for you. So take a moment to tell him right now that you repent of your adulteries and that you want to come back home.

---

[10] Hosea 3:4–5 echoes the message of Amos 9:11–15, that the Lord's judgment on Israel was a necessary precursor to his rebuild. It would bring them back to God's Temple and to God's Messiah.

[11] These chapters of judgment should cause you to fear the Lord, but they shouldn't make you doubt his love towards you. Hosea 3:5 invites us literally to *"come in fear to the Lord and **to his goodness**"*.

The Divorce Court
(Hosea 4:1–5:15)

*Hear the word of the Lord, you Israelites, because the
Lord has a charge to bring against you.*

(Hosea 4:1)

I don't spend a lot of time in divorce courts, but every time I
do I leave feeling incredibly sad. It always reminds me of Tom
Cruise in the movie Cocktail, when he tells his ex-girlfriend to
stop crying because, *"Relationships always end badly - otherwise
they wouldn't end."* Somehow nothing feels sadder than love
turned to bitterness.

Despite the pain of it, the Lord drags Israel into the divorce
court at the start of chapter 4. It's impossible to miss the change
of tone here. The first three chapters of Hosea date back to the
first few years he prophesied, while he was still living in the
northern kingdom of Israel and his family challenges could be
witnessed by all his neighbours. The final eleven chapters date
back to the four decades that he carried on prophesying to Israel
from the new base he established in the southern kingdom of
Judah.[1] These chapters all attempt to convince the reluctant
people of Israel to admit that his troubled relationship with
Gomer is a picture of their own troubled relationship with God.
Hosea starts with two chapters that create a courtroom setting
in which the Lord can give a detailed list of Israel's adulteries.
He has plenty of legal grounds to divorce her.

---

[1] We can tell this from the way that 1:1 dates Hosea's ministry only to 753 BC
in Israel, but to 715 BC or later in Judah. We can also tell it from the way that
from now on he makes lots of references to Judah.

In 4:1–3, Hosea lists the sins that have led to the drought that is causing so much suffering in Israel. Their land was prosperous before they exchanged the Lord's ways for the ways of their idols – swapping *faithfulness, love* and *the knowledge of God for cursing, lying, murder, stealing* and *adultery*. These things have robbed them of rain and have crippled their agrarian economy. These courtroom proceedings are of their own making.

In 4:4–6, Hosea pinpoints the root cause of Israel's spiritual unfaithfulness.[2] We ought to find these verses pretty challenging, because Hosea says that it is the neglect of Scripture. The ideas on which we feed our minds start very quickly to dominate the way we view the world, and the way we view the world starts even more quickly to dominate our actions. The priests and prophets of Israel are therefore most to blame for her adulteries, just as preachers and pastors are most to blame for the sins of the churches they lead.[3] The Lord warns us solemnly in 4:6 that *"My people are destroyed from lack of knowledge."* Ignorance of the Scriptures isn't bliss. It is always spiritually fatal. There is nothing neutral about deciding to take our diet from the media – TV, print, digital or social. Our spiritual well-being depends on our commitment to feast on the Word of God instead.[4]

In 4:6–14, the Lord speaks judgment over the priests of Israel. Since they have rejected his Word, he will reject them. Since they have exchanged the glory of the real God for the worship of disgraceful idols, he will bring disgrace down on them. From 4:9 onwards, the Lord includes in these curses

---

[2] The *mother* in 4:5 is the nation of Israel. She is depicted as a woman, just like Gomer.

[3] Training up more leaders isn't the solution. Training up more of the right kind of leaders is the solution. Hosea 4:7 warns us that more of the wrong kind of leader will actually result in our churches getting worse.

[4] This is why the famine of God's Word that was predicted in Amos 8:11–14 was such a terrible punishment. Put more positively, this is also why faithful Bible teaching is so powerful to transform a church and nation.

the people that the priests have led astray. Since they have gone after fertility gods, they will fail to harvest enough food. Since they have slept with shrine prostitutes at pagan shrines, their own daughters will be reduced to prostitution, selling themselves for such a pittance that their wages will not even put food on the table. Since they have rejected the Scriptures which would have given them knowledge, the Lord will befuddle their minds with wine. Since they have committed spiritual adultery with their idols, he will hand their nation over to a demon of prostitution so that all their daughters-in-law cheat on their sons.[5]

Divorce courts are often the scene of bitter custody battles, so Hosea turns in 4:15–19 to his new neighbours in the southern kingdom of Judah and pleads with them to remain faithful to the Lord. They must not fool themselves that, if only they meet Israel halfway in her compromise, they will be able to bring her home. That is utter folly, like a Christian who expects that she will save an unbeliever if she marries him.[6] Hosea warns that such wishful thinking will only lead Judah astray. If Israel could be brought back to him that easily, there would be no need for her to be destroyed! But there is need. God warns Judah to save herself by staying away from the idols of Bethel and Gilgal.[7]

In 5:1–7, the Lord exposes the guilt of Israel still further.[8]

---

[5] When we resist the Holy Spirit, we can open ourselves up to evil spirits. In 4:12 and 5:4, the Lord speaks twice about Israel being in thrall to a *rūach zenūnîm* – that is, *a spirit of prostitution*.

[6] Or like a Gospel-believing church that hopes to bring other churches back to God by pursuing false unity. True believers used the oath *"as surely as the Lord lives"* (1 Samuel 20:3, 21), so the Lord warns Judah in 4:15 not to make any alliance with Israel that involves pretending that her people are true believers.

[7] *Bethel* means *House of God*, so the Lord often refers to it in the book of Hosea by its ancient name of *Beth Aven*, meaning *House of Wickedness*. He sees this as a far more appropriate name for the city. See 5:8; 10:5.

[8] We do not know what happened at Mizpah and Tabor (5:1), but it clearly marked a new low for Israel.

There is deliberate ambiguity in the Hebrew word *yāda'* in 5:4. Is he saying that they have failed to *acknowledge* him by running off with their idols, or is he saying that their idolatry has prevented them from *knowing* him? The answer is, both. However many flocks of sacrifices they slaughter at their religious festivals, he is no longer listening. Their marriage is over.[9]

In 5:8–15, the Lord therefore predicts the destruction of Israel. In her ignorance, she will turn to Assyria for help, little suspecting that Assyria is the empire that will destroy her![10] She will sound trumpets across the land to gather troops for battle, but it will be too late. The Lord who roared like a lion at the beginning of Amos has made up his mind to destroy her in order to rebuild a truly godly nation out of the Israelite survivors.

In 5:15, the Lord ends his courtroom speech by slotting the final piece into the jigsaw of his judgment. Many people are confused when they read Hosea. If God is as committed to unfaithful Israel as Hosea was to Gomer, why is he in the divorce court at all? The Lord explains. His forgiveness cannot be granted without repentance, and he knows Israel will not repent until he sends her into exile. She has already begun to lead Judah astray with her sin, so there is no time to lose in proceeding with the plan.[11]

Hosea's courtroom scene is over. Israel has been proved to be as much a serial adulterer as Gomer. In the next chapter we will see Israel's response. Can this marriage be saved?

---

[9] Israel's ignorance did not make its people innocent. Hosea 5:5 echoes Amos 1–2, that God will judge those who arrogantly ignore his Word for doing what their consciences told them full well was wrong.

[10] This prophecy was fulfilled in 2 Kings 15:19–20 and 17:3.

[11] Hosea mentions Judah being infected by Israel's sin in 5:5, 10 and 12–14. Judah had moved boundary stones by sinfully seizing territory from Israel (1 Kings 15:16–22; Deuteronomy 19:14; 27:17).

Real Repentance
(Hosea 6:1–7:16)

"What can I do with you?... Your love is like the morning mist, like the early dew that disappears."

(Hosea 6:4)

There is a famous story about a man who stopped Martyn Lloyd-Jones in the street to tell him how much his sermon had moved him the previous evening. The man was not a Christian, but he had wept and sobbed his way through the entire message. He had felt a bit put out when Lloyd-Jones failed to call for people to come forward then and there. *"You know, doctor, if you had asked me to stay behind last night I would have done so."* Lloyd-Jones smiled back, *"Well, I am asking you now, come with me now."*

Suddenly the man started back-pedalling, *"Oh no, but if you had asked me last night I would have done so."* Lloyd-Jones was very firm in his reply:

> *If what happened to you last night does not last for twenty-four hours I am not interested in it. If you are not as ready to come with me now as you were last night you have not got the right, the true thing. Whatever affected you last night was only temporary and passing, you still do not see your real need of Christ.*[1]

If we ever needed proof that Martyn Lloyd-Jones was correct and that superficial repentance can save no one, look no further

---

[1] Martyn Lloyd-Jones shares this story in his book *Preaching and Preachers* (1971).

than Israel's response to God's accusations in the divorce courtroom. On the surface, their response in 6:1–3 sounds very promising. They confess that their sin has provoked the Lord to strike them. They resolve to turn back to him, convinced that he might yet spare them from exile. But look a bit more closely and it is clear that their repentance is not real. They expect that after two or three days they will have their revival. Picturing their restoration as a sunrise in the darkness, they expect that they can get it overnight and then move on.

The Lord therefore spends these two chapters calling Israel to repent of their sham repentance.[2] Their hearts have not truly changed towards him. It is entirely superficial. The Lord likens their love to the early morning dew that evaporates by breakfast and to the early morning mist that is gone by the time most people open their curtains. This leads into one of the most famous verses in the whole of Hosea: *"I desire mercy, not sacrifice, and acknowledgement of God rather than burnt offerings."*

Jesus explains for us what this verse means in two of his clashes with the Jewish leaders. When the Pharisees complain that he is friends with tax collectors and sinners, he quotes this verse to rebuke them in Matthew 9:13: *"Go and learn what this means: 'I desire mercy, not sacrifice.'"* When they complain that he is allowing his disciples to pick food on a Sabbath walk, he quotes the verse again in Matthew 12:7: *"If you had known what these words mean, 'I desire mercy, not sacrifice,' you would not have condemned the innocent."* What Jesus is saying is that man-made repentance is always superficial. It produces lots of resolutions and looks down on those who fail to keep them, but it never results in real heart change. Self-reform is no substitute for knowing God. Trying harder is no substitute for receiving his love. Real repentance means allowing God's Spirit to do a deep

---

[2] His main focus is on the northern kingdom, but he also warns that Judah has a similar problem (6:4, 11).

and lasting work in our hearts. It requires humility and it is the first sign that revival has begun.

The Lord therefore lists several signs that Israel's repentance is really nothing of the kind. It is now some time after 740 BC (we can tell that from the way Hosea speaks in 6:8 about the band of murderers from Gilead who murdered the king of Israel that year and established a new dynasty under the army general Pekah[3]), so Israel is less than twenty years away from its destruction. That explains the urgency in the Lord's voice as he points out what is lacking in their response to him.

From time to time they actually seem plausible in their repentance, but then they give the game away by lying and stealing (7:1–2), or by goading one another on to sexual immorality and drunkenness without any provocation from the pagans (7:3–7),[4] or by listening to the ideas of foreign idolaters, little noticing that it is making their worldview less and less biblical and therefore sapping them of what little strength they have (7:8–10).[5] At other times of supposed repentance, God has found them cosying up to Egypt and Assyria, or crying out to pagan idols, seeking help from anyone but the Lord (7:11–16).[6] All of this is proof that their repentance is a superficial sham. Since it is short-lived, so will be their future.

A lot of what the Lord says to Israel in these two chapters is pretty bleak. You won't find many of these verses on the inside of Christian greeting cards. But in a strange way I find

---

[3] 2 Kings 15:25. We do not know the precise sins of the priests of Shechem in the hill country of Ephraim. Did they murder people with literal violence or simply by telling them whatever they wanted to hear?

[4] Hosea is right to prophesy in 7:5 that the kings of Israel mock God. Not a single king in the entire history of the northern kingdom followed him. Hosea is also right to talk in 7:7 about the people of Israel *devouring their rulers*. In the 31 years from 753 to 722 BC they went through six kings, five dynasties and four royal assassinations.

[5] 7:10 repeats 5:5. Our Bible ignorance does not make us innocent. God judges us by what we do know.

[6] Hosea says in 7:11 that this is pigeon-brained. Our only hope lies in the Lord.

what the Lord says here enormously encouraging. Let me give three reasons why.

First, the Lord encourages us here that we cannot save anybody. That's really good news. If we honestly believed that we could cajole people into repentance, we would feel under enormous pressure to twist their arms into praying a prayer of salvation. These chapters set us free from all that. They tell us that we can't save anyone. Our job is to communicate God's Word faithfully and to pray for our hearers. It's the Holy Spirit's job to bring them to repentance. Our fruitfulness is just as much reliant upon God's grace as our salvation.

Second, the Lord encourages us that he really wants to save people. Don't miss it when he tells the people of Israel twice in 6:11 and 7:1 that he wishes to heal and restore them. Don't miss it when he says for a third time, in 7:13, that he longs to redeem sinful people.

Third, the Lord says that the main thing that is stopping him from saving people is the fact that we fail to rely on the work of his Spirit. Today he still says of many Christians what he says of Israel in 7:9: *"Foreigners sap his strength, but he does not realize it. His hair is sprinkled with grey, but he does not notice."* These chapters tell us that when we rely on our own strength, seeking to convert unbelievers by mimicking them, we simply become weaker.[7] When we rely on programmes and human strategies, we become like weak old men and women, but when we rely on partnership with God's Spirit we become extraordinarily effective. He works in people's hearts to bring them to real repentance.

So don't settle for a superficial response to God, either in your own heart or in the hearts of others. Ask the Lord to help you to surrender to his Spirit's power to do a deep work within your own heart, and ask him to empower you by that same Spirit to bring true repentance to those around you.

---

[7] The *half-baked loaf* in 7:8 represents believers who are only semi-different from the world. Mimicking unbelievers converts no one, but daring to be different enables God's Spirit to convert people through us.

True Knowledge
(Hosea 8:1–9:17)

Israel cries out to me, "Our God, we acknowledge you!"

(Hosea 8:2)

The little Hebrew word *yāda'* turns up almost 1,000 times in the Old Testament. It means *to know*, and it is a key word in Hosea. The prophet warns us in 4:6 that lack of knowledge is going to destroy Israel, and in 6:3 that obtaining knowledge is its only hope of salvation.[1] Having taught the Israelites the real meaning of repentance in chapters 6 and 7, the Lord now gives them a similar lesson about true knowledge.

The word *yāda'* carries a much broader meaning than the English verb *to know*. It can be translated three ways, and very often in the Old Testament it means all three things at the same time.[2] We can translate Israel's prayer in 8:2 as *"Our God, we know about you"*, in the sense of understanding what he is like, or as *"Our God, we acknowledge you"*, in the sense of submitting to that understanding, or as *"Our God, we experience you"*, in the sense of enjoying the fruit of surrendering to who the Lord

---

[1] Lack of knowledge also destroys Israel in 2:8; 4:1; 5:4, and knowledge saves Israel in 6:6. Ignorance is therefore anything but bliss. Our knowledge of God dictates whether he blesses or curses us.

[2] This is why George Lucas chose to use its noun form as the name of the greatest Jedi Master in the *Star Wars* movies. Yoda knows all about the force, he submits to the force and he constantly uses the force.

really is.[3] The Lord uses the word in these chapters to inform the Israelites that they do none of these three things.

The people of Israel claim to know all about God, but they are fatally ignorant of his character. They have rejected his Law (8:1) and have therefore lost all sense of his definition of good and bad (8:3).[4] They have neglected the Hebrew Scriptures for so long that, on the few occasions that they try to read them, it feels like browsing the foreign-language section of a bookstore (8:12). They have forgotten what God is like to the extent that when they talk about him they recite a mishmash of lies (7:13 and 8:14). When prophets such as Amos and Hosea try to bring them back to the Scriptures, they dismiss them as madmen (9:7).[5] Since they have rejected God's invitation to come and learn all about him, the Lord therefore declares he is about to reject them as a nation (9:17).

The people of Israel claim to acknowledge God, but in reality they resist what little they know about him. They know he wants to be worshipped at the Temple in Jerusalem, yet they have set up alternative shrines in their own land (8:1). They know that he wants them to be ruled by David's dynasty, yet they have broken away from Judah and chosen strange kings of their own (8:4). They know that the Lord forbids anyone to make an image of him, since his glory is far too great to be captured in metalwork or wood or stone, yet they have erected images of him as a young bull throughout their land (8:4–6).[6] As a result, the altars on which they offer sin offerings are actually sins themselves (8:11). Because they do not acknowledge the

---

[3] Yāda' is used to describe Adam sleeping with Eve in Genesis 4:1 and 25. It means more than book learning!

[4] The days of Gibeah in 9:9 refers to an absolute low point in Israel's moral history, when the Benjamites there tried to gang-rape a Levite and ended up gang-raping and killing his concubine instead (Judges 19–21).

[5] 'Ish hārūach in 9:7 is literally a man of the Spirit. Those who don't really know God often dismiss Spirit-filled believers as a bunch of maniacs.

[6] 1 Kings 12:28 suggests that the people of Israel didn't think they had stopped worshipping the Lord at all. They thought their golden-calf idols were accurate representations of the Lord.

Lord, constantly raging against him (9:7), rebelling against him (9:15) and resisting him (9:17), he is about to ruin them.[7]

The people of Israel claim to experience God, but he and they are living separate lives. They have turned their backs on the covenant he made with their ancestors at Mount Sinai every bit as much as Gomer turned her back on her wedding vows (8:1). Israel is utterly promiscuous with her spiritual affection – worshipping fertility gods at her threshing-floors (9:1),[8] worshipping images at Gilgal (9:15) and even travelling long distances to worship the idols of Assyria (8:9).[9] Her people have become like their ancestors, who bowed down to idols at Baal Peor in Numbers 25 and became as vile as the objects that they worshipped.[10] The Lord will make them as barren as their lifeless images (9:11–16).[11] Since they love foreign gods so much and desire to experience the Lord so little, he will send them far away from his Temple and into foreign exile.[12]

What makes these two chapters so utterly tragic is that the people of Israel have no idea about any of this. They genuinely think in 8:2 that they know about the Lord, that they acknowledge the Lord and that they are experiencing the Lord. That's why these verses ought to challenge us, as

---

[7] Note the depth of God's anger about this in 9:15. He doesn't just hate their sin. He hates them.

[8] *The bread of mourners* communicates that this has made their whole harvest unclean (Numbers 19:14–15).

[9] Amos 4:4 and 5:5, and Hosea 4:15, tell us that at this time Gilgal was a major centre of idolatry within Israel.

[10] Numbers 25 was another terrible low point in Israel's history, on a par with Judges 19–21. Far from living in a golden age, with God on their side, they needed to see that theirs was one of Israel's vilest generations.

[11] 2 Kings 17:15. Becoming like what we worship means that living for money, fame, sex or power makes us increasingly shallow. Living for the Lord makes us increasingly glorious (2 Corinthians 3:16–18).

[12] The hovering *eagle* or *vulture* in 8:1 (they are the same word in Hebrew) speaks of imminent attack from Assyria. *The king of princes* or *the great king* in 8:10 was one of the titles of the king of Assyria (10:6 and Isaiah 36:13). Hosea talks about Egypt in 7:16; 8:13; 9:3 and 9:6 because many of Israel's survivors fled there.

Christians and as churches. Have we contented ourselves with something less than genuinely knowing God ourselves? A. W. Tozer contends that

> *The Church has surrendered her once lofty concept of God and has substituted for it one so low, so ignoble, as to be utterly unworthy of thinking, worshipping men. This she has not done deliberately, but little by little and without her knowledge; and her very unawareness only makes her situation all the more tragic. The low view of God entertained almost universally among Christians is the cause of a hundred lesser evils everywhere among us... If we would bring back spiritual power to our lives, we must begin to think of God more nearly as He is... What comes into our minds when we think about God is the most important thing about us.*[13]

That's what the Lord is warning against when he states in 8:7 that the people of Israel *"sow the wind and reap the whirlwind"*. If we fail to know God as he really is, our sin is multiplied back to us many times over.[14] This is as true for us today as it was for ancient Israel. If you don't believe me, just paraphrase the curse in 9:11–14 and ask if it applies to you or your church: *You will see no converts; when you think you see a convert, they will not follow through on their decision; even when someone does, they will have so little experience of the Spirit that their discipleship will be dead.* Are you sure that Hosea is someone else's mail?

The remedy is simple. Get to know the Lord. For me, this meant a period of four years when I resolved to read the Bible for more time each day than I watched television, listened to the radio and surfed the internet put together. For you, it may merely require getting up a little earlier or spending your

---

[13] A. W. Tozer in *The Knowledge of the Holy* (1961).

[14] The word *zāra'* in 8:7, meaning *to sow* or *to scatter*, is the root of the name Jezreel. See 1:4–5.

morning commute reading Scripture instead of tapping on your smartphone. Get to know what God is really like and submit to what you find. Instead of judging his Word, allow it to judge you, then ask him to fill you with his Spirit and to turn all of this head knowledge into genuine friendship with him.

God's people are destroyed for lack of knowledge, but they are saved through proper knowledge of the Lord. So whatever it costs you, acquire the true knowledge of God.

Soft Ground Drinks Rain
(Hosea 10:1–15)

*Break up your unploughed ground; for it is time
to seek the Lord, until he comes and showers his
righteousness on you.*

(Hosea 10:12)

While I have been writing these chapters on Hosea, there has been flash-flooding in my part of London. It has been raining heavily, and there are simply too many driveways and patios and paved-over areas for the water to drain away. The soil is so hard from the past few weeks of sunshine that it fares no better. It refuses to soak up the rainwater.

The people of Israel understood this problem far better than we do. Their agrarian economy depended on their soil soaking up every precious drop of rain that fell from the sky, so the Lord uses this as a picture to answer the greatest conundrum of the book of Hosea. If the Lord truly loves the Israelites and truly longs to bless them, why doesn't he forgive and restore them straightaway? Why the need to send them into exile?[1]

The key verse that answers this conundrum is 10:12: *"Sow righteousness for yourselves, reap the fruit of unfailing love, and break up your unploughed ground; for it is time to seek the Lord, until he comes and showers his righteousness on you."*

The fact is, we are told in 10:1–2, the hearts of the people of Israel were so hard towards God that they could not receive his mercy and forgiveness. Although the Lord had planted them

---

[1] The talk of *sowing* and *reaping* in 10:12–13 deliberately echoes 8:7. Israel can still sidestep God's judgment.

in the Promised Land as a flourishing vine, their prosperity had made them spiritually calloused.[2] Hosea prophesies literally in 10:2 that *"their heart is divided"*. They were so distracted by their possessions and by their busy religious programmes that only something terrible would jolt their attention back onto the Lord. He longed to bless them and to shower them with his forgiveness, but the problem was on their side. They could no more respond to his grace than a patio can soak up heavy rainfall.

This is why, we are told in 10:3–5, the people of Israel resisted the Lord's many calls to repent and return to him. They are on their nineteenth king and their ninth dynasty in only two centuries, yet instead of seeing their frequent civil wars as God's judgment against them and turning south back to Jerusalem, they laugh off their need for a king. Every news story seems to bring fresh evidence of lying politicians, bitter litigation and the failure of their idols to deliver on their promises, yet they simply pick themselves up and carry on as if these things were not the Lord shouting for their attention.[3]

That's why the Lord tells them in 10:5–11 that he will take them into exile as an act of mercy. Their hearts will never become soft enough to receive his mercy and forgiveness any other way.[4] Unless somebody snatches their idols from them and executes their kings, they will never reunite themselves with Judah to worship at the Temple in Jerusalem as devoted followers of the Messiah. The Lord was right about this. The exile in Assyria really was the only thing that brought the survivors of

---

[2] The Lord often likens Israel to a vine in the Scriptures. See Genesis 49:22; Psalm 80:8–16; Hosea 14:7; Isaiah 5:1–7; Jeremiah 2:21; Ezekiel 17:5–8; Matthew 21:33–45; John 15:1–5.

[3] The fact that they fear for the idols that have promised to protect them is pretty damning! Yet still they fail to grasp that this is the fruit of turning *Bethel (House of God)* into *Beth Aven (House of Wickedness)*.

[4] *The days of Gibeah* marked a terrible low point in Israel's history. See 9:9 and Judges 19–21.

Israel back to him. He proclaims that this is his plan: *"I will drive Ephraim... and Jacob must break up the ground."*[5]

The nineteenth-century evangelist Charles Finney preached a very famous sermon on this chapter. He argued that

> *The mind of man is often compared in the Bible to ground, and the Word of God to seed sown therein, the fruit representing the actions and affections of those who receive it... Sometimes your hearts get matted down, hard and dry, till there is no such thing as getting fruit from them till they are broken up, and... fitted to receive the Word.*[6]

Charles Finney was right. Hard-heartedness towards God can be just as big a problem for us, but here's the good news: The prophet Hosea says that we don't have to wait for God's judgment to soften us. We can plough up the hard soil of our hearts ourselves! That's why what happened to the northern kingdom of Israel is so tragic. If they had listened to Hosea in 10:12 and ploughed up the hard soil of their hearts, God would have freely rained his mercy and forgiveness down on them.[7] Instead, we are told in 10:13–15 that they simply increased the size of their army and fortified their cities. God had given the people of Israel the option of revival without ruin: *Blessing or curse – you decide.* But, tragically, they chose to take the second option.[8]

Praise God, we can still choose the first option ourselves, both personally and as churches. If we plough the hard soil

---

[5] It is now after 730 BC, and Judah has begun to pursue the same idolatry as Israel (2 Chronicles 28:1–25). Therefore Hosea 10:11 prophesies that Judah will have to share in Israel's judgment too.

[6] This sermon forms the third of the lectures in his famous *Lectures on Revival* (1835).

[7] *Showers of righteousness* in 10:12 refers to God mercifully forgiving our sin as a result of our repentance.

[8] *Shalman* in 10:14 is short for Shalmaneser, the name of several kings of Assyria.

of our own hearts to adjust our lives to God's Word willingly, we need never feel the sharp and deadly ploughshare of his judgment. Charles Finney continues:

> *If you mean to break up the fallow ground of your hearts, you must begin by looking at your hearts: examine and note the state of your minds, and see where you are. Many never seem to think about this. They pay no attention to their own hearts, and never know whether they are doing well... Do not be in a hurry. Examine thoroughly the state of your hearts, and see where you are... Take up your individual sins one by one, and look at them... It will be a good thing to take a pen and paper, as you go over them, and write them down as they occur to you. Go over them as carefully as a merchant goes over his books; and as often as a sin comes before your memory, add it to the list. General confessions of sin will never do. Your sins were committed one by one and as far as you can come at them, they ought to be reviewed and repented of one by one.*

This may sound strange to you, but I have done it several times and I have found it an incredibly helpful exercise. Listing all my sins of commission (the wrong things that I do) and all my sins of omission (the right things that I don't do) has been very painful, but ploughing is always a painful process for the soil. I have found it to be worth it. It is a very powerful step towards becoming more fruitful. I really recommend it to you.

Jesus quotes from 10:8 in Luke 23:28–31 to warn the first-century Jews that their nation is in the same predicament as ancient Israel. Unless they soften their hearts through reading Scripture, through reflection and through repentant prayer, they are about to be destroyed. Jesus still quotes these verses to many Christians and many churches today. He tries to capture our attention through our personal struggles and our church decline.[9]

So break up the hard ground of your heart. Recognize that only soft ground is able to drink up rain. The Lord wants to shower you with mercy and forgiveness, if you will let him. He doesn't want you to choose the path of judgment: *Blessing or curse – you decide.*

---

[9] Jesus also echoes 10:8 in some of his other New Testament warnings. See Revelation 6:15–17.

A Whole Lot of History
(Hosea 11:1-11)

*When Israel was a child, I loved him, and out of Egypt
I called my son.*

(Hosea 11:1)

One Direction aren't alone in telling the one they love that
they've got a whole lot of history together. They aren't alone in
declaring that they could be the greatest team the world has
ever seen. The Lord sings the same song here, in chapter 11,
in order to convince the people of Israel to take him up on his
offer of mercy and forgiveness without the need for exile. Time
is running out for them but he is still there for them, just as he
always has been.[1]

In 11:1-4, the Lord begins the song by looking back to
when Israel was a child. Like any proud father, he looks back
fondly on the early days of baby Israel being added to his family.
There were only seventy people in Jacob's household when
he settled them in Egypt but they quickly grew into a nation
of over a million. God sent Moses to tell Pharaoh that they had
outgrown their Egyptian nursery: *"Israel is my firstborn son, and
I told you, 'Let my son go, so that he may worship me.' But you
refused to let him go; so I will kill your firstborn son."*[2]

The lyrics of this love song become very tender when the

---

[1] Hosea 11-14 is quite different from Hosea 4-10. The motif for Israel in these
final four chapters is no longer that of an adulterous wife, but that of a wayward
son.

[2] Exodus 4:22-23. The Lord also describes himself as the Father of Israel in
Deuteronomy 32:6.

Lord reminisces about how he taught the toddler Israel to walk. *"I led them with cords of human kindness, with ties of love,"* he remembers, as he thinks back to the pillar of cloud and fire that showed them which way they ought to go during forty years in the desert. He never forced them to follow him – the choice between his blessing and his curse was theirs to take from day one – yet he always made the choice easy for them. *"To them I was like one who lifts a little child to the cheek, and I bent down to feed them."* Whether it was bread or quail or water from the rock, Israel could not have wished for a better Father.

Suddenly the love song changes key. Despite all that he did for them, the Israelites responded with rebellion. They worshipped the harvest god Baal and the other idols of the Canaanites that God dispossessed before them. They were staggeringly ungrateful. He was the perfect Father to them but they responded like the Prodigal Son.

In 11:5–7, the Lord sings the second verse of his love song and it doesn't sound very much like a love song at all. The English playwright William Congreve claimed that *"Hell hath no fury like a woman scorned."*[3] Well, it seems pretty clear that heaven does. The Lord spells out his determination to bring the Prodigal Son back to his senses. Foreign invaders will sack Israel's cities, ridding the land of the false prophets who have prophesied comfort instead of confrontation.[4] Although they call him the Most High God, rather like an estranged son who talks of "Dad" but never rings him, the Lord will expose their dysfunctional family for what it is. Only a handful of Israelites will survive to be slaves in Assyria or to reverse the Exodus by going back to Egypt.

In 11:8–11, the third verse of the song makes it sound a bit more like a love song again. As the Lord looks back over

---

[3] He says this in his tragic play *The Mourning Bride* (1697).

[4] The Hebrew word *bad* in 11:6 means either the *keep* of a fortified city or a *false prophet*. Whichever is intended, the Lord says literally that they will be *eaten* or *gobbled up* in the destruction.

his history with Israel, he declares that he cannot simply treat them like Admah and Zeboyim, the sister cities of Sodom and Gomorrah that he destroyed without survivors, never to be built again.[5] The Lord is not a man so overcome with anger towards his child that he forgets his former love. If they are unwilling to plough up the hard ground of their hearts, he will plough up their hearts for them through the exile so that he is able to change his tune over them. *"My heart is changed within me; all my compassion is aroused. I will not carry out my fierce anger, nor will I devastate Ephraim again."* The Lord's love song therefore ends with a promise that he will roar like a lion – not in judgment, as in Amos 1:2, but to rally their survivors back from Egypt and Assyria to resettle them in the Promised Land.[6]

If this were a complete description of the love song, it would be very beautiful but it would leave many questions unanswered. The biggest would be the one that has run throughout this book: If the people of Israel are as guilty as the Lord says they are, how can he forgive them? Surely justice demands that he treat them in the same way as Admah and Zeboyim, or even worse, since they have chosen to rebel against him despite having far greater revelation of him. That's a really important question, so make sure that you don't miss the answer that the Lord gives throughout his love song.

The answer starts in the very first sentence of the song. The Lord says that Israel is his son, and we know from the New Testament that he also has another, better Son. Hosea 11:1 is quoted in Matthew 2:15 and applied to Jesus as one of the many parallels that the gospel writers draw between the life of Jesus and the history of Israel – that he is the true

---

[5] Genesis 14:8; Deuteronomy 29:23. The Lord mentions these two cities, instead of the more famous Sodom and Gomorrah, in order to emphasize that he erased even their memory from the earth.

[6] The Hebrew word for *dove* in 7:11 and 11:11 is *Jonah*. Just as the prophet Jonah was rebuked by God and sanctified during his mission to Assyria, so would Israel be. Its people would come home different.

seed of Abraham, who went down to Egypt as a refugee and who was baptized in the River Jordan as his own equivalent of crossing the Red Sea, emerging so sinless from his forty days of temptation in the desert, corresponding to Israel's forty years, that he was able to declare himself to be God's true vine, the true and better Israel.[7]

The first time I read Matthew's quotation, I have to confess that I thought he was misquoting Hosea. I didn't know the Bible well enough at the time to realize that this theme runs right through the Old and New Testaments. The only reason why God is able to forgive the people of Israel is that another Israel has agreed to bear their punishment for them. Under the Law of Moses, the fixed penalty for any son who rebelled against his parents was death.[8] In order to forgive Israel, God did not turn his back on these verses of Scripture and on justice. Instead, he turned his back on his Son.

That's the paradox towards the end of this love song: *"I am God, and not a man – the Holy One among you."* The death and resurrection of Jesus is the only reason why the Holy God is able to dwell among sinners. The incarnation of Jesus is the only reason why the human race is able to be forgiven and set free. When God sings this love song today, he has to change the words. He has to sing, *"I am God **and** a man."*[9] Having sung this love song, he came down to earth in person and wrote the final verse of the song with his own blood. It can be found in Romans 6:23, where the Lord sings over his people that:

> *The wages of sin is death, but the gift of God is eternal life in Christ Jesus our Lord.*

---

[7] Matthew 1:1, 17; 1 Corinthians 10:2; Matthew 4:1–11. Compare John 15:1 with Hosea 10:1.

[8] Deuteronomy 21:18–21. This corresponds to Romans 6:23 in the same way that Deuteronomy 21:22–23 corresponds to Galatians 3:13.

[9] We are told in 1 Timothy 2:5 that Jesus is still a man today. He saved us by becoming one of us.

The Day Comes
(Hosea 11:12–13:16)

They will fall by the sword; their little ones will be dashed to the ground, their pregnant women ripped open.

(Hosea 13:16)

When I was about twenty, I was pressured to go on a blind date by a friend. I didn't want to, so I took the coward's way out. I agreed to go but set the date a long way in the future. The date was so many weeks away that, to my mind, it felt like a polite way of saying "no". Never again. You see, there is a problem with dates a long way in the future. The present catches up with them eventually. However far off, the day still comes.

The people of Israel were being about as intelligent as I was as a twenty-year-old. They had listened to God's love song but had decided not to bother ploughing up the hard soil of their hearts. They had concluded that these warnings of judgment described a day a long way off in the future. Chapters 12 and 13 therefore warn that the day will come.

We know Hosea wrote these two chapters less than five years before Israel was destroyed, because in 10:14 he mentions the actions of King Shalmaneser V of Assyria, who only came to the throne in 727 BC.[1] Instead of facing up to their imminent slaughter, we are told in 11:12–12:6 that the people of Israel still think that they can save themselves by playing Egypt and Assyria

---

[1] Although it is technically possible that Hosea is referring to the actions of Shalmaneser IV in 10:14, few people would remember the actions of a king who had been dead and buried for almost 50 years.

off against one another.[2] They think that they can escape the Day of Judgment through clever diplomacy and by weaving a web of lies, just like their ancestor Jacob when he tried to gain God's blessing by disguising himself as his brother and lying to his father. Jacob reaped disaster and so will his children. At least Jacob worshipped God at Bethel, rather than one of their golden calves, and at least he finally repented of struggling against God and started pleading with him for mercy.[3] Time is running out for the Israelites to do the same, because the Lord has put a date against their judgment in his diary.[4]

In 12:7–14, we are told that the people of Israel have not turned from the sins that Hosea confronted in his earlier prophecies. They are still using corrupt business practices. They are still convinced that their wealth can bribe any judge to look the other way – even the Lord on Judgment Day.[5] They are still busy with their empty worship services and with their idols at Gilgal. Instead of repenting when the Assyrians annexed Gilead and the rest of Israel's territory east of the River Jordan in 732 BC, they refused to learn their lesson. Therefore Gilgal is about to become a pile of rubble too.[6]

Once again, the Lord reminds Israel of their history

---

[2] 2 Kings 17:3–4. Hosea likens Israel's foolish foreign policy to trying to catch the wind. He includes the southern kingdom of Judah in this, since 2 Chronicles 28:1–25 says their new king was like the kings of Israel.

[3] Genesis 25:26; 28:11–22; 32:24–32. Hosea is not saying that Jacob overcame the Lord by wrestling, but by stopping wrestling, by admitting his weakness and by begging for the Lord's undeserved favour!

[4] The Hebrew words that Hosea uses for *love* and *justice* in 12:6 are the same words used in Micah 6:8. Micah had recently started prophesying to the southern kingdom, so he may have influenced Hosea.

[5] The Hebrew word for *merchant* in 12:7 means literally a *Canaanite*. Since they are behaving as sinfully as the trading nations that the Lord drove out of the Promised Land, they will soon be driven out too.

[6] 2 Kings 15:29. Hosea 12:11 should therefore be translated, *"Was Gilead wicked? Yes, it's people **were** worthless."* The reference to piles of stones defiling ploughed ground links back to 10:12 and warns that Israel has missed her moment. There is a play on words with *Gilgal* in Hebrew, since the word for a *pile* is *gal*.

together.[7] He used the prophet Moses to bring them up out of Egypt and to care for them in the desert. Why then are they not listening to his prophets now? He took their ancestor Jacob to far-away Mesopotamia to labour hard for the perfect wife, so he will take them into far-off exile in the same direction in order to turn them into the kind of Bride that he is looking for.

In 13:1–8, we are told that the people of Israel spent their last days hardening their hearts instead of ploughing them. Not only have they multiplied their idols, but they have now even started offering human sacrifices on their altars, like the vilest of pagans.[8] In their prosperity they have forgotten God, and in their troubles they have cried out for their idols to save them, instead of to the Lord who is the only Saviour of the world. There was a time when Ephraim was the mightiest tribe in Israel,[9] but as a result of their sin the Lord has set a day to attack them like a leopard, a lion and a bear combined![10]

In 13:9–16, the Lord therefore describes the Day of Judgment that is drawing near on the calendar.[11] Amos never named the nation that would destroy Israel, referring vaguely to somewhere *"beyond Damascus"*, since that day of disaster was over three decades away. In contrast, Hosea names Assyria nine times in his book, and the Hebrew word he uses in 13:7 for *"I will lurk"* looks very similar to the Hebrew for Assyria. The people of Israel have been very foolish to imagine that the Day of the Lord will either never come or else

---

[7] These verses still apply to church leaders today. If we hold gifted prophets at arm's length and keep them on the edge of church life, we miss out on the direction and protection that God wants them to give us.

[8] The Hebrew text of 13:2 is slightly ambiguous about this, but it is stated clearly in 2 Kings 17:17.

[9] Genesis 48:20; Jeremiah 31:9. Ephraim means *Doubly Fruitful*, so Hosea 13:15 uses the Hebrew verb at the root of his name to declare that Ephraim's fruitfulness is over.

[10] Since Israel is the Lord's son, it is fitting that he should feel like a bear bereaved of her cubs.

[11] A literal translation of 13:9 is *"You have destroyed yourself, Israel, but in me is your help."*

be good news for them when it does. God compares them to a baby that lacks the sense to recognize that it has come full term inside its mother and so dies in the womb.[12] Hosea warns the people of Israel not to be so senseless. Their day will surely come. *"The guilt of Ephraim is stored up, his sins are kept on record."*

Very shortly after Hosea prophesied these words, King Shalmaneser of Assyria was furious to catch the king of Israel negotiating a secret treaty with Egypt. He invaded Israel and besieged Samaria in 724 BC. After two years of siege, during which it is said that the people of Israel became so hungry that parents murdered and cooked their own children, the city finally fell in 722 BC. Most of the men of Israel were put to the sword. The pregnant women were fatally stabbed in the belly. Most of the remaining women and children of Israel were thrown to their deaths from the city walls.[13] Only a tiny proportion were deported as captives to Assyria or fled as fugitives to Egypt. Their land was resettled with pagans from another part of the empire.

The day had come. Amos and Hosea had always said it would, and they were vindicated terribly. But don't miss the glimmer of hope as we end this final prophecy of judgment. The Lord promises another day – a day of resurrection for Israel: *"I will deliver this people from the power of the grave; I will redeem them from death. Where, O death, are your plagues? Where, O grave, is your destruction?"*

The apostle Paul quotes this verse when he talks in 1 Corinthians 15:55 about our own resurrection from the dead, because the Lord is always the God of death and resurrection. He doesn't just have a Day of Judgment; he also has a Day of Restoration. These chapters are bleak but they are not hopeless. The Lord will put Israel to death in order to resurrect it as the glorious nation that he always intended it to be.

---

[12] The New Testament also likens God's judgment to the suddenness of childbirth. See 1 Thessalonians 5:3.

[13] 10:14–15; 2 Kings 17. Note that the king of Israel was captured *before* the siege, fulfilling Hosea 13:10.

The Return (Hosea 14:1–9)

"I will heal their waywardness and love them freely,
for my anger has turned away from them."

(Hosea 14:4)

Hosea wrote the final chapter of his book of prophecies after Israel was wiped off the map. We can tell that from the fact that 1:1 tells us that he continued prophesying until at least 715 BC, seven years after Israel was destroyed. The change of tone here is therefore deliberate. Hosea is now speaking to the handful of Israelites who survived.

In 14:1, Hosea asks them to face up to what has just befallen their nation. Note the past tense. *"Return, Israel, to the Lord your God. Your sins have been your downfall!"* Hosea says that Israel was destroyed because its people refused to plough up the hard soil of their hearts, so the Lord had to sharpen the ploughshare of his judgment in order to churn up their hearts for them. Now that the job is over, the Lord repeats that all his promises of restoration are theirs for the taking: *Blessing or curse – you decide.*

That's why, in 14:2, Hosea instructs them in how to repent. He tells them to *"Take words with you and return to the Lord"*, because repentance isn't just about feeling sorry for our sins. It is about voicing how we feel to the Lord. It is also about siding verbally with the Lord against ourselves, even when we do not feel grieved by our sins; in fact, we rather like them.[1] The journey of genuine repentance begins with more than a feeling.

---

[1] This is common and yet ridiculous. We are reminded in 14:1 that even pleasant sins destroy us.

It starts when we use our voices to confess that the Lord hates the sins we love and to ask him to change our hearts to hate those sins too.

Proverbs 18:21 teaches us that our mouths are a vital weapon in returning to the Lord: *"The tongue has the power of life and death."* Romans 10:9–10 adds a bit more detail: *"If you declare with your mouth, 'Jesus is Lord,' and believe in your heart that God raised him from the dead, you will be saved. For it is with your heart that you believe and are justified, and it is with your mouth that you profess your faith and are saved."* So Hosea is echoing the whole of Scripture when he says that coming back to God begins with our mouths: *"Say to him: 'Forgive all our sins and receive us graciously, that we may offer the fruit of our lips.'"*[2]

In 14:3, Hosea continues helping the survivors of Israel to write their own script of repentance. He highlights three things in particular that they need to say to God. First, they need to repent of their reliance on false saviours – for them it was reliance on Assyria or on military might, but for us it might be such things as living morally, attending the right church, getting baptized, signing the right statement of faith or following a gifted leader. These are good things in and of themselves, but they are all toxic when we start to treat them as semi-saviours instead of relying on Jesus alone.[3] Second, Hosea tells them to repent of their wrong view of the Lord, since we can only be saved by God if we come to who he really is. Third, he tells them to repent of the self-centred worldview that treats the poor and helpless as somebody else's problem.

In 14:4–8, Hosea encourages the people of Israel by telling them what the Lord will say to them if they respond to his call to

---

[2] 14:2 says literally *"that we may repay you with our lips, like sacrifices of bulls"*. That's an ancient Israelite way of saying that the real sacrifice God is after from his people is words of grateful worship for their salvation.

[3] Since the Israelites are now in exile, these false saviours are ways of getting back to the Promised Land. Cosying up to their captors or planning an insurrection will not bring them back home. Only the Lord can.

real repentance. However difficult the book of Hosea has been to read in places, it was all worth it to arrive at the gracious promise in 14:4: *"I will heal their waywardness and love them freely, for my anger has turned away from them."* The Lord says that, now that he has dispensed justice to Israel, the first part of his plan is over. He has ploughed up their stony hearts, so they are now able to return to him. Now that he has forced them to eat their fill of his Plan "B", they are able to choose more wisely and lay hold of his Plan "A". The Lord's promise can just as easily be translated as *"I will heal their backsliding"*, so this is far more than the offer of a second shot for Israel. It declares that the Lord has wrought such a deep change in their hearts that they are now ready to choose godliness, *"for it is God who works in you to will and to act in order to fulfil his good purpose"*.[4]

This change in their hearts paves the way for an amazing promise of fruitfulness. The Lord mixes his metaphors in his eagerness to describe such fertility. He will respond to their repentance by becoming like morning dew that makes them blossom back in the Promised Land, and by becoming like underground rivers that make them grow tall like the mighty cedars of Lebanon. He will make them as splendid as an olive tree, as fertile as a field of corn and as sought-after as the vines that produce the famous wines of Lebanon. After their years of grief and separation, they will rejoice in conversation with the Lord. They will marvel out loud to the Lord, as they do in 14:8, that they ever abandoned a God like him for their measly old idols. He will laugh in reply that he is only just getting started on his great plans for them: *"Your fruitfulness comes from me."*[5]

---

[4] Philippians 2:13. The Hebrew word *meshūbāh* in 14:4 literally means *apostasy* or *backsliding*.

[5] The Hebrew verb that is used in 14:8 for God *caring for* Israel looks very similar to the Hebrew word for Assyria and it is the same word that was used in 13:7 to describe God *lurking* like a leopard to attack them. The Hebrew word for *fruitfulness* in 14:8 is the root of the name *Ephraim*, which means *Doubly Fruitful*.

In 14:9, Hosea therefore ends his book of prophecies with a final appeal to the survivors of Israel: *"Who is wise? Let them realize these things. Who is discerning? Let them understand. The ways of the Lord are right; the righteous walk in them, but the rebellious stumble in them."* Not all of the survivors of Israel would make it back home from their Assyrian exile, but only those who learned the lessons that God was trying to teach their nation. They must therefore be wise and discerning and respond wholeheartedly to these fourteen chapters of prophecy. The Lord's ways are right – the people of Israel have proven that by going off after disastrous ways of their own – so Hosea ends his book by asking them to make a clear choice. Unless they choose to walk in God's ways, instead of persisting in rebellion, they will fall again beyond all recovery.

The survivors of Israel were in exile for having ignored the words of Amos and Hosea, but now God allows them to make a fresh decision. They are like Gomer, when Hosea bought her back from her pimp and offered her a chance to restart their marriage. Their national disaster was the Lord's way of opening up a new doorway of hope for their nation.[6] He humbled Israel in order to bring his people back to his great plans for them. That's why he ends by offering them the same choice again that he offered them long ago at Mount Sinai. *Blessing or curse – you decide.*

---

[6] 2 Chronicles 30:1–11, Ezekiel 37:15–28 and Luke 2:36 all tell us that many Israelite survivors made it home and were reunited with Judah. Forget myths about the "Ten Lost Tribes". The Lord brought them home.

Part Two:

Assyria

The Man Who Said "No"
(Jonah 1:1–3)

The word of the Lord came to Jonah son of Amittai:
"Go to the great city of Nineveh"... But Jonah ran
away from the Lord.

(Jonah 1:1–3)

You wouldn't have liked the Assyrians. Nobody did. The inhumanity of their legal system suggests that they didn't even much like one another. People had their ears, noses and lips cut off for relatively minor offences. Husbands were permitted by law to beat up their adulterous wives and to castrate their lovers. People who committed capital offences (and there were a lot of those) were usually skewered on poles and left to die slowly on the city walls. There's a reason why Nahum 3:1 calls Nineveh *"the city of blood"*. The Assyrians were barbaric, even by the brutal standards of their age.

When it came to waging war, the Assyrians invented a whole new scale of brutality. They pioneered the practice of mass deportations. They skinned their captives alive and created mountains of their severed heads. They cut open pregnant women and threw babies and children from the tops of city walls onto the rocks below so that they would not grow up to avenge their dead fathers. They put hooks and ropes through the noses and lips of their prisoners of war, often after gouging out their eyes and cutting out their tongues beforehand. Their aim was to spread terror among their enemies, and it worked.

Frankly, every time I read the ancient accounts I feel pretty terrified of them too.[1]

That's why many people imagine that Jonah said "no" to God's call to go and prophesy to Nineveh because he was scared of the Assyrians. Yet Jonah 4 says this wasn't the reason. It was something far simpler. He said "no" because he hated the Assyrians. He simply didn't want them to be spared from destruction, and he certainly didn't want to help in their salvation. He came from the town of Gath Hepher on the far northern border of Israel, so he knew that his home town would be the first to be conquered if and when the Assyrians invaded Israel.[2] We are meant to sympathize with his logic and to consider whether we are ever like him ourselves. The truth is, all of us are tempted to say "no" to God at times. The book of Jonah shows us why we do and why we mustn't.

The first reason we often say "no" to God is that we are already doing something else. Although it may not appear in your English translation, the first word of the book of Jonah is *and*. It indicates to us that we are only picking up with Jonah partway through his story. We can fill in the blanks from 2 Kings 14:25, where Jonah prophesies to King Jeroboam that the Lord is with him to push back the Arameans and reconquer the northern borderlands of Israel and its territory on the east side of the River Jordan. When Jeroboam believes him and succeeds in extending his borders, Jonah becomes a national hero. That's why the book starts with *and*. Jonah has become a big-shot prophet.

It is much harder to say "yes" to God when we are successful. In our early days, it is easier because we have much less to lose. It requires far more courage for a church leader to make radical

---

[1] See Amos 4:2; Hosea 10:14–15; 13:16; Nahum 3:10, 19.

[2] Jonah wasn't wrong. Gath Hepher was sacked along with the other cities of Zebulun when the Assyrians annexed Galilee from Israel in 732 BC. It had been under Aramean rule for 100 years until very recently, so he felt very sensitive about his home town's vulnerable border position (1 Kings 15:20; 2 Kings 15:29).

changes to a congregation that is growing fast than to one that is struggling. It took Philip more humility in Acts 8 to leave a city in revival to go and meet an Ethiopian on a desert road than it would have done if the church in Samaria had been dragging its feet. Jonah must have felt the same. Why send a national hero like him to Nineveh while importing a foreigner like Amos to preach to Israel?[3]

The second reason we often say "no" to God is that we don't see the world the same way that he does. That's part of what he meant when he warned us in Hosea 4:6 that *"My people are destroyed from lack of knowledge."* The Lord says two things here that prompt Jonah to say "no" to him. First, he calls Nineveh *"the great city"*, which reinforces Jonah's view that its people are a threat to Israel. Second, he mentions that *"its wickedness has come up before me"*, which hardens Jonah in his view that its people do not deserve to be saved.[4] Before we rush to judge him, it's worth noting that the idea that God wants to save people from nations other than Israel was pretty radical at the time.[5] It seems obvious to us today, but to Jonah it must have felt like a massive curveball. His reaction reminds us that we can all develop no-go areas in our minds. If it isn't a particular ethnic group for you, it may be members of the gay and transgender community, or Muslims, or people much richer or poorer or older or younger than you are. Not all of us are as obedient as David Wilkerson was when God called him, out of nowhere, to leave suburbia in order to go and minister to the gangs of New York City.[6]

---

[3] 2 Kings 14:25 indicates that Jonah burst onto the scene as a prophet no later than 790 BC. The events of his book appear to have taken place sometime between then and the arrival of Amos in Israel in 760 BC.

[4] In addition to their infamous cruelty, the Ninevites were rebellious, sexually immoral, exploitative and idolatrous (Nahum 1:11, 14; 3:4, 16).

[5] It should have been obvious from Genesis 12:2–3; 1 Kings 17:8–24; 2 Kings 5:1–15 and 1 Chronicles 16:7–36, but it wasn't. The people of Judah still forget it in Malachi 1:5. Guard your own vision.

[6] He tells his amazing story of what happens when we say "yes" to God in *The Cross and the Switchblade* (1962).

The third reason we often say "no" to God is that we get caught up in other things. I find it fascinating that Jonah does not resist God's command to go by staying, but by going somewhere else! The Lord uses the Hebrew word *qūm* to tell Jonah in 1:2 to *get up* and go to Nineveh, and precisely the same word *qūm* is used in 1:3 to say that Jonah *got up* and went to Tarshish! This may well be the single biggest reason why most of us say "no" to God. We have so many great ideas of what we want to do for God that we have no time left to say "yes" to his own plans for us. As a rich trading station on the southern tip of Spain, Tarshish must have sounded much more attractive to Jonah than Nineveh.[7]

The book of Jonah shows us that the Lord knows best and that we will never truly be fruitful until we shelve our own plans and say "yes" to whatever call he gives us. He knew best when he told Noah to build a boat many miles from the sea, when he told Abraham to swap his house in the greatest city in the world for a nomad's tent in Canaan, when he told Moses to take on the most powerful ruler in the world with nothing but the wooden staff in his hand and when he told Joshua to conquer Jericho by shouting. He knew best when he told Jonah to go and prophesy to Nineveh and, guess what, he knows best when he interrupts whatever you and I are doing today.

So as we begin reading Jonah, take a quiet moment to reflect. What successes in the past are holding you back from saying "yes" to God's fresh call in the present? What blind spots in your view of the world are preventing you from saying "yes" to God's call for you to pioneer an unlikely breakthrough? In what ways are you so busy with plans of your own that you have no room left to say "yes" to the better plans God wants to give you? In what ways are you like Jonah, the man who foolishly said "no" to God?

---

[7] *"Ships of Tarshish"* bring back exotic cargo in 1 Kings 10:22 – gold, silver, ivory, apes and baboons.

Three Sides to a Story
(Jonah 1:4–17)

Jonah was in the belly of the fish three days and
three nights.

(Jonah 1:17)

There is something very unusual about Jonah as a prophet. How can I put it? He doesn't exactly do a lot of prophesying. He speaks one line of prophecy in 3:4, which amounts to only five words in Hebrew and only eight words in English. The rest of the time he largely spends running away and complaining. That ought to strike you as odd.

But Jonah truly deserves his place among the Minor Prophets because he acts out his prophecies instead of speaking them. His famous first chapter isn't just a great children's story. Jonah is acting out a prophetic picture for us on three different levels.[1]

First, we are meant to see what happens in Jonah 1 as a prophetic picture of *God's people*. Since the name Jonah means *Dove* in Hebrew, the Lord provided us with a clue when he used the prophet's name to tell us in Hosea 7:11 that *"Ephraim is like a dove, easily deceived and senseless."* Jonah lacks common sense in this chapter, but it is all for a reason. The Lord is using him, in spite of himself, to offer a stern rebuke to his nation.

Jonah epitomizes the religion of Israel. He is devout on the

---

[1] We also saw this in Hosea 1–3. What a prophet does is as important as what a prophet says.

outside but rebellious on the inside.[2] We can tell he isn't really interested in pursuing a relationship with the Lord, because we are told three times that he is trying to run away from him.[3] He wants the trappings of missionary work in Tarshish without the challenge of actually having to partner with God. He substitutes Tarshish for Nineveh in the same way that the people of Israel substituted their golden calf at Bethel for the Temple in Jerusalem. Just like Israel, Jonah is unaware of how much his rebellion is weakening and impoverishing him.[4] At the end of the chapter, the Lord arranges a free ride for him all the way to Nineveh, but he has to pay a costly fare to get himself to Tarshish under his own steam.

Jonah's storm mirrors the national calamity that is heading Israel's way. The pagan sailors cry out to their own idols, but Jonah mimics Israel's spiritual deadness by going to sleep instead of praying to the Lord. The captain's rebuke is as much for the whole northern kingdom as it is for Jonah: *"How can you sleep? Get up and call on your God!"*[5]

Despite Jonah's sin, the Lord remains in charge of the situation.[6] When the sailors cast lots to find out who has caused the storm, the Lord fixes the outcome to force Jonah to face up to his actions. He finds deliverance by confessing to the pagans that he has failed in his calling – *"I know that it is my fault that*

---

[2] This is the tragic irony of Jonah. He thinks he is a big-shot prophet, but he is actually just as bad as Israel.

[3] This is impossible (Psalm 139:7–10). It is also ironic. The same Hebrew word used in 1:2 for Nineveh's wickedness coming up *before* the Lord is also used three times in 1:3 and 10 for Jonah fleeing *before* the Lord.

[4] Even if he misses it, we are meant to spot his downward spiral when we are told that *he went down to Joppa, went down below deck and sank down to the roots of the mountains* (1:3, 5; 2:6).

[5] Jonah is on his own in his cabin. There is no mention in the whole book of his having a friend. This partly explains why he was spiritually asleep. Praying and worshipping with others helps us to come alive.

[6] The same is true of the sleeping Western Church. Because it failed to go to the nations with the Gospel so that they could be saved, the Lord has brought the nations of the world to Western cities instead.

this great storm has come upon you" – and by embracing God's death-and-resurrection pathway.[7] All of this mirrors what Israel needs to do to avoid its own impending destruction.[8]

There is also a second side to the story. We are also meant to see this chapter as a prophetic picture of *God's power to save.* Since we are likely to feel as little love for the faceless thousands of Assyrians as Jonah, the Lord introduces us to a group of salty sailors and their captain so that we will feel in miniature his love for the whole world.[9] These pagans are devout. They cry out to their idols and are conscience-stricken about having to throw Jonah overboard. They are the kind of people who would be saved if only Jonah and his fellow Israelites woke up to the Gospel harvest all around them.

Hosea taught us that salvation comes through knowledge of the Lord, and it doesn't take much of it to save this bunch of pagans. The moment they cajole a basic Gospel statement out of Jonah – *"I worship the Lord, the God of heaven, who made the sea and the dry land"* – they immediately respond in faith to the little they have heard. They give up trying to save themselves through their own strength on the oars and confess instead that the Lord is sovereign over everything – the storm that blows, the lots they cast and the fate of the Hebrew that they are throwing overboard.[10] They cry out to the Lord as they offer Jonah as a sacrifice to appease his anger and, when the storm stops suddenly, their salvation is spiritual as well as physical:

---

[7] This shows why Israel needed to be judged by God in order to find its way back to him. Before the storm comes, the Lord appears weak to Jonah and the sailors (1:10). In the storm they discover his power (1:9).

[8] When a nation is in turmoil, we ought to at least consider the possibility that the turmoil might be the result of churches failing to speak out the Gospel. Jonah was awakened by the storm, and so must we be.

[9] The Hebrew word for *sailors* in 1:5 means literally *salty men*. Israel was to be salt and light to the nations but slept instead (Matthew 5:13–16). Therefore God will find salty men and women among the pagans.

[10] Proverbs 16:33. This is vital because salvation comes through faith that Jesus is *Lord* (Romans 10:9).

"The men greatly feared the Lord, and they offered a sacrifice to the Lord and made vows to him."[11] As a missionary to the pagans, Jonah demonstrates what God can do through us when we educate unbelievers about him.

The third side to the story is that we are meant to see this chapter as a prophetic picture of *God's means of salvation.* How can these pagan sailors be saved so easily? How can such a disobedient prophet be forgiven by the Lord? The answer is found in a statement that Jonah probably does not even realize is prophecy as he says it. When he tells the sailors to seek salvation by throwing him overboard, the Lord uses it to prophesy the death and resurrection of his Son, Jesus the Messiah. Whatever else may be his failings, Jonah is at least willing to sacrifice his own life to save the pagan crew, so God uses him as a symbol of the loving sacrifice of Jesus for the world. There are no fish in the Mediterranean Sea large enough to swallow a man, but the Lord demonstrates his sovereignty in our salvation by providing one at the exact spot it is needed. Jonah spends three days and nights in its belly as a symbol of Christ's burial and resurrection.

Jesus spoke about the three sides to this story. He described the shortcomings of Israel, he proclaimed the Holy Spirit's power to save and he declared that what happened to Jonah was a prophecy of his own work to save us. He told the crowds in Matthew 12:38–41 that:

> *As Jonah was three days and three nights in the belly of a huge fish, so the Son of Man will be three days and three nights in the heart of the earth. The men of Nineveh will stand up at the judgment with this generation and condemn it; for they repented at the preaching of Jonah, and now one greater than Jonah is here.*

---

[11] The sailors address God by his covenant name *Yahweh* in 1:14. The Lord treats their obedience to the prophet's instruction that there can be no salvation without blood sacrifice as genuine faith in the Messiah.

Jonah may be very foolish in this chapter, but God uses him to prophesy loud and clear all the same. God is far more powerful to save than you realize. All you have to do is open your mouth and give him a few words to use. Because of the great sacrifice that was prophesied by Jonah in the storm, God's salvation is never far away from anyone.

What's That Smell?
(Jonah 2:1–10)

From inside the fish Jonah prayed to the Lord his God.
(Jonah 2:1)

There are plenty of sweet-smelling miracles in the Bible. There's the fresh bread that the Israelites ate for forty years in the desert, there's the olive oil that Elisha told a widow would not run dry, there's the water that Jesus turned into expensive wine and there's the great fish that swallowed Jonah. Don't be so overcome by the stench of the fish's belly that you miss the sweet aroma of these ten short verses.

Many people do miss it. This is the point at which they check out of the story. Since it is impossible for a human to survive for three days in the belly of a whale, they conclude that the book of Jonah must be a parable rather than a real event in history.[1] They treat it like the moment when Pinocchio is swallowed by a whale in the Disney movie – entertaining and enlightening, but entirely fictional. Conservative scholars tend to respond by telling the story of James Bartley, an English whaler who fell overboard off the coast of the Falkland Islands in 1891, was swallowed by a sperm whale and was cut out of its stomach when his crewmates harpooned it thirty-six hours later. Although his skin had been permanently bleached by the acids in the whale's stomach, he lived to tell the tale for forty-

---

[1] The Hebrew text of Jonah does not actually tell us that he was swallowed by a whale. The word *dāg* simply means *fish*. The Greek word *kētos* in Matthew 12:40 means *large sea creature*. It may well have been a whale, but Scripture does not actually specify what sea creature God used to perform this miracle.

three years.[2] They therefore argue that Jonah must be viewed as history.

Both sides are missing the point. It is profoundly impossible for a person to survive for three days in the belly of a sea creature. Even if the story of James Bartley is true (and the historical evidence suggests it isn't) it proves nothing, since Jonah was in the fish's belly for twice as long as the English whaler. We are to view these events as historical because Jesus does so in Matthew 12:38–41, pointing out that his Father proves his Gospel to the world by performing the impossible.[3] Jesus healed the blind, the deaf, the lame and the leprous in order to demonstrate that he had not given up on them. He raised the dead to life in order to proclaim that the Gospel is a promise of resurrection. In the same way, the Lord performed a miracle for Jonah in order to prophesy to Israel and Nineveh and the rest of the world that there was hope for them. If they surrendered to the prophet's Gospel message, they could all enjoy the sweet smell of salvation.

These verses carry the sweet smell of *a new Jonah*. The prophet was rebuked by a pagan sailor for his prayerlessness in chapter 1, but here we find him praying fervently in the fish's belly. It is not a prayer for God to save him from the fish, but a prayer of thanks that God has saved him from the sea, and a complete recalibration of his life's priorities. Jonah confesses that, as he sank down to the bottom of the Mediterranean Sea, he realized that his greatest joy was his experience of the presence of the Lord. That's significant because we were told three times in chapter 1 that he tried to run away from the presence of the Lord, so this prayer marks a major turnaround in the prophet's

---

[2] This incident was reported in the English newspaper *The Yarmouth Mercury* on 22nd August 1891. Hailed as a true story at the time, modern investigations suggest that it was a sailor's yarn.

[3] This miracle does not make Jonah any less historical as a book than the healing miracles of Jesus make the gospels unhistorical. The God of the impossible used it to back up his prophet's message.

attitude. He has realized that he wants to know God more than anything in the world.

These verses also carry the sweet smell of *a new Israel*. We discovered in Amos and Hosea that one of Israel's biggest sins was turning away from the Temple in Jerusalem and worshipping idols at shrines across the northern kingdom. Jonah personified this sin in chapter 1, so now he personifies his nation's repentance by turning his face back to the Temple in Jerusalem. *"I have been banished from your sight; yet I will look again towards your holy temple... When my life was ebbing away, I remembered you, Lord, and my prayer rose to you, to your holy temple."* If we are in any doubt that his "resurrection from the dead" is a prophecy about what will happen to his nation if it repents, our doubts are removed at the end of his prayer: *"Those who cling to worthless idols turn away from God's love for them. But I, with shouts of grateful praise, will sacrifice to you."* Jonah is not just describing his own path back to wholehearted faith in the Lord, but pointing the way for his nation to follow. He confesses that God has judged him for his sin and believes that God will save him if he turns back to the Temple in Jerusalem.[4]

These verses also carry the sweet smell of *a new Nineveh*. When Jonah recommits himself to God's purposes for his nation, he finds faith that God will use someone from Israel to save the cruel Assyrian city.[5] Their sinful actions flow from their worship of brutal deities such as Ashur and Ishtar and Nergal, but if they renounce their worthless idols, God's mercy is theirs for the taking. If they repent of their sin and ask the

---

[4] In Amos 4, the Israelites refused to attribute their misfortunes to God's hand of judgment against them. In contrast, even though the sailors threw him overboard, Jonah attributes their action to God's hand in 2:3.

[5] Jonah uses the Hebrew word *she'ōl* in 2:2, which can either mean *the realm of the dead* or *hell*. David prophesied in Psalm 139:7-10 that, even if we try to flee from the presence of the Lord to *she'ōl*, he can rescue us from there. Having experienced what it will be like for Israel and Nineveh unless they repent, and having experienced the grace that could be theirs, Jonah recommits his life to prophesying to them.

Lord to save them, he will perform the same miracle for them that he performed for Jonah. Having saved his prophet from certain death, he will save their city from certain destruction. Jonah therefore vows to stop running away from God's plan to save the nations. He will go to Nineveh and prophesy whatever words God gives him. *"What I have vowed I will make good. I will say, 'Salvation comes from the Lord.'"*

As a consequence, the final verse of Jonah 2 carries the sweet smell of *a new hope for the world*. As Jonah wipes the vomit from his clothes on the closest beach to Nineveh, he testifies to God's power to save. There are no whale-sized creatures in the Mediterranean Sea, but the Lord brought one through the Strait of Gibraltar to the right spot at the right time in order to save him when he was thrown overboard, then he directed it to the far north-eastern corner of the sea and instructed it to vomit Jonah onto dry land.[6] Don't miss the way that this detail proclaims that God is in complete control. Whether it is a prophet who spends three days and three nights inside a fish, or a Messiah who spends three days and three nights inside a tomb, the Lord will do whatever it takes to save the world and no power of hell can ever thwart his saving plan.

The final words of Jonah's prayer mean literally, *"Salvation belongs to the Lord."* They add to the confession of faith that he made to the sailors in 1:9, that God created the world and is sovereign over everything that happens in it. Now he proclaims that God wields this sovereignty in order to save the world that he has made.

What's that smell? It's the sweet scent of salvation for Jonah, for Israel, for Nineveh and for the whole world. Enjoy the aroma as the prophet washes vomit from his clothes.

---

[6] Nineveh was 400 miles away from the Mediterranean coastline, so the fish vomited Jonah on the beach closest to it and he had to walk from there. The fish had to vomit him onto dry land because most people in the ancient world could not swim. Had the Lord not commanded this, Jonah would probably have drowned.

Word Power (Jonah 3:1–10)

Forty more days and Nineveh will be overthrown.

(Jonah 3:4)

Who do you think was the most successful Gospel preacher in the Bible? It wasn't John the Baptist, who gathered crowds by the River Jordan. It wasn't Peter, who preached a sermon twenty-seven verses long on the Day of Pentecost and saw 3,000 people saved and baptized. Every preacher in the Bible is beaten hands down by Jonah.

Jonah only preaches five words in Hebrew or eight words in English: *"Forty more days and Nineveh will be overthrown."*[1] His sermon is surly and taciturn, as if preached through gritted teeth, indicating that his repentance in the fish's belly was short-lived.[2] It reminds me of the way my children apologize to one another when I force them to do so against their will. But here's the thing: Jonah's reluctance doesn't stop the Lord from converting the entire city of Nineveh. That's the power that God's Word carries to save.

The odds are hugely stacked against Jonah. Nineveh straddled the junction of the River Tigris and River Khoser, making it the largest and most prosperous city in the world. Three times in the book of Jonah it is hailed as *"the great city"*, and 3:3 emphasizes that *"Nineveh was a very large city; it took*

---

[1] Even if this is an abridged account of Jonah's sermon, it is abridged in order to emphasize that it was paltry and inadequate. We discover in chapter 4 how reluctant Jonah was to preach it at all.

[2] Note how much 3:1–2 echoes 1:1–2. Whenever we disobey God, we waste chapters of our lives.

three days to go through it."[3] Even if we take this to mean that the city took three days to explore rather than to traverse, it was still enormous by the standards of its age. It was home to anywhere up to a million people, so Jonah's hurried words of prophecy were likely to be lost in the clamour of the city.[4]

Add to this the fact that Nineveh was also enormously sinful. It was not yet the capital, but it was already the most influential city in the Assyrian Empire. It embodied everything we read about their cruelty. This was a city that castrated adulterers and skewered people on poles for insulting the king, so we might have expected it to respond to Jonah's stark and threatening sermon by castrating and skewering him too. Instead, they do the very last thing we expected. They take God at his word and repent wholeheartedly. Then they take the words of Jonah's sermon directly to their king.[5]

Unlike the kings of Israel, who ignored the words of Amos and Hosea, the Assyrian king reacts swiftly. He doesn't just command his citizens to fast from food and to wear sackcloth under their clothes. He commands them to make all of their animals fast and wear sackcloth too! He leads the entire city in a united act of repentance. *"Let everyone call urgently on God. Let them give up their evil ways and their violence. Who knows? God may yet relent and with compassion turn from his fierce anger so that we will not perish."*

All of this is meant to convince us that God can save people through us too. We can all share the Gospel more adequately than Jonah, so we can all expect God to save people through us

---

[3] See 1:2; 3:2 and 4:11. Nineveh was also one of the most ancient cities in the world (Genesis 10:11–12).

[4] Historians are divided over the population of ancient Nineveh. It is possible that 4:11 describes the total population, but it is equally possible that *"120,000 people who cannot tell their right hand from their left"* refers only to the babies and infants in the city.

[5] Nineveh was not yet the formal capital of Assyria, but the king was evidently in the city. This was either Adad-Nirari III (811–783 BC) or one of his sons, Shalmaneser IV (783–773 BC) or Ashur-Dan III (773–755 BC).

when we share. This chapter warns us not to make the same false assumption as the people of Israel, that the unbelievers all around us are not interested in our message. The Hebrew words that are translated as *"a very large city"* in 3:3 mean literally *"a great city belonging to God"*. In other words, this godless city wasn't godless at all. It was just waiting for a Gospel preacher to arrive.[6]

The king's decree can also be translated literally as *"Let everyone call violently on God. Let them repent of their evil ways and of the violence of their hands."* In other words, God used even the violence of the Assyrians to bring them to salvation! In the same way, he uses the devout faith of Muslims, the superstition of Reiki healers, the passion of partygoers and the curiosity of scientists to save them too. When we doubt that God can save people through us, our doubt is not in ourselves. Our doubt is in the power of his Word.

This chapter is also meant to convince us that God can work through us to save people from any nation or any sector of society. The Ninevites worshipped savage idols, yet God was able to save them despite the gaping holes in Jonah's message. He omits to tell them that God is the Creator of the universe (see 1:9), that he loves them and will forgive them if they throw away their idols (see 2:8–9), or that they need to offer a blood sacrifice that points towards the death of the coming Saviour (see 1:12).[7] Nevertheless, God is able to use his fumbling message to save an entire city that knows very little about him. Even the mighty king of Assyria exchanges his royal finery for sackcloth and grovels in the dust for God to save him. That's the irresistible power of God's Word.

---

[6] That's why Jonah is such a tragic book. Imagine what God might have done had many other Israelites gone to preach the Gospel in pagan cities. Imagine what he might do if many Christians did the same today.

[7] Strangely, Jonah does not even mention his miraculous deliverance from death in the belly of a sea creature. Perhaps his bleached skin proclaimed this for him, but there is nothing in the text to indicate that it did.

If we want to see people saved ourselves, all we have to do is ensure that what we are preaching is actually God's Word. Jonah's sermon is short on detail, but it is extremely courageous. When we share the Gospel, things are often the other way round. We share plenty of detail about God's love and mercy, but we fear to describe his righteous anger towards sin. We tend to talk about how much conversion to Christ will improve people's lives, without telling them that it is the only way in which they can escape God's impending judgment that is bearing down upon them.[8]

When Billy Graham was asked to explain how he had seen so many tens of thousands saved through his Gospel preaching, he dated all of his successes back to a decision to preach the Word of God in all of its offensive glory:

> *As that night wore on, my heart became heavily burdened. Could I trust the Bible?... I had to have an answer. If I could not trust the Bible, I could not go on... "O God! There are many things in this book I do not understand. There are many problems with it for which I have no solution. There are many seeming contradictions. There are some areas in it that do not seem to correlate with modern science."*
>
> *I was trying to be on the level with God, but something remained unspoken. At last the Holy Spirit freed me to say it. "Father, I am going to accept this as Thy Word – by **faith**! I'm going to allow faith to go beyond my intellectual questions and doubts, and I will believe this to be your inspired Word." When I got up from my knees... I sensed the presence and power of God as I had not sensed it in months. Not all my questions were answered, but a major bridge had been crossed. In*

---

[8] This is the message that was modelled to us in Amos 5:4, 6 and 14 – *"Seek good, not evil, that you may live."*

my heart and mind, I knew a spiritual battle in my soul
had been fought and won.[9]

So share the Word of God with people. Don't share parts of it.
Share it all. If you want to lead people to salvation, Jonah says
that all you need is the raw power of God's Word.

---

[9] Billy Graham recalls this as his major turning point in his autobiography *Just
As I Am* (1997).

The Lives of Others
(Jonah 4:1–11)

But to Jonah this seemed very wrong, and he
became angry.

(Jonah 4:1)

Most of us are very grateful when God extends his grace towards us. We are less grateful, however, when he extends it towards the lives of others. We might have expected Jonah to be elated that his five words had saved a city, making him per word the most successful evangelist of all time. But he wasn't. He was furious with the Lord.

We have already seen that one of the most remarkable words in Amos 7 is *nāham*, which means *to change one's mind*. When Amos prayed for Israel, we are told twice that *"The Lord changed his mind"* and poured out his lavish mercy on a sinful nation. Jonah does not pray for Nineveh but its citizens pray for themselves and, as a result, the word *nāham* appears again in the final two verses of Jonah 3. The king says literally, *"Who knows? God may yet **change his mind** and with compassion turn from his fierce anger so that we will not perish."* He is right. *"When God saw what they did and how they turned from their evil ways, he **changed his mind** and did not bring on them the destruction he had threatened."*[1]

The prophet is furious. He refuses to believe that God has actually decided to forgive the Assyrians instead of destroying them. He prophesied that God would destroy the city after forty days, so he builds himself a shelter outside the city walls and watches from

---

[1] Jonah repeatedly emphasizes God's sovereignty (1:4, 15, 17; 2:10; 4:6, 7, 8). God only "changes his mind" because he has purposed that his perfect plans for the world will be triggered through our prayers.

a distance.[2] Once again, he epitomizes the entire northern kingdom as he refuses to extend God's grace towards the lives of others. Although the Lord revealed himself to Moses in Exodus 34:6–7 as *"a gracious and compassionate God, slow to anger and abounding in love, a God who relents from sending calamity"*, Jonah complains when the Lord displays the same character towards those who live outside the borders of Israel.[3] He betrays a callous nationalism in 4:2 when he refers to Israel literally as *"my land"*, and in 4:3 when he tells the Lord that he would rather die than see God's mercy extended towards the pagan nations.[4] He even attempts to rewrite his own story by claiming that his flight to Tarshish was a noble action to promote the welfare of God's chosen people.[5]

The Lord uses his sulking prophet as a parable of Israel's sinfulness.[6] He causes a leafy plant to grow up over Jonah to shade him from the sun, then sends a worm to kill it and causes the sun to shine so hard on the prophet's head that he declares for a second time that he would rather die than have to live within God's plan.[7]

[2] The Hebrew word for *shelter* in 4:5 is *sukkāh*, the same word that is used for David's fallen *shelter* in Amos 9:11. This is intentional, emphasizing how different Jonah's vision for the Gentile nations is from the Lord's.

[3] The Hebrew word for *relents* in 4:2 is *nāham*. The word for *calamity* is *rā'āh*, which is also used to describe the *evil deeds* of the Ninevites in 1:2; 3:8 and 3:10. Those who try to make a distinction between the "vengeful God" of the Old Testament and the "loving God" of the New Testament don't understand the book of Jonah, since he complains here that the God of the Old Testament is too loving! See Acts 5:1–11 and Hebrews 13:8.

[4] Jonah has witnessed God's total sovereignty over the actions of sea creatures (1:17) and pagan sailors (2:3), yet he is still too blind to see that God is passionately concerned about the fate of every single human being.

[5] This and Jonah's courage in 3:4 show us that he did not flee to Tarshish for fear that he would be killed by the Ninevites. He fled for fear that God would actually save them! Jonah's home town of Gath Hepher was on the northern border of Israel and felt threatened by Assyria, so he wanted them destroyed.

[6] The fact that he built his shelter *"east of the city"* meant that the city walls offered him no protection from the noonday sun or from the hottest breezes. Jonah lacked common sense as well as compassion.

[7] The first time, Jonah claims to be annoyed for the sake of God's people. The second time, it is obvious that he is actually annoyed at his own inconvenience. He wants the world to revolve around him, not his Creator.

In 4:9, the Lord repeats the question that he asked Jonah in 4:4: *"Is it right for you to be angry?"* When Jonah insists that it is right and wishes himself dead for a third time, the Lord uses his love for the plant to expose his lack of love for the 120,000 innocent babies and toddlers who live in Nineveh.[8] Since the Hebrew word for the leafy plant means literally *a plant that makes you want to vomit,* we are meant to view this as a picture of Israel's nauseating self-centredness.[9] They don't just want the Lord to bless them. They also want him to curse everybody else. They don't want God to prosper them for the sake of reaching the Gentiles, but at the expense of the Gentiles.

The Lord's final words to Jonah are therefore a prophetic warning to the entire northern kingdom of Israel. He refuses to tolerate their selfish attitude any longer. He is God of all the earth, not just of Israel.[10] He created their nation by promising Abraham in Genesis 12 that *"I will make you into a great nation, and I will bless you... and all peoples on earth will be blessed through you."* If they are willing to embrace this Plan "A", he will bless them and use them as his team of willing missionaries throughout the earth. But if, like Jonah, they insist on his Plan "B" for their nation, he will curse them and use their destruction as a warning to the nations. The Lord issues the same warning through Jonah that he issued through Amos and Hosea: *Blessing or curse – you decide.*

These words are also a prophetic warning to the Church today. Many Jews have counted themselves out of Israel's story and many Gentiles have counted themselves in, but the basic

---

[8] The same Hebrew word *hūs* is used for Jonah *having compassion* on the leafy plant in 4:10 and the Lord *having compassion* on Nineveh in 4:11.

[9] The Lord does not mention the guilty men and women in the city, focusing solely on the innocent infants and animals (Isaiah 7:14–16). He does so in order to refer literally to *"twelve times ten thousand people"*, emphasizing that his salvation plans extend far beyond the 12 tribes of Israel.

[10] Genesis 18:25; Joshua 3:11; Psalm 47:7; 97:5; Isaiah 54:5; Micah 4:13; Zechariah 4:14; Revelation 7:9–10.

choice for God's people remains the same.[11] He wants to bless his obedient Church and send them out as missionaries to the nations so that people everywhere will respond to his Gospel. If the Church refuses and seeks to grow fat on his blessings instead of sharing them with unbelievers, he will destroy and scatter them.

The book of Jonah does not tell us whether or not the prophet repented of his self-absorption and of his ungodly hatred towards the pagans. This is deliberate, since it invites the reader to write their own chapter 5. Will we be distracted by the equivalent of Jonah's leafy plant – self-indulgent trinkets that ultimately do not matter – or will we follow the example of Jesus by pouring out our lives for the world?[12]

Personally, I think there was a happy ending to Jonah's story. Since all the other Minor Prophets appear to have compiled their own books of prophecy, there is no reason to assume that Jonah was an exception. It seems then that he portrays himself so honestly for the sake of his countrymen because he wanted his own failures to instruct Israel. Furthermore Hosea 11:11, which was written shortly after the book of Jonah, can be translated as a promise that Israel will repent during their exile and come back either *"like a dove from Assyria"*, or *"like Jonah from Assyria"*.

Whether or not the prophet Jonah repented, he hands us his pen and asks us to write our own chapter 5. Will you embrace God's Plan "A" to reach unbelievers through you, or will you choose his Plan "B" of self-absorption and of discipline by God. The book of Jonah warns us to make our choice wisely: *Blessing or curse – you decide.*

---

[11] The Church has not replaced the Jewish nation. The Lord still continues Israel's story through those Jews and Gentiles who accept Jesus as Israel's Messiah. Compare Exodus 19:5–6 with 1 Peter 2:5–12.

[12] Jonah's escape from the fish's belly prefigures the death and resurrection of Jesus, but his response to the sinfulness of Nineveh is nothing like Jesus' response to sinful Jerusalem in Luke 13:34 and 19:41–42.

Watch and See
(Nahum 1:1–15)

Look… Judah… No more will the wicked invade you;
they will be completely destroyed.

(Nahum 1:15)

Nahum never met Jonah. He prophesied in around 630 BC, so he was born about a century after Jonah died.[1] Nevertheless, the two men were close partners in three ways.

First and most obviously, both men prophesied against the city of Nineveh. Second, both men appear to have been Galilean northerners. Since the name Nahum means *Comfort* in Hebrew, many believe that the town of Capernaum in Galilee means *The Town of Nahum* rather than *The Town of Comfort*.[2] Third, although both men prophesied to Nineveh, they were very conscious that they were doing so for the sake of the twelve tribes of Israel. Jonah recorded his own successes and failures as a missionary to Nineveh in order to convict the northern kingdom of Israel that it needed to repent of resisting God's plan to save the nations through them. Nahum says nothing in his book to suggest that he went in person to Nineveh. He appears to have prophesied to the Assyrians via open letters from Judah, expecting the people of the southern kingdom to learn as much

---

[1] Nahum's prophecies are undated, but 3:8–10 mentions the fall of Thebes, which took place in 663 BC, and 1:11 talks about a strong Assyrian ruler, the last of whom died in 627 BC. Since Nahum treats the fall of Nineveh as an imminent event, he therefore probably prophesied these chapters in c. 630 BC.

[2] Nahum is described as an *Elkoshite* in 1:1, but nobody knows if this refers to his home town or to his clan.

from his predictions as the Ninevites. The big theme of Nahum 1 includes them: *Watch and see.*

The people of Judah had been watching the city of Nineveh for over a century since it repented under Jonah. The Lord had done more than simply spare it in response to its repentance. He had turned it into by far the world's most powerful city. The people of Judah had watched in horror as the reforms of King Tiglath-Pileser III (745–727 BC) turned him into one of the greatest military commanders in history. They had seen him conquer most of the known world and then turn his greedy eyes towards Israel.

The people of Judah had watched Tiglath-Pileser conquer and destroy the kingdom of Aram in 732 BC. Later that same year, they had seen him strip Israel of Galilee in the north and of its territory east of the River Jordan. They had seen the way the king of Israel tried to take advantage of Tiglath-Pileser's death by signing a treaty with Egypt to fight together against Assyria, and how the new king Shalmaneser V heard the news in Nineveh and marched south-west to besiege Samaria. They had looked on in horror as he captured Israel's capital in 722 BC, wiping out the ten northern tribes and carrying off the few survivors into captivity. Two decades later, it had been Judah's turn to be invaded. They had watched King Sennacherib conquer most of their territory, before being repulsed by a last-minute miracle through the prayers of the prophet Isaiah and King Hezekiah in 701 BC. Nahum knows that the people of Judah feel that they have been watching and seeing the evil deeds of Nineveh for far too long.[3]

That's why he prophesies in 1:2–8 that what they watch and see is all about to change. It has not escaped the Lord's notice that Nineveh is just as sinful now as it was before Jonah preached the Gospel in the city. The people of Judah must not

---

[3] 2 Kings 15:29; 16:9; 17:3–6. So Jonah was right: Gath Hepher did fall to the people of Nineveh.

mistake God's patience for passivity. *"The Lord is a jealous and avenging God... The Lord is slow to anger but great in power; the Lord will not leave the guilty unpunished."* Nahum describes the wrath of God bursting forth from Jerusalem and north towards Nineveh – past Mount Carmel and Bashan, to the west and east of Lake Galilee, and over the mountain ranges of Lebanon.[4] The people of Judah are about to witness God's patience coming to an end.

Although these verses describe the fate of the Assyrians, Nahum makes it clear that he is describing these things for the sake of the people of Judah. He uses God's covenant name *Yahweh*, meaning *the Lord*, because these events will teach Israel the true character of its God. He is love, but that doesn't mean tolerance. It means fierce vengeance towards anyone who harms the people he has made and fierce jealousy towards anyone who worships a false idol instead of their true Lord.[5] It means that the Lord patiently stores up his wrath against his enemies and appoints a Day of Judgment to deal with them.[6] It means that he longs to save people from the judgment that is coming, but that he will not hold back his hand from those who spurn his offer of salvation. So Nahum turns to the people of Judah with a promise: *"The Lord is good, a refuge in times of trouble. He cares for those who trust in him."* Then he turns

---

[4] Bashan, Carmel and Lebanon were famous for their rainfall and fertility. The fact that their rivers will run dry and their fields wither therefore proclaims the Lord's power to destroy prosperous Nineveh.

[5] God's character is described in 1 John 4:8 and 16 *and* in Exodus 20:5 and 34:14. Only grasping one half of God's character gives us a false view of him. The Bible condemns this as idolatry.

[6] Nahum 1:2 tells us literally that the Lord *keeps in reserve* his wrath against his enemies. This is a very important principle that is repeated in Psalm 10:11–14 and 94:7–10; Ezekiel 8:12–18 and 9:9–10; and Zephaniah 1:12–18. Although Nahum is never quoted in the New Testament, Paul appears to have this verse in mind in Romans 2:5. When God appears to have overlooked people's sins, don't be fooled. He is storing up a pay packet to dispense on the payday that he has set for them (Romans 6:23; 1 Timothy 5:24).

north-east with a warning: *"But with an overwhelming flood he will make an end of Nineveh."*[7]

In 1:9–15, Nahum uses this promise as a springboard from which to prophesy that God is about to delight the people of Judah by destroying evil Nineveh. The Lord has not failed to notice King Ashurbanipal's wicked plans or the heavy burden that he has placed on Judah by turning it into one of his vassal territories.[8] Nahum talks to Nineveh and predicts its doom in 1:11–14, before turning to the people of Judah in 1:15 and predicting that they will rejoice over its destruction.[9] He echoes the words of Isaiah 52:7, spoken over sixty years earlier, when he prophesies that a messenger will come to Jerusalem with a message of peace. Their one-time invader will be no more. The Lord will proclaim his message of salvation to the people of Judah.[10]

The kingdom of Aram had failed to repent when Amos prophesied, and it had been destroyed. The kingdom of Israel had failed to repent when Amos, Hosea and Jonah prophesied, and it had been destroyed too. The city of Nineveh had repented at the preaching of Jonah, but its change of heart had been short-lived. By the time of Nahum, its actions were as cruel as ever. That's why the Lord tells the people of Judah to watch and see. They are about to witness one of the most sudden downfalls in world history.

---

[7] We will discover what this cryptic warning means when we look at 2:8 together.

[8] 2 Chronicles 33:10–13. Nahum 1:11 must be referring to King Ashurbanipal (669–627 BC), since he was the last great king of Assyria and was even more brutal than his predecessors to the cities that he conquered.

[9] The Hebrew text does not include the words *"O Nineveh"* in 1:11 and 14 and *"O Judah"* in 1:12, but they are included in many English translations for the sake of modern readers to explain what Nahum is saying. The words *"O Judah"* do appear in the Hebrew text of 1:15 and they form the great crescendo of chapter 1.

[10] There are several subtle prophecies about Jesus in these verses. The *seed* of Nineveh will be destroyed so that the seed of Abraham can flourish (1:14 and Galatians 3:16) and come to preach the Gospel to the people of Judah (the singular participle in 1:15 points to Matthew 4:17 and Mark 1:15).

The Impossible
(Nahum 2:1–13)

The river gates are thrown open and the palace collapses.

(Nahum 2:6)

The Lord loves to prophesy the impossible and then do it. He told Noah to build a big boat on dry land because flood waters were coming. He promised Abraham a son, despite the fact that he was in his nineties and his wife in her eighties. He promised Moses that he would use him to free the Israelites from slavery, armed only with a staff. None of these prophecies appeared any more unlikely than the prophecies of Nahum. The Assyrian Empire seemed so invincible that the fall of its capital sounded impossible.

Nineveh was enjoying a golden age. Its citizens had never had it so good. Sennacherib had officially made their city his new capital in around 700 BC and its fortunes had skyrocketed under King Ashurbanipal, who reigned from 669 BC to 627 BC and who conquered Egypt, making the Assyrian Empire the largest that the world had ever seen. Nahum's predictions therefore appeared ridiculous to the people of Judah, let alone to the people of Nineveh. That's why they demonstrate that God is in control of history.

In 2:1–2, Nahum predicts that an attacker will advance against Nineveh. This seemed laughable in 630 BC since there was no candidate for the role but, sure enough, when Ashurbanipal died his empire was plunged into civil war. A man named Nabopolassar took advantage of this anarchy to have himself crowned as a rival king in the city of Babylon. He recruited as allies the many disgruntled people groups across the empire and marched out in 612 BC at the head of an army of Babylonians, Medes, Persians, Parthians, Scythians and Cimmerians. The Battle of Nineveh had begun.[1]

In 2:3–4, Nahum predicts something even more unusual. He prophesies that the army that will destroy Nineveh will be dressed in scarlet uniforms and will carry red shields. Again, this was odd, since no army in the world fought in scarlet in 630 BC. It was only after Nahum prophesied these verses that Nabopolassar created his new Babylonian army and decided that it would fight in scarlet so that his soldiers' wounds would be invisible to the enemy. It is little details such as these that make the book of Nahum so important to us today. It reminds us of the words of Amos 3:7 and of Joshua 21:45: *"The Sovereign Lord does nothing without revealing his plan to his servants the prophets"*, and *"Not one of all the Lord's good promises to Israel failed; every one was fulfilled."*

In 2:5–8, Nahum predicts how Nabopolassar will capture the city of Nineveh. The very idea seemed impossible, since everyone thought it was so well fortified and so well supplied by river that it could withstand any length of siege. Nahum predicts that the city will fall when *"the river gates are thrown open"* and when it becomes *"like a pool whose water is draining away"*. Listen to how the ancient historian Diodorus Siculus says that Nabopolassar and his allies finally captured the city in July 612 BC:

> *Because of the strength of the walls they were unable to do any harm to the men in the city; for neither engines for throwing stones, nor shelters for undermining the walls, nor battering-rams for knocking down walls had as yet*

---

[1] The Lord *restored the splendour of Israel* (2:2) by raising up Babylon to destroy the one who had destroyed them. Babylon would then destroy Judah, paving the way for a reunification of the 12 tribes after their exile.

been invented at that time. Moreover, the inhabitants of the city had a great abundance of all provisions, since the king had taken thought on that score. Consequently the siege dragged on, but... after there had been heavy and continuous rains, it came to pass that the River, running very full, flooded a portion of the city and swept away the walls for a distance of three kilometres. At this the king, believing that the oracle had been fulfilled and that the river had plainly become the city's enemy, abandoned all hope of saving himself... The rebels took the city by forcing an entrance where the wall had fallen down.[2]

Nobody could have predicted that the rivers of Nineveh would turn against it and wash away its great city walls. Nobody, that is, except for the Lord, who also prophesied in 1:8 that *"with an overwhelming flood he will make an end of Nineveh"*.[3] The book of Nahum therefore reminds us that the God of Israel is also the Lord of history.

In 2:9–10, Nahum predicts that it will take several days to plunder the city of Nineveh of its seemingly endless storerooms of silver and gold. Again, this is confirmed by tablets dating back to the time of its fall: *"They carried off the vast booty of the city and the temple and turned the city into a ruin heap."*[4]

In 2:11–13, Nahum predicts that the city of Nineveh will be destroyed utterly. This must have seemed ridiculous to the Assyrians, since ancient cities that were captured in battle tended to be restored fairly quickly. The city of Babylon, for example, 250 miles to the south, had been captured and destroyed and rebuilt many times. However, the Babylonians

---

[2] Diodorus Siculus wrote this in c. 45 BC in his *Historical Library* (2.27.1–3).

[3] Diodorus Siculus also confirms what Nahum prophesied in 1:10. The Assyrians were so complacent that many of them were drunk when Nabopolassar and his allies attacked them.

[4] This quote comes from the *Fall of Nineveh Chronicle*, which is now on display in the British Museum in London.

were so determined to wipe out any trace of Nineveh that they carried off its rubble to build new cities elsewhere. Even today, there is little to see in the abandoned ruins of Nineveh across the River Tigris from the Iraqi city of Mosul. That's what happens when the Lord curses a city with the words, "'I am against you,' declares the Lord Almighty... 'The sword will devour your young lions. I will leave you no prey on the earth.'"[5] Our choice between his blessing and his curse really matters because what the Lord speaks he always fulfils.

Nahum predicts terrible judgment, but so did Jonah over a century earlier. The Lord gives this stark warning because he still wants the people of Nineveh to repent and avoid becoming shocking proof that he is serious when he warns that he has set a Day of Judgment for the world. The key verse in the whole of this book is the promise of salvation in 1:7 – "The Lord is good, a refuge in times of trouble. He cares for those who trust in him" – and this could still have been the experience of the Ninevites had they repented as wholeheartedly as their ancestors in the time of Jonah. Instead, they laughed off the threat of God's judgment and therefore chose to meet him as their Judge instead of as their Saviour.

When they got what they wanted, their sudden destruction horrified the world. Even in far-away Greece, Nineveh became proverbial for complacency and folly. The poet Phocylides told the Greeks to learn from its stupidity: "A small town on a rugged headland that takes good note of the law is far more fortunate than the great but foolish city of Nineveh."[6]

Nahum wants us to heed the same warning ourselves: *Blessing or curse – you decide.*

---

[5] King Ashurbanipal's empire seemed as invincible as a lion (2:11–12), but it was no match for the Lion of the Tribe of Judah (Revelation 5:5).

[6] Phocylides said this in c. 530 BC, quoted here in Dio Chrysostom's *Discourses* (36.13).

Casualty (Nahum 3:1–19)

*Nothing can heal you; your wound is fatal… for who
has not felt your endless cruelty.*

(Nahum 3:19)

When my youngest son Ethan was aged two, he had an accident
with a heavy door and partially severed his thumb. I wasn't
present when it happened, but I came running when I heard
his piercing scream. One look at his mangled hand and I leapt
into action. I phoned for an ambulance and put his thumb on ice
while we waited. When the ambulance took too long to arrive, I
jumped in the car and drove him to the hospital myself. Nobody
had to tell me to drive like a madman or to leave my car in an
illegal parking bay. When you see a wound like that, you want to
get to casualty right away.

That's how Nahum wants the city of Nineveh to react to
his stern words of prophecy. The Lord derives no pleasure from
destroying sinful cities, so the prophet hopes that his words will
spur the Ninevites into action to deal with their sin. His third
and final chapter describes their gaping wound in great detail
in order to send them running to God's casualty ward. If they
repent quickly and wholeheartedly, as in the days of Jonah, it is
not too late for them to become part of God's Plan "A" instead of
his Plan "B".

In 3:1–3, the Lord therefore confronts the people of Nineveh
with their barbaric cruelty towards their defeated enemies. He
calls them *"the city of blood… never without victims… piles of
dead, bodies without number"*. They have made a terrible mistake
by seeking to terrify their conquered peoples into submission by

cultivating a reputation for irrational violence and sudden acts of cruelty, because in so doing they have turned the Lord who saved them in the days of Jonah into their sworn enemy today. How can they hope to receive mercy on the Day of Judgment when they have shown no mercy at the end of their sieges – skinning people alive, gouging out their eyes or displaying their severed heads on a pole? How can they hope to find forgiveness when they have cut open pregnant women and thrown babies down from the walls onto the rocks below? How can they hope to find salvation when the Lord has heard King Sennacherib's boast that *"I cut them down with the sword, allowing no one to escape. I impaled their corpses on stakes all around the city"*?[1] Unless they run to his casualty ward quickly, the Lord warns that the Babylonians will soon be making the exact same boast about them.

In 3:4, the Lord confronts the people of Nineveh with their insatiable greed. Long gone are the days when they worshipped the Lord. Now they lust after their demon-gods and their magic spells in the same way that a prostitute longs for wealthy lovers.[2] Their lust for the false god of war has driven them to conquer for the sake of conquering. Their wars have long since ceased to be defensive. They are now attempts to enslave the entire world. Unless the Ninevites run to God's casualty ward quickly, their wound will therefore fester and destroy them. They will be defeated and put to utter shame.

In 3:5–7, the Lord confronts the people of Nineveh with their pride. They may think they are invincible and that God will never punish them for their sin, but that proud thought attracts a terrible curse from the Lord in 3:5: *"'I am against you,' declares the Lord Almighty. 'I will lift your skirts over your face. I will show the nations your nakedness and the kingdoms your shame.'"*

---

[1] He makes this boast about Babylon on the *Sennacherib Prism*, now found at the British Museum in London.

[2] See also 1:14. We are told in Isaiah 14:12–17 that Satan himself was the true power behind the throne of Assyria. Isaiah calls the king of Assyria *the king of Babylon* because that was one of his greatest conquests.

Nineveh has acted with the barefaced arrogance of a prostitute, so God will put it to shame like a prostitute too. Unless they run into his casualty ward quickly, their city will be destroyed suddenly and nobody will mourn its passing.

These words are stern and abrasive, but they are intended to spur the people of Nineveh into action. God loves the Assyrians more than I love my son Ethan, so he does whatever it takes to drive them into his casualty ward. These threats point them back to his promise in 1:7: *"The Lord is good, a refuge in times of trouble. He cares for those who trust in him."* It need not be this way for them if they receive him as their Saviour.

The Lord can tell that his offer of mercy is falling on deaf ears. That's why he changes his tone in 3:8–13 and starts to warn the people of Nineveh that the doors are closing on his casualty ward. The Lord reminds them how they sacked the Egyptian capital city of Thebes in 663 BC.[3] It was defended by the waters of the River Nile, just as Nineveh was defended by the River Tigris and the River Khoser.[4] It had strong alliances right across the region, just as Nineveh had strong alliances with many of its subject peoples. If Thebes fell to the Assyrians in spite of all this, the people of Nineveh must not fool themselves that their city is impregnable.[5] Their fortresses will fall as easily as ripe fruit from a tree. Their army will be overpowered like an outing of old women.[6] Their gates and their walls will be swept away.

---

[3] The Lord refers to Thebes in Hebrew as *Nō 'Āmōn*, meaning *the City of Amon*, since that was the name of the idol whose temples dominated the city. The ruins of the temples still survive at Luxor and Karnak.

[4] The Lord emphasizes that the River Nile is greater than the River Tigris and the River Khoser put together by referring to its waters twice in 3:8 literally as *a sea*.

[5] The Assyrians threw babies down from the walls of the cities they captured so that none of them would grow up to avenge their city. This was a bad miscalculation, since it turned the Lord into their Avenger (1:2).

[6] Most English translations paraphrase the Lord's words in 3:13 because they offend our sense of gender equality, but he declares literally, *"Look at your troops – they are all women!"* See also Jeremiah 51:30.

Their only hope of survival is to run into God's casualty ward fast and to repent as they did in the days of Jonah.

Even as he says this, the Lord can tell that the people of Nineveh have no intention of doing so. He therefore ends in 3:14–19 with a final threat of destruction. He commands them to prepare for a siege, strengthening the brickwork that he knows will let them down when the river breaks its banks and washes their defences away. He warns the king of Assyria to wake up his captains, to steady his officials and to rally his soldiers for battle.[7] But it is all too late for them. The final words of Nahum sound the closure of God's casualty ward: *"Nothing can heal you; your wound is fatal. All who hear the news about you clap their hands at your fall, for who has not felt your endless cruelty?"*[8]

In July 612 BC, the Babylonians captured and destroyed the city of Nineveh. The king of Assyria committed suicide and, when his successor attempted to rally what was left of his army, the survivors were slaughtered by the Babylonians at the Battle of Carchemish in 605 BC. Nineveh and its empire seemed invincible when Nahum prophesied in around 630 BC, but within twenty-five years it was totally destroyed.[9]

The southern kingdom of Judah had been told to watch and see what happened to their former enemy. This book of prophecies was written as much for them as for the people of Nineveh. Nahum therefore expects his readers to run to God's casualty ward themselves. He warns us to deal quickly with our own sins. *Blessing or curse – you decide.*

---

[7] Diodorus Siculus tells us that the Assyrian leaders were drunk and asleep when the Babylonians attacked. The reference to *shepherds* reminds us that when church leaders sleep it is fatal for their churches too.

[8] In case you are interested, my son Ethan made a complete recovery. Go to casualty straightaway!

[9] This fulfilled the prophecy in 1:14 that no survivors would be left to rebuild Nineveh.

Part Three:

Judah

Sin Spreads (Micah 1:1–16)

Samaria's plague is incurable; it has spread to Judah.
It has reached the very gate of my people, even to
Jerusalem itself.

(Micah 1:9)

Sin spreads. That's pretty obvious when we read the prophecies of Micah. The sins that destroyed the northern kingdom of Israel and the mighty empire of Assyria quickly infected the southern kingdom of Judah too. In Part 3 of this commentary, we will look at how Judah responded to the terrible disaster that befell the northern kingdom. Much of the time it doesn't make for happy reading, but these books are also full of hope.

In 1:1–2, we find that Micah prophesied from around 740 to 686 BC. That's why his book is described as *"the vision he saw concerning Samaria and Jerusalem"*, since the northern kingdom has not yet fallen in its opening chapters. Micah came from Moresheth Gath, a village in the foothills of Judah, so his prophecies have a distinct southern flavour when compared to those of Hosea or Jonah.[1] He dates his ministry via the kings of Judah, not of Israel. He describes his prophecies as the words of *"the Lord from his holy temple"* in Jerusalem. Nevertheless, he starts by prophesying to the northern kingdom and he insists that what he says is for the benefit of all the nations of the earth. Sin spreads without borders, so these words are relevant to everybody everywhere.

In 1:3–7, Micah prophesies to the northern kingdom of

---

[1] The full name Moresheth Gath is used in 1:14 when Micah prophesies that King Sennacherib and his Assyrian army will sack his home town in 701 BC.

Israel. What he says is nothing new. His contemporaries, Hosea and Isaiah, speak the same message of judgment in greater detail in their own books of the Bible, but as a third witness in his own generation against the sins of the northern kingdom, he confirms that Israel is on the brink of Judgment Day. Micah pictures the Lord marching down the mountain slopes from the Temple in Jerusalem towards the northern capital Samaria, like molten wax running down a candle or like water rushing down rapids. Since Samaria had pursued sin and idolatry instead of obedience to the Lord, it would be destroyed by the Assyrians in 722 BC. Since the Israelites had refused to accept their calling to be God's Vine, the Lord would clear the land of them and turn it into wasteland only fit for planting vineyards.

In 1:8–16, Micah laments that the contagion of Israel's sin has now spread south across the border into Judah. We were prepared for this devastating news in 1:5, when Micah warned that Jerusalem has become as bad an influence on Judah as Samaria is on Israel, but we are still supposed to find it very shocking. The prophet grieves that *"Samaria's plague is incurable; it has spread to Judah. It has reached the very gate of my people, even to Jerusalem itself."* Unless we take steps to check its progress, sin spreads.

Micah lists many towns and villages by name to underline just how much sin has spread from Jerusalem to the whole of Judah. We miss it in our English translations, but Micah uses clever puns to ram home the fact that every southern town and village has become infected with the same sin that has been the downfall of the northern kingdom. To understand these verses, I find it helps for us to imagine how Micah might make similar puns about our own cities today. He would have said something like: London will be left alone and done for; Paris will be unable to parry the blows that will fall on her; Berlin will burn; Warsaw will see war; Amsterdam will be damned and Helsinki will sink down to hell. Micah does in Hebrew with the names of the towns and villages of Judah what I just did in English with European capitals.

Gath sounds like the Hebrew word for *tell*, so Micah asks for no one to tell the Philistines who live there about Judah's misery. Knowing that God's enemies are gloating will only make this torment worse. Beth Ophrah means *House of Dust*, so Micah calls its citizens to repent in the dust. Shaphir means *Pleasant*, so he describes its unpleasant fate. Zaanan sounds like the Hebrew word for *exit*, so he predicts that no one will exit from its ruin.[2] Maroth means *Bitterness*, so Micah prophesies its bitter judgment. Lachish sounds like *to the chariot* in Hebrew, so he advises any righteous person left in the city to take to their chariot and flee its destruction.[3] Akzib means *Deceit*, so he warns that it will prove deceptively weak as a fortress city.[4] Mareshah sounds like the Hebrew word for *conqueror*, so he says it will be conquered. This list of place names is meant to emphasize how widespread sin is throughout Judah. God's judgment will be just as widespread too.

Micah's message to Judah is sobering and serious, but don't miss the fact that it is also full of God's love towards them. For a start, it assures the people of Jerusalem in 1:3 that he still dwells among them in his Temple at the heart of their city. Micah addresses Jerusalem as *"Daughter Zion"* in 1:13 in order to convey God's continued love towards the city. Furthermore, although *"I"* clearly means Micah in 1:8, it is equally clear that *"I"* refers to the Lord himself in 1:6–7 and in 1:15. These verses emphasize that God has not given up on his people. He still

122

---

[2] There are no puns in Hebrew for Beth Ezel, Moresheth Gath or Adullam. Micah was evidently inspired by God to prophesy against those towns but could not think of any suitable play on words.

[3] We do not know how Lachish led the rest of Judah into sin, but we do know that it suffered terribly at the hands of the Assyrians in 701 BC. Sennacherib's *Lachish Reliefs* have pride of place in the British Museum.

[4] Don't be surprised that Micah refers to *"the kings of Israel"* in 1:14. The Lord never fully recognized Israel's split into two kingdoms, so he continues to use the word *Israel* to refer to the southern kingdom.

calls them back to himself because his true desire is for them to repent quickly and be saved.[5]

Micah must have prophesied the words of this opening chapter to Israel and Judah early on in his ministry, between 740 and 722 BC. It appears to be part of a larger prophecy which extends into chapters 2 and 3. We must therefore read these verses in the context of 2:12–13, where the Lord promises to gather all of the twelve tribes of Israel back to himself under a new and better King – the coming Messiah. If the Lord sounds fierce in his anger towards Judah at the outset of the third section of this commentary, it is therefore only because he loves the people of Judah so much that he is planning to send his own Son to come and die for their salvation. As we begin a new section of this commentary, looking at the Minor Prophets who addressed the southern kingdom of Judah, we find that the coming Messiah finally begins to step onto the stage.

Sin spreads. That much is obvious in the prophecies of Micah, but don't miss the flipside of the prophet's message. He tells us that wherever sin spreads, God's judgment swiftly follows, but he also tells us that wherever God's judgment spreads, God's mercy follows too. The Lord still loves his people. He has not given up on them. He is about to reveal the mighty way in which his mercy spreads even faster than our sin.

---

[5] For similar affectionate language towards Jerusalem, see 4:8; 2 Kings 19:21; Psalm 9:14 and Isaiah 1:8.

Head Down
(Micah 2:1–3:12)

Her leaders judge for a bribe, her priests teach for a price, and her prophets tell fortunes for money.

(Micah 3:11)

When Kaiser Wilhelm II became ruler of Germany, he declared himself the champion of justice and kindness towards the poor:

Called to the throne of my fathers, I have taken over the government, looking to the King of all kings, and have vowed to God, following the example of my father, to be a righteous and gentle prince, to foster piety and the fear of God, to maintain peace, to further the welfare of the country, to be a help to the poor and oppressed, and to be to the righteous man a true protector.[1]

Vladimir Lenin saw things rather differently after the outbreak of World War One. He declared that *"One slave-owner, Germany, is fighting another slave-owner, England, for a fairer distribution of the slaves."*[2]

Kaiser Wilhelm and Vladimir Lenin saw things very differently because they lived in very different worlds. It is helpful to note that, in the same way, Micah lived in a very different world from Hosea and Isaiah. Whereas the other two prophets were city-dwellers, Micah came from the countryside. Moresheth Gath was a farming community in the Shephelah, the

---

[1] The Kaiser said this in a proclamation on 18th June 1888.

[2] Lenin said this in a café conversation with Valeriu Marcu in early 1917.

foothills that lay between Hebron and the Mediterranean Sea. Whereas the other two prophets appear to have been relatively well off financially, this also suggests that Micah was poor. It was harder to get rich as a farmer in the hills than it was as a merchant in the city, so Micah was more like Lenin than the Kaiser. He was a commoner who felt it acutely whenever Judah's leaders mistreated the poor.

In 2:1–5, Micah prophesies against the leaders of Judah's economy. However strongly you may feel today about greedy oligarchs and fat-cat bankers, things were far worse back then. The richest citizens spent the dark hours inventing new ways in which to rob the poor, only to spend the daylight hours putting those schemes into action. The government did nothing to prevent them from seizing people's houses, from taking over people's fields or from robbing people of whatever they had inherited from their parents. The Law of Moses spoke sternly against this, but the rulers of Judah looked the other way and allowed the rich to get ever richer at the expense of the poor.[3]

The Lord had outlawed their shady business practices at Mount Sinai. He had commanded the Israelites in Deuteronomy 27:17 to climb a mountain and to shout over the Promised Land that *"Cursed is anyone who moves their neighbour's boundary stone!"* It is therefore significant that Micah 1:2–3 depicts the Lord as calling from the summit of Mount Zion. He spoke the first time from Mount Sinai to make a covenant with his people. He speaks this second time from Mount Zion to enforce the terms of that covenant. Since the southern kingdom of Judah has chosen his Plan "B" instead of his Plan "A", he is about to destroy them and to drive them out of the Promised Land.[4]

---

[3] Leviticus 25:10–28; Numbers 36:1–7; Deuteronomy 19:14; 1 Kings 21:1–3. *"Because it is in their power to do it"* in 2:1 emphasizes that not every economic practice that is legal is necessarily right.

[4] Although God addresses *Jacob* and *Israel* throughout these verses, he clarifies in 3:10–12 that by this he primarily means the southern kingdom of Judah.

In 2:6–11, Micah prophesies against the false prophets of Judah. They have become like the imposters appointed at Bethel by the kings of Israel.[5] They have led the people of the southern kingdom astray by failing to warn them that their sins are storing up judgment for them, fearing that if they talk about God's anger, they will provoke Judah to reject him as impatient and vindictive. The Lord reminds them that this is utter folly. His Word is powerful to save whenever it is faithfully delivered: *"Do not my words do good to the one whose ways are upright?"* If they speak the truth in love, they will see many people saved, but as it is they speak whatever they think the sinful people want to hear. *"If a liar and deceiver comes and says, 'I will prophesy for you plenty of wine and beer,' that would be just the prophet for this people!"*

We ought to find it very challenging when the Lord warns that those who fail to speak the truth for fear of offending their hearers become accomplices in the sins of their hearers. Micah is telling us that when pastors fail to pastor and when prophets fail to prophesy, whole church congregations are led astray, and that when congregations fail to speak the Word of God to unbelievers, whole nations are led astray. He is saying that whatever is embodied in church leaders will be embodied first in the Church and then in the world. It's like the old proverb says: *"A fish always rots from the head down."*

In 3:1–12, Micah turns on Judah's leaders as a whole.[6] He accuses the rulers and princes of devouring the people instead of helping them.[7] He accuses the prophets of saying whatever the highest bidder wants to hear. He accuses the

---

[5] 1 Kings 12:31–32; Amos 7:10–17.

[6] Micah talks about the *leaders* and *rulers* of Judah, but not about the king. Since the godly King Jotham ruled from 740 to 732 BC and the evil King Ahaz ruled from 735 to 715 BC, with three years of joint rule, Micah probably spoke these words under Jotham – a godly king who was too weak to control his officials (2 Chronicles 27:1–2).

[7] Contrast 3:1–3 with Acts 20:28 and 1 Peter 5:1–4. Christian leaders will have to give an account to the Chief Shepherd, Jesus, as to whether they have served or lorded it over their congregations.

rulers of despising justice, the judges of taking bribes and the priests of selling out on the Gospel.[8] What is worst of all is that these leaders are largely unaware of their sin.[9] Like Kaiser Wilhelm, persuading himself that he is the righteous servant of God, they are convinced that the fact God dwells among them in the Temple means that he is on their side, so Micah prophesies that Jerusalem will be utterly destroyed.[10] Its prophets will fall under the same curse as those of Israel in Amos 8:11–14. They will hear no words from God. They will be unable to say with Micah, *"But as for me, I am filled with power, with the Spirit of the Lord, and with justice and might, to declare to Jacob his transgression, to Israel his sin."*[11]

But what's this? In the middle of this terrible exposé of the sins of Judah's leaders comes a prophecy in 2:12–13 about the arrival of a new and better King. Micah prophesies that after the destruction of the southern kingdom, the Lord will bring the survivors of the twelve tribes of Israel back from exile to the Promised Land. He will appoint over them a new King – the Messiah, who begins to feature more explicitly in the Minor Prophets from this moment onwards, and who will be for them a better Shepherd, a better Leader and a better Head. Fish may rot from the head down, but the flipside is also true. Everything will change for God's people when they have *"the Lord at their head"*.

So if you are a leader, be warned. God is watching. He has given you the perfect Leader in Jesus his Son. If you let him, he will empower you through his example and his Spirit to transform your own community from the head down.

---

[8] 3:10 reminds us that good ends never justify evil means – especially when it comes to building the Church.

[9] This is also obvious from 1:5. Their self-righteous reaction to God's warnings was *"Sin? What sin?"*

[10] We are just as foolish when we think that God's presence at our church meetings guarantees that he is pleased with us. See 1 Corinthians 1:7; 3:16–17; 5:4; 11:17, 27–30!

[11] This is a great mission statement for any Christian leader: Spirit-filled and unafraid to preach God's Word.

The New Jerusalem
(Micah 4:1–5)

The law will go out from Zion, the word of the Lord from Jerusalem.

(Micah 4:2)

There's a brilliant scene in the classic 1980s' movie *Crocodile Dundee*. A huge man named Donk is taking money from every man in the bar by placing a pint of beer on his head and betting that none of them can make him spill it. No matter how hard they punch him, he doesn't spill a drop until it is Dundee's turn. While Donk is tensing his muscles and preparing to resist a punch, Dundee lands a big wet kiss on his lips. Donk is so surprised that he spills the entire glass on his head and has to hand over all of his money.

The first five verses of Micah 4 remind me of that scene. We have read enough of the Minor Prophets by now to know what we ought to expect in a book of prophecies like this one: back-to-back oracles of judgment with a final glimmer of hope at the end (like Amos or Hosea), or back-to-back oracles of judgment with barely any hope at all (like Nahum). We therefore start chapter 4 bracing ourselves to receive yet another blow of judgment. We are meant to feel as surprised as Donk when the Lord ambushes us with a kiss instead. Micah 4 and 5 are brimful of his hope and of his love.

These five verses promise that *God's judgment will not be the end of the story*. Chapter 3 ended with a prediction that Jerusalem would become a heap of rubble, but now Micah reveals that *"in the last days"* it will be rebuilt.[1] Since we know that Judah eventually returned from exile, we can easily miss how surprising these words were. It was very unusual. The sin that caused the destruction of Judah would not have the last word. The prophet announces that God's mercy will triumph over his judgment.

These five verses promise that *God will build a new and better Jerusalem.* Again it is easy to miss the full weight of what Micah is saying here unless we slow down to consider the geography of Israel. Jerusalem was built on five hills, the highest of which was Mount Zion. At only 765 metres above sea level, it was 60 metres shorter than the nearby Mount of Olives, over 1,000 metres shorter than Mount Zaphon, the largest mountain in the region, and less than a tenth of the size of Mount Everest in the Himalayas. It was a very precious mountain to the people of Judah, but on a global scale it was puny. Be surprised, then, when Micah prophesies that *"the mountain of the Lord's temple will be established as the highest of the mountains".*[2] The Lord isn't simply promising to rebuild Jerusalem here. He is saying that he will make it vastly better than before.

The New Testament writers have this prophecy in mind when they tell us that the Church is the "New Jerusalem" and the "New Mount Zion". They unpack Micah's words when they tell us that we *"have come to Mount Zion, to the city of the living God, the heavenly Jerusalem"* and that *"the Jerusalem that is above is free, and she is our mother".* They echo these verses when they talk about *"a mountain great and high"* on which is built *"the Holy City, the new Jerusalem, coming down out of heaven from God".*[3] So Micah is promising much more here than simply the

---

[1] Peter announced in May 30 AD that *"the last days"* have begun (Acts 2:14–17). Hebrews 1:2, James 5:3 and the rest of the New Testament echo this. *"The last days"* therefore refers to the whole of AD history.

[2] The Temple was actually built on Mount Moriah, but the whole of Jerusalem is often referred to as *Zion*, since that is the highest of its five hills.

[3] Galatians 4:25–26; Hebrews 12:22; Revelation 3:12; 21:2, 10. We are also told that the Church is God's new Temple in 1 Corinthians 3:16–17; 2 Corinthians 6:16; Ephesians 2:21–22 and 1 Peter 2:5.

return of the survivors of Judah after their exile. He is saying that through his Messiah the Lord will build a new and better capital city for his people. The New Jerusalem will become the centrepiece of the whole earth.

These five verses promise that *God will save the nations through Jerusalem*. Micah prophesies that *"the law will go out from Zion, the word of the Lord from Jerusalem"* and that as a result people from many nations will stream up the slopes of the city to worship the Lord. We are meant to see this as a miraculous work of God, since rivers naturally flow downhill, never uphill. What is more, these five verses are repeated almost word for word in Isaiah 2:1–5. Some scholars argue that Micah copied Isaiah and other scholars that Isaiah copied Micah, but all of them miss the point. Last month one of my Spirit-filled friends prophesied over me a promise from God that was identical to one that I received two years ago from somebody he has never met before. Neither of them copied the other. They were both simply inspired by the same Holy Spirit. Although it is technically possible that Micah and Isaiah collaborated on these verses, we are much more meant to see it as another miracle that confirms these words are true. This is not simply Micah's wishful thinking. God has confirmed his vision through Isaiah too.

This vision was fulfilled initially when Jesus died on a cross and three days later was raised to life outside the walls of Jerusalem. He told his followers to wait in Jerusalem to be anointed with the Holy Spirit and then to take the Gospel out from Jerusalem to every nation of the world.[4] The promise is reaching its ultimate fulfilment right now, however, as we share the Gospel in the most global generation in history.[5] These verses

---

[4] Acts 1:4, 8. The word for *teach* in 4:2 is the Hebrew verb *yārāh* and the word for *law* in 4:2 is its Hebrew noun *tōrāh*, meaning *teaching*. We need to teach people about Jesus if we want to inspire them to follow him.

[5] At the time of Micah, Judah's great hope was to extend its borders back to those of its heyday under David and Solomon, but God promises something far better – the salvation of the nations that David and Solomon longed to

warn us not to tone down the offence of the Gospel, like the false prophets in 2:6–7, but to trust that God will use our faithful message to save the nations. Earthly empires are founded by force, but God's Kingdom is founded by his miraculous power.[6]

As a result, these five verses promise that God *will grant his people a new and better Promised Land.* Joshua had to teach the Israelites to fight to conquer Canaan, but the Messiah will go one better. He will do all of the conquering for us, making us more than conquerors, enabling us to turn our wartime weapons into peacetime farm tools and enjoy God's blessings without any fear of being destroyed by the evil one.[7]

Micah is as surprised as we are by the amazing mercy of this prophecy. Like Donk in *Crocodile Dundee,* he was expecting the Lord to deliver another blow of judgment, not a kiss of mercy such as this. He is so surprised that he leads Judah in a prayer of repentance and of national reconsecration to the Lord. *"All the nations may walk in the name of their [false] gods, but we will walk in the name of the Lord our [real] God for ever."*[8]

Since we live in the last days that are described in these five verses, we ought to pray the same prayer ourselves. Tell the Lord that you renounce everything that would stop you from being part of his New Jerusalem. Tell him you are willing to lay down anything that might prevent you from taking his Word out from Zion to the nations of the world.

---

see through the Temple but never did (1 Chronicles 16:7–36; 1 Kings 8:41–43; Amos 9:11).

[6] In 4:1, *nāhar* means *to flow like a river.* Reliance on anything but God's strength is like pushing water uphill.

[7] Living under your own vine and fig-tree was a Hebrew metaphor for peaceful enjoyment of the Promised Land (1 Kings 4:25; Zechariah 3:10). Micah isn't entirely like Lenin: property still exists in his paradise.

[8] This is the main difference between Micah's version of the prophecy and its parallel in Isaiah 2:1–5. Isaiah exhorts the people of Judah to respond this way, whereas Micah actually leads them in a prayer of doing so.

King David II
(Micah 4:6–5:15)

*Bethlehem Ephrathah, though you are small among
the clans of Judah, out of you will come for me one
who will be ruler over Israel, whose origins are from
of old, from ancient times.*

(Micah 5:2)

The surprises continue in the rest of Micah 4 and 5. God's mercy does not simply triumph over his judgment. It triumphs in a manner beyond Judah's wildest dreams. The nation looked back with nostalgia to its golden age under King David, so the Lord makes them a stunning promise here: a better age is coming under King David II.

In 4:6–8, the Lord looks back to three great moments in the life of David. The first recalls the way in which a ragtag army of debtors and discontents gathered to David while he was an outlaw hiding in the cave of Adullam. The Lord has already hinted in 1:15 that he is going to repeat that story by telling us that *"the nobles of Israel will flee to Adullam".* Now he explains what he means here. He is going to gather the exiles of Judah out of their distress and turn them into another ragtag army that will follow his Messiah.[1]

The second moment recalls the way that David captured Jerusalem and turned it into his capital. The Jebusites who lived there were so confident they could beat him that they bragged

---

[1] The Lord uses feminine singulars in 4:6 and 4:7a to emphasize his love for Judah. He promises literally to gather *her* that is lame, *her* that is exiled and *her* that I have brought to grief.

in 2 Samuel 5 that even the blind and lame among them could defend the city. The Lord therefore promises that, though the exiles will return with the same limp of humility that he imparted to Jacob at the Jabbok River, the Messiah will lead his lame army to victory and re-establish them as a strong nation on his New Mount Zion.

The third moment recalls the early days of David, when he tended his father's sheep in the fields around Bethlehem. One of the areas he must have frequented was known as Migdal Eder in Hebrew, or *The Watchtower of the Flock* in English, so the Lord refers to that area in order to promise that Bethlehem will produce a second great king for Jerusalem. Despite its smallness, it will be the birthplace of King David II.[2]

In 4:9–13, the Lord warns that the path towards this will not be easy. The nation of Judah will go into exile in Babylon because of its sin. Its king will be deposed by the Babylonians.[3] Even after its return from exile, it will remain a province of a foreign empire and will have no king. The pagan nations will gloat that David's dynasty has had its day, little knowing that this is all part of God's plan to redeem his people through King David II.[4] He will use the centuries of anguish to sort the wheat from the chaff across the earth so that, when the Messiah comes, his chosen people will be ready.

In 5:1–4, the Lord looks back on three more moments in the life of David. The first recalls his sufferings. In the same way that David was unjustly hated by Saul, despised by Nabal

---

[2] See Genesis 35:19–21. This may well be where the angels found the shepherds in Luke 2:8–20.

[3] The city of Babylon was still subject to the Assyrian Empire when Micah spoke these words in c. 715 BC. The people of Judah barely gave Babylon a second thought (Isaiah 39:3), and neither Amos nor Hosea name it as Judah's destroyer. Nevertheless, the Holy Spirit inspires Micah to prophesy what Babylon will become.

[4] Revival requires us to walk God's death-and-resurrection pathway. Jesus' enemies gloated over his death (4:11) yet discovered that it was all part of God's perfect plan (4:12) when he rose again to judge them (4:13).

and imprisoned by the Philistines, the Messiah's pathway to the throne will not be an easy one. The New Testament never directly quotes or applies Micah's prophecy that *"They will strike Israel's ruler on the cheek with a rod"* to the life of Jesus, but we discover in the gospels that he was beaten exactly as the prophet had foretold.[5]

The second moment recalls the birth of David. He was born a commoner in Bethlehem – or to use its ancient name, Ephrath or Ephrathah – a village so insignificant that when a ruler visited it everybody asked him what on earth he was doing there![6] It couldn't have been expected to produce one king, let alone two. Nevertheless, the Lord prophesies that the Messiah will come from the same nowheresville as David. He also predicts something even more surprising. King David II will not merely be a better human king. He will be the Son of God, the one who existed eternally before the creation of the world.

The New Testament quotes this prophecy explicitly in Matthew 2:3–6, when the Jewish rabbis use it to answer King Herod's question about where the Messiah will be born. It is also echoed indirectly in John 8:58 and 17:5, when Jesus claims to have existed from eternity, and in John 10:11–15 when he claims to be the Good Shepherd. Since Bethlehem means *House of Bread* and Ephrathah means *Fruitfulness*, John 6:35 and 15:16 may also echo this prophecy when Jesus claims to be the Bread of Life, who came to earth to make God's people fruitful forever.

The third moment recalls the many years that David spent caring for his father's sheep. The Old Testament presents him as a devoted shepherd-king in 1 Samuel 17:15 and Psalm 78:70–72, so Micah promises that King David II will be an even better Shepherd-King towards God's people. Israel and Judah will both have to go into exile before they will be reunited as one nation,

---

[5] Matthew 27:30; Mark 15:19; John 18:22; 19:3.

[6] 1 Samuel 16:1–5.

but when they return the Messiah will shepherd them in the mighty power of God's name. No longer will they face danger and distress. They will rest securely as they watch their Messiah conquer every last corner of the earth.

In 5:5–15, the Lord warns again that the path towards the Messiah's coronation will not be easy. The southern kingdom of Judah will be invaded by the same Assyrians who destroyed the northern kingdom in 722 BC. Their land will be occupied, their army defeated, their fortress cities destroyed and their nation brought to the brink of destruction before the Lord grants them an eleventh-hour deliverance.[7] The Lord knows that they will only throw away their idols and their magic spells if he humbles them completely. He therefore promises to do whatever it takes to get them ready for King David II. He will turn them into a devoted nation that brooks no compromise with sin.

I find these two chapters very surprising, but not as surprising as the way in which the Jewish rabbis responded to them in Matthew 2. They know that Micah has prophesied a new and better king for Israel. They are able to quote chapter and verse to Herod, and the appearance of the Magi and of a bright star in the sky ought to convince them that King David II has finally been born. Despite all this head knowledge, however, Matthew says they were *"disturbed"* by the news. They were so upset that God might upset the apple cart of their man-made religion that they were unwilling to travel six miles south from Jerusalem to ponder what the arrival of the baby Jesus might mean.

So don't settle for head knowledge of these two chapters. Humble yourself and confess to God that you need his Messiah. Surrender your whole life to serving King David II.

---

[7] This took place under King Sennacherib of Assyria in 701 BC. See 2 Kings 18–19. *Nimrod* in 5:6 was the ancient founder of Assyria (Genesis 10:8–12). Very appropriately, his name is Hebrew for *Rebellion*.

Courtroom Drama
(Micah 6:1–7:7)

*The Lord has a case against his people; he is lodging
a charge against Israel.*

(Micah 6:2)

We don't really know what we are asking for when we complain
that God ought to be more lenient towards our sin. Many people
have the same attitude as the German poet Heinrich Heine, who
boasted on his deathbed that *"Of course God will forgive me:
that's his job."*[1] But think for a moment about what that would
mean. What about all the ways we have offended God by acting
like little gods? What about all the people we have wronged?
Do we really want a God who is willing to turn a blind eye to
people's sin?

The newspapers make it pretty clear that we don't. They
rage against high-court judges who give people a mere slap on
the wrist for their crimes, and they despise corrupt rulers who
acquit their guilty cronies. That's why it is good news when
Proverbs 17:15 assures us, *"Acquitting the guilty and condemning
the innocent – the Lord detests them both."*

It's good news, but it also means in Micah 6 and 7 that
Judah is in serious trouble. Its people have ignored the prophet's
warnings of judgment and his promises of mercy, so the Lord
speaks to them in these two final chapters like the prosecutor
in a courtroom. In 6:1–5, he summons the mountains and the
hills to act as the jury, since they have witnessed his kindness to

---

[1] Quoted by Sigmund Freud in his book *The Joke and Its Relation to the
Unconscious* (1905).

the twelve tribes of Israel over many centuries. He reminds the people of Judah that he rescued them from slavery in Egypt, led them through the desert, protected them from their enemies and brought them into the Promised Land.[2] Since he has only ever acted righteously towards them, the base ingratitude of their sin against him is totally inexcusable.[3]

In 6:6–8, Micah stands up in the courtroom to defend his client Judah. Unfortunately, he has not got very much that he can say. We can tell that he is prophesying after 715 BC, since Hezekiah is the last of the kings mentioned in 1:1 and since Jeremiah 26:18 recalls that *"Micah of Moresheth prophesied in the days of Hezekiah king of Judah."*[4] These verses come after the twenty years in which King Ahaz led Judah so far into idolatry that parents slaughtered their own children as sacrifices to the idol Molech.[5] Micah has to confess that the defence therefore has no case at all. This courtroom drama predicts what it will be like on the Day of Judgment when every sinful mouth is silenced.[6]

Micah confesses that there are not enough sacrificial animals in the fields of Judah and not enough oil on its shelves to atone for all its sin. Even if sacrificing a firstborn son could atone for their transgressions, they have already sacrificed their firstborn sons to Molech! This is of course a prophecy that God is able to atone for our sin through the sacrifice of his own firstborn Son – but how could we ever expect such mercy from

---

[2] *Balak, Balaam, Shittim* and *Gilgal* all refer to the events of Numbers 22–25 and Joshua 2–5.

[3] Looking back on Church history and on our own personal history with God is more than an interesting pastime. It helps us to cultivate a proper attitude of gratitude towards God.

[4] Jeremiah 26 quotes from Micah 3:12, which was actually prophesied to King Jotham. Its point is simply that some of Micah's toughest prophecies were to King Hezekiah yet the godly king did not arrest him.

[5] 2 Kings 16:1–4; 23:10; 2 Chronicles 28:1–4. King Ahaz ruled from 735 to 715 BC.

[6] Romans 3:19 says God gave us his Law *"so that every mouth may be silenced"* while there is still time to repent.

the God our actions have offended? Micah can only point out to his client Judah how far short it has fallen from God's standards: *"He has shown you, O mortal, what is good. And what does the Lord require of you? To act justly and to love mercy and to walk humbly with your God."*

The Lord loves mercy but he also loves justice. He will never turn a blind eye to our sin. The penalty for sin is death, so somebody must die – either us or God's innocent Son.

In 6:9–16, the courtroom drama lurches back into a stark description of the problem. The Lord is still the prosecutor, and he produces a catalogue of sins. The way that the people of Judah exploit one another proves that their true god is money. They carry around two sets of weights for their scales: one that weighs too little so that they can short-change their customers and one that weighs too much so that they can overcharge them. They lie and deceive and bully each other for profit. They fool themselves that God cares how they act in their leisure time, but not in the workplace. They are wrong. He has punished them in the way that he always punishes those who worship money: by making them dissatisfied with what they have, cursed in their investments and so afraid of losing their wealth that they hoard it instead of enjoying it.[7] The Lord warns that he is about to ruin Judah for aping the sins of the northern kings Omri and Ahab. He will destroy their precious idol to bring them running back to him.[8]

In 7:1–7, Micah tries again to defend his client Judah. Once more he has no case to argue. He complains that he is like a man who looks for grapes in a vineyard after the harvesters have been through. However hard he looks, he cannot find any reason why the Lord ought to overlook his client's sin. Not a

---

[7] This is God's *rod* of discipline in 6:9, but the people were too foolish to repent under it.

[8] The cut-throat, hard-ball capitalism of our generation is therefore entirely self-defeating. We don't lose by forfeiting money to serve the Lord. We discover the secret of true contentment (Philippians 4:11–12).

single person in the southern kingdom is righteous. They are ambidextrous at sin: both hands are equally adept at doing bad. Rulers steal from their subjects, judges auction off their verdicts and the rich foist an unjust economic system on the poor. As for the common people, they are just as bad. Friends lie to one another, lovers betray one another and families turn on one another. Judah is rotten to the core. Its people have no hope of being declared righteous by God.[9]

If you find all this a bit depressing, it's because you are meant to. God wants to bring you to a point where you recognize that he will never sweep your sin under the carpet. He wants to bring you to the same conclusion as Micah in 6:7, that only the sacrifice of his Son can ever be enough to offset your rebellion against him. He wants to bring you so low that you will say with Micah in 7:7, *"But as for me, I watch in hope for the Lord, I wait for God my Saviour; my God will hear me."* These verses aren't meant to depress us. They are meant to show us how much we need Jesus to be our Saviour. They are meant to persuade us to lay hold of him as the only sufficient sacrifice for sin.

At the beginning of the Bible, in Genesis 2:17, God warns that the penalty for sin is always death. He still means it. He is far too committed to justice to turn a blind eye to sin. That's why he confronted it head on by sending his Son to die our death for us. The apostle Paul explains in Romans 3:25–26 and 6:23 what God is trying to convey to us by pledging to be both just and merciful in Micah's courtroom drama:

> *God presented Christ as a sacrifice of atonement, through the shedding of his blood – to be received by faith. He did this...* ***to be just and the one who justifies*** *those who have faith in Jesus... For the wages of sin is death, but the gift of God is eternal life in Christ Jesus our Lord.*

---

[9] Jesus quotes from 7:6 in Matthew 10:35–36, so these verses describe our own generation too.

Back to Plan "A"
(Micah 7:8–20)

Who is a God like you, who pardons sin and forgives the transgression of the remnant of his inheritance?

(Micah 7:18)

Yesterday I paid my ten-year-old son to do the gardening for me. I had a book to write, so it seemed like a good idea at the time. When I took a break and went outside I discovered a disaster. He had got carried away squaring off the edging of the path and had dug away a massive section of the lawn. I tried not to discourage him, but on the inside I was horrified. One hour of foolishness had made my garden an eyesore.

I couldn't ignore the problem. I had to do it justice, so I paid him the amount of money I had promised, then informed him that his day's work was not yet done. He had to go to the compost heap and retrieve all the turf that he had cut and thrown away. He needed to relay it so that my disfigured lawn could be restored. That was the voice of justice, but now for mercy. I told him that I would give up on my writing and roll up my own sleeves to help him. I would spend the next hour showing him how to relay the turf, and I would take upon myself the task of watering it daily, instead of him, until the grass had put down roots and begun to grow again.

That's a very trivial example, but it illustrates in miniature why the final thirteen verses of Micah are full of hope for the people of Judah. The Lord cannot deny his own character by turning a blind eye to justice when we sin. He always faces up to the very real consequences and imposes the full legal penalty for the many ways in which we have defiled his creation. But he always extends his hand of mercy too. Micah's prophecies that the Son of God will come to earth as our Saviour unlock God's mercy towards Judah. These final thirteen verses tell us what happens whenever someone asks God to roll up his sleeves and come to their aid.

In 7:8–10, Micah prophesies that, whenever we repent of our sin, God's mercy always triumphs over his judgment. Judah's enemies may gloat over its destruction, but if its people confess their sin, like the prophet in 7:7, and ask the Lord to save them, he will do more than give them a second chance to get it right.[1] He will step down into their darkness and become their light. He will step into the courtroom and bring new evidence that turns around their lost cause: the innocent blood of his only Son.[2] Though Judah has fallen, this means its people will rise again. Though Judah looks abandoned, this means that God will vindicate them and let them see the downfall of their enemies.[3] These verses are true for all of us. Whenever we repent and gladly choose to follow Jesus along God's death-and-resurrection pathway, we always experience revival.

In 7:11–13, Micah prophesies that, whenever we repent of ruining what God has given us, he rolls up his sleeves and helps us to rebuild what is left of our forgiven lives. The people of Judah deserved their land to be destroyed by the Assyrians in 701 BC and by the Babylonians in 586 BC, but the Lord promises to do more than just deliver them. He also promises to help them rebuild. He pledges to enlarge the borders of their nation and to

[1] *My enemy* takes a feminine verb and pronoun in the Hebrew text of 7:10. The suffix for *your* in 7:10 and 11 is feminine too. This is therefore meant to be a conversation between the cities of Jerusalem and Babylon.

[2] Note that 7:9 says that God's mercy is all about *"his righteousness"* and not our own. Romans 1:17 explains that *"in the gospel the righteousness of God is revealed – a righteousness that is by faith from first to last"*.

[3] In 2 Kings 18:33–35, King Sennacherib of Assyria effectively asks the people of Judah in 701 BC the question that Micah describes in 7:10: *"Where is the Lord your God?"* He soon finds out.

help them win converts to their Messiah from every nation of the world. That's what it means for God's mercy to triumph over his judgment. His compassion restores whatever his justice has destroyed – and much, much more.

This was wonderful news for the people of Judah and it is just as wonderful for you and me today. If you feel as though your life has been ruined by sin, God promises to forgive you and to help you fix it by his power. If you have already benefited from his rebuild, take a look at the Church, which has been decimated in the West through the sins of its leaders. They have diluted the Gospel to avoid offending people. They have worshipped the idols of numbers and embraced this world's definition of success. Some of them have even sold out their calling for money, sex and power. These verses are therefore for such a time as ours. If we truly repent and ask the Lord to revive our churches, the Messiah who laid down his life to make the Church his spotless Bride will help us rebuild its walls with a renewed passion for holiness and help us bring many nations to faith in his undiluted Gospel. He will enable the Church to say, *"Do not gloat over me, my enemy! Though I have fallen, I will rise!"*

I love the moment in the movie The Taking of Pelham 123 when Denzel Washington asks John Travolta if he has a Plan B, and he quickly shoots back, "*Of course not. My Plan B is always to enforce Plan A!*" It reminds me of the promise here, in 7:14–17. The moment Jerusalem turns and pleads with the Lord in 7:14 to become its Shepherd again, he declares that all the curses of Deuteronomy have been deactivated and that all the blessings of Deuteronomy are now back on.[4] He declares that he has brought the nation of Judah back from his Plan "B" and into his glorious Plan "A". He promises in 7:15 to renew the miracles that he performed for their ancestors long ago during the Exodus

---

[4] The Hebrew suffix for *your* in 7:14 is masculine, so this is Jerusalem replying to the Lord.

from Egypt.[5] Micah celebrates in 7:16–17 that this guarantees that God will help them conquer their enemies, as he did in the days of Joshua.[6] We ought to be celebrating with Micah too. He is telling us that a revived Church will always result in a revived world.

In 7:18–20, Micah brings his book of prophecies to its final crescendo. His name means *Who Is Like the Lord?*, so he ends his book with a breathless prayer, *"Who is a God like you, who pardons sin and forgives?... You do not stay angry for ever but delight to show mercy."* We have to agree with Micah. There is no one like the Lord, willing to pay such a heavy price to ensure that mercy triumphs over judgment. There is no one like the Lord, drawing the survivors of Israel and Judah close to him while catapulting their sins far away. There is no one like the Lord, remembering his covenant of mercy and forever bringing repentant people out of his Plan "B" and back into his Plan "A".[7]

The message of Micah is twenty-seven centuries old, yet it could not be more relevant to us today. God still reaches out to us with the same choice: *Blessing or curse – you decide.*

---

[5] Miracles were a key feature of the Messiah's ministry and that of his early followers. These verses promise that they ought to be a key feature of our own ministry too (John 14:12).

[6] It is significant that *Carmel*, *Bashan* and *Gilead* were all areas of the northern kingdom now under Assyrian rule. Plan "A" brings certain victory, just as surely as Plan "B" brings certain misery.

[7] These final three verses give us two big reasons to be confident that God will restore us to his Plan "A" if we repent – he is always faithful to his character (7:18) and to his promises (7:20).

Insect Army (Joel 1:1–20)

What the locust swarm has left the great locusts have eaten; what the great locusts have left the young locusts have eaten; what the young locusts have left other locusts have eaten.

(Joel 1:4)

If you are old enough, I am sure that you'll remember where you were when you heard about the terrorist attack on the Twin Towers in New York City. On Tuesday, 11th September 2001, I was working for a soft drinks company and one of my colleagues leapt up from his desk and started shouting out the news. Listening to the screams on the radio, we all felt like crying. Later that evening, my fiancée and I had planned to launch a new Bible study group in her home. We had to let group members share their shell-shocked feelings for the first hour before we could turn them to God's Word and to prayer. Tremors seized everybody on that day. It was truly a day that shook the world.

The southern kingdom of Judah had its own Twin Towers moment in 701 BC. Something unthinkable happened and it sent their nation reeling. The Assyrians had agreed to leave Judah alone after the destruction of the northern kingdom, just so long as they paid them an annual tribute. When they defaulted on the tribute at the start of 701 BC, the Assyrian response was swift and devastating. King Sennacherib invaded Judah at the head of a vast army that trampled every field and orchard and captured every fortified city except for Jerusalem. The people of Judah were horrified. That's why the Lord sent the prophet Joel to explain to them what had happened and how they needed to respond.

The book of Joel is undated. It requires a bit of detective work to date it based on what the prophet says. Some scholars date it as early as 900 BC, since it includes many themes that are developed by the other prophets.[1] Other scholars date it as late as 400 BC, since it addresses elders and priests but not kings. I hope to show you that the context, especially in chapter 2, points very strongly to the years leading up to 701 BC. Joel prepares God's people for their 9/11 moment. Take a good look at the Church in the West and you will see how relevant his prophecies still are to the people of God today.

Joel gave the prophecy in chapter 1 a few years before 701 BC, and most probably before 715 BC. He addresses an earlier national crisis, when a swarm of locusts swept through Judah, destroying all the fields of crops, all the vineyards and all the fruit trees. Joel helps the people respond to the devastation that was wrought by this insect army.

In 1:2–12, Joel helps them see the Lord's hand in the disaster. Joel means *The Lord is God*, so he tries to convince them that what has happened cannot be an accident: it must be the hand of the Lord.[2] Joel calls on the old men of Judah to testify that there has never been such a plague of locusts in their lifetime.[3] He predicts that the children of Judah will never see a plague of locusts like it again in their own lifetime. The Lord is trying to capture Judah's attention by snatching wine from every drunkard's lips, grain and drink offerings from every greedy priest, wheat and barley from every idolatrous farmer, and figs,

---

[1] The main problem with this view is that Joel never lists the sins of Judah. He clearly assumes that we already know their sins in detail from having read the writings of the other prophets.

[2] Joel was a very common name in ancient Israel. Twelve other Joels are mentioned in the Old Testament.

[3] The Hebrew word *zeqēnīm* in 1:2 can either mean *elders* (as in 1:14) or *old men* (as in 2:16).

olive oil, dates and pomegranates from every busy housewife. The Lord has judged the nation of Judah in order to bring it back to his glorious Plan "A".

A plague of locusts is a terrible thing. Billions of locusts band together to cover hundreds of square miles and to consume thousands of tons of crops each day. It was a plague of locusts that humbled Pharaoh in Exodus 10 and a plague of locusts that was listed among God's curses for disobedient Israel in Deuteronomy 28: *"You will sow much seed in the field but you will harvest little, because locusts will devour it... Swarms of locusts will take over all your trees and the crops of your land."* Joel therefore urges the people of Judah to recognize that the hand of God is behind their national disaster, proving to them that they have left his path of blessing and have forfeited his Plan "A". Joel pleads with them to *"mourn like a virgin in sackcloth grieving for the betrothed of her youth"* because this is only the beginning of God's Plan "B". Unless they weep before God like a young bride whose fiancé has died on his way to the altar, something far worse is about to happen to them.[4]

It is amazing how resistant God's people can be to the suggestion that God is judging them. In the past seventy years, the number of people who attend church on a Sunday in the United Kingdom has plummeted by almost 90 per cent, yet believers put a brave face on the problem and carry on with barely a tear. In 1:13–20, Joel pleads with the priests to lead their nation back to God.[5] If they put on sackcloth and weep over the sins of Judah, their repentance will be infectious. They will be able to summon the elders and the people of Judah to the

---

[4] Joel uses vivid images to stir our emotions: she wears sackcloth instead of a wedding dress to mourn her virginity instead of fertility. That's how Joel says we also ought to mourn for the unfruitful Bride of Christ.

[5] Like Micah, Joel uses puns in his prophecies. The Hebrew word for *field* sounds like *destroyed* in 1:10, and the Hebrew word for *Almighty* sounds like *destruction* in 1:15.

Temple for a national day of fasting and repentance.[6] He warns them that unless they lead God's people into such prayers of repentance for their empty barns, their hungry cattle and their dried-up rivers, Judah will reap an even greater day of disaster – the one we read about in chapter 2: *"Alas for that day! For the day of the Lord is near; it will come like destruction from the Almighty."*[7]

We are living through our own version of what happened to Judah in the days of Joel. Mark Sayers observes that

In the West we are witnessing a number of disappearances. The ongoing disappearance of the Judeo-Christian worldview from Western culture. The disappearance of a large segment of believers, who across the Western world are leaving churches, walking away from active faith, or faith altogether during their young adult years. The disappearances of thousands of churches across the West, as churches close or begin the process of winding down, and as the heavily represented builder and boomer generations within the church enter their twilight years and pass from this life. The disappearance of a mode of church engagement characterized by commitment, resilience, and sacrifice among many Western believers. In its place a new mode of disengaged Christian faith and church interaction is emerging. This new mode

---

[6] It is unusual that Joel fails to mention the king in 1:13–14. Rather than proving that he prophesied after Judah's return from exile, however, it suggests to me that he prophesied during the reign of the evil King Ahaz (735–715 BC). Ahaz was too busy sacrificing his children to Molech to lead his nation back to the Lord.

[7] The mention of dried-up rivers in 1:20 shows us that Judah had already begun to reap even greater disaster. The devastation of the plague of locusts had now been compounded by a terrible drought. One of the biggest lessons of Joel is that God's judgment does not automatically lead to repentance. We have to choose.

is characterized by sporadic engagement, passivity, commitment phobia, and a consumerist framework.[8]

Let's therefore be quicker to grieve and repent over the sins of God's people than the people of Judah. Let's call others to pray with us, like Joel in 1:2–18, but let's also be prepared to pray on our own if we have to, like Joel in 1:19–20. *"To you, Lord, I call,"* he prays by himself when his nation refuses to listen. Let's recognize God's hand at work behind the disappearing Church and let's weep like a bereaved bride for its revival.

---

[8] Mark Sayers in his book *Disappearing Church* (2016).

Human Army (Joel 2:1–27)

The day of the Lord is coming... A large and mighty army comes.

(Joel 2:1–2)

After Joel prophesied about the locust army and prayed for the Lord to revive his nation, things suddenly began to look up for the southern kingdom of Judah. The evil King Ahaz died and was succeeded by his son, the godly King Hezekiah, the one about whom 2 Kings 18 says, *"Hezekiah trusted in the Lord, the God of Israel. There was no one like him among all the kings of Judah, either before him or after him. He held fast to the Lord and did not stop following him; he kept the commands the Lord had given Moses."*

149

King Hezekiah did as Joel prophesied. He called the people to assemble at the Temple to confess their sin and recommit themselves to pursuing God's Plan "A" for their nation.[1] As a result, Judah enjoyed fourteen golden years of blessing from 715 to 701 BC. Then Hezekiah did something stupid. He thought that he knew better than the prophet Isaiah.

The city of Babylon and the nation of Egypt were assembling a coalition of armies to resist Assyrian rule. King Hezekiah felt very flattered to be wooed by their envoys, so he sinfully boasted to them about his nation's prosperity. When the Lord sent the prophet Isaiah to confront him with his sinfulness, he refused to repent. He convinced himself that no harm could ever befall Judah during his own lifetime. Although Isaiah warned him to stay out of the coalition, he burned his bridges by refusing to

---

[1] 2 Kings 18; 2 Chronicles 29–31.

pay any further tribute to Assyria in 701 BC.[2] Neither Babylon nor Egypt was able to prevent Sennacherib's retaliation. The Assyrian invasion spelled even greater disaster for Judah than the plague of locusts a few years earlier. Happily, Joel had already predicted that this would happen and how Judah ought to respond.[3]

In 2:1–11, Joel explains that the Assyrian invasion is *"the day of the Lord"* that he warned about in 1:15. This is good news. Although the land will be overrun by the largest and strongest army so far known to man, Joel predicts that the real force at work behind it won't be Sennacherib, but the Lord.[4] Sennacherib will believe himself to be at the head of the army, but God will be leading him by the nose in order to fulfil his Plan "B" promises to complacent Judah. *"The Lord thunders at the head of his army; his forces are beyond number, and mighty is the army that obeys his command. The day of the Lord is great; it is dreadful. Who can endure it?"* Only those who recognize that the sounding of the *ram's horn* in 2:1 links what is happening to the work of Jesus, the slaughtered Lamb. What looks like disaster for God's people is all part of his long-term plan for their salvation.[5]

Joel tells the people of Judah to face up to the scale of God's judgment towards them. They must not downplay the might of the Assyrian army. Joel compares it to the locust army that

---

[2] 2 Kings 20:12–19; Isaiah 20:1–6; 30:1–5; 31:1–3; 39:1–8. I explain in *Straight to the Heart of Isaiah* how we know that all of these events took place before 701 BC, even though the story is told in a topsy-turvy way.

[3] Note that Joel doesn't say that the events of 701 BC *have* happened, but that they *will* happen. He appears to have prophesied these verses ahead of time, at the same time as chapter 1, under King Ahaz (735–715 BC).

[4] Joel's prediction in 2:2 that this army will be the strongest army ever assembled in history is a clue that Sennacherib and his Assyrian army are a prophetic picture of Satan and his demon army. We will explore this further in the next chapter. The events of 701 BC are meant to encourage beleaguered Christians today.

[5] This isn't an Assyrian battle trumpet, but the ancient Israelite equivalent of an air-raid siren. Amos 3:6 reminds us that the sounding of the *shōphar* was one of the most terrifying sounds to fill an ancient city.

devastated their land a few years earlier, turning land as fertile as the Garden of Eden into a desert wasteland where nothing grows. The Assyrian foot soldiers will be as fast as horses and as nimble as chariots. They will barely miss a step clambering over Judah's city walls. Joel therefore tells the people to rush quickly to God with their problem. It's the same for us. Only if we recognize that God is behind the decline of the Church will we repent of our sin and receive revival from his willing hand.[6]

That's why, in 2:12, the Lord urges the people of Judah to repent of their sin. He spoke these words through Joel before the invasion came so that they would know what to do when the Day of the Lord finally arrived.[7] It is not too late for them to go back to his Plan "A" for their nation. *"'Even now,' declares the Lord, 'return to me with all your heart, with fasting and weeping and mourning.'"* He still speaks those same words to us today.

In 2:13–17, Joel encourages the people of Judah to respond to God's gracious words towards them. He urges them to offer real repentance that is more than superficial because God isn't looking for the torn clothes of an ancient mourner, but for a heart that is genuinely contrite over sin. If the leaders of Judah sound the ram's horn trumpet a second time to call their nation back to God, Joel promises that they will find him still to be the gracious God that Moses met at Mount Sinai. He will still be for them *"the Lord, the Lord, the compassionate and gracious God, slow to anger, abounding in love and faithfulness, maintaining love to thousands, and forgiving wickedness, rebellion and sin"*.[8]

Having used the vivid picture of a grieving bride in 1:8, Joel stirs our emotions here in 2:16 through another vivid picture.

---

[6] Revelation 2:5 tells us that only Jesus closes down churches, never the Devil.

[7] For other references to *"the Day of the Lord"*, see Isaiah 13:6–9; Ezekiel 13:5; 30:3; Amos 5:18–20; Obadiah 15; Zephaniah 1:7, 14; Zechariah 14:1; Malachi 4:5; 1 Corinthians 5:5; 1 Thessalonians 5:2; 2 Peter 3:10.

[8] Exodus 34:6–7. This expression of God's character ties in with Jonah 4:2, just as the talk of God *relenting* from his judgment in 2:14 (*nāham*) ties in with Jonah 3:9–10 and 4:2.

This time, he says that Judah's peril is so serious that even newly-wed couples disappearing into their bridal chambers ought to put off consummating their marriage until later so that they can pray. Eager bridegrooms, nursing mothers, elderly grandparents and busy priests ought to drop everything in order to devote themselves to doing what matters most: praying urgent prayers of national repentance. If they pray such prayers, the Lord will not have to risk the nations misunderstanding his Plan "B". He will restore his people back to Plan "A".[9]

In 2:18–27, Joel therefore encourages the people of Judah that the Lord will listen to them if they repent wholeheartedly. He will send the Assyrian army back north with its tail between its legs, decimating its ranks along the way.[10] He will restore the nation of Judah back to the blessings of his Plan "A", causing their barns and vats to overflow with grain and wine and oil. He will grant them all the blessings that are listed in Deuteronomy 28 and none of the curses. He will turn their disaster into their salvation.

So pray. Pray prayers of repentance for your own sin, for the sins of your church and for the sins of the Church right across your nation. Drop whatever you are doing and ask God to forgive his people and restore them to his Plan "A". If you are willing to confess that you are under God's curse because of sin then, through the slaughtered Lamb, all his blessings are yours for the asking. *Blessing or curse – you decide.*

---

[9] Note the way that Joel teaches us to pray in 2:17. We ought to remind the Lord that, whenever the Church looks weak, unbelievers conclude that he is either non-existent, too weak or too uncaring to save his people.

[10] See 2 Kings 19:35–37. The promise in 2:20 that the army will drown in the Dead Sea and the Mediterranean continues to liken the Assyrian army to a plague of locusts. See Exodus 10:19 and 14:26–28.

Spirit-Filled Army
(Joel 2:18–32)

*"Afterwards, I will pour out my Spirit on all people...
and everyone who calls on the name of the Lord will
be saved."*

(Joel 2:28, 32)

When William Booth arrived in London in 1865, the British Church was much like Judah in the book of Joel. It had a veneer of godliness but it was sinful at its heart. That's why its attendance numbers had plummeted in recent years. Six years earlier, Charles Darwin had published *On the Origin of Species*, giving the educated classes a convenient excuse for abandoning their dwindling faith in God. As for the common people, they had long since rejected the Church as a hotbed of oppression and hypocrisy. William Booth reflected later that in his early days of preaching, *"The respectable portion of the community were too proud to enter [Gospel-preaching churches] and the lower orders were as positively opposed to anything of that kind as they could possibly be."*[1]

But William Booth believed the promises of God in Joel 2. He believed that the Lord always makes his people fruitful if they confess their sins and return to him with all their hearts (2:18–24).[2] He believed that the Lord lifts their shame and routs the demon armies that stand against them (2:19–20).[3] He believed

---

[1] William Booth in his pamphlet *How We Began* (1886).

[2] Just as all needed to repent in 1:2–2:17, so do all enjoy the blessings that come through repentance in 2:18–32.

[3] Joel cannot simply be talking about the Assyrians in 2:20 because their army was not drowned in the sea. Acts 2:17–21 says it refers to our own battle too. See Exodus 14:26–31; Jeremiah 51:63–64; Mark 5:12–13.

that the Lord always revives his repentant people – described by Joel as granting them *"abundant showers, both autumn and spring rains"* (2:23).[4] He believed that the Lord promises, *"I will repay you for the years the locusts have eaten"* (2:25).[5] Instead of looking at his backslidden nation and throwing his hands up in despair, he looked at the promises in the book of Joel and believed that God had set the stage for a great national revival.

Most of all, William Booth believed in Jesus as the Saviour of the world. Joel has already hinted at the importance of the coming of the Messiah by referring to the blowing of the *ram's horn* in 2:1 and 15. Now he drops another big hint for his readers in 2:23. The Hebrew phrase *nāthan lākem hamōreh litsedāqāh* can either be translated *"he has given you the autumn rains because of his righteousness"* or *"he has given you the Teacher of Righteousness"*. Peter goes with the second reading on the Day of Pentecost when he quotes from 2:28–32 in Acts 2:17–21 and applies it to the Christians in Jerusalem. These five verses are so important that in Hebrew texts they form a separate chapter 3, turning what we call Joel 3 into Joel 4. They contain amazing promises for us in our own day, so let's read these five verses slowly and carefully.

Joel begins by telling us that these five verses are for *afterwards*. In other words, they are not for the post-invasion people of Judah but for people who put their faith in the Messiah many centuries later. Peter makes this explicit when he says that Joel is talking about what will happen *"in the last days"* – in other words, throughout the whole of AD history, from the ascension of Jesus until his second coming. These words are therefore equally God's promise for our own day: *"I will pour out my Spirit on all people."*

---

[4] Israelite farmers relied on the autumn rains to help their newly planted seeds to grow, and on the spring rains to help their mature plants to bear ample fruit. Both were vital to a successful harvest.

[5] The Lord states again in 2:25 that *he* humbles his people in order to revive them. Don't blame it on the Devil. Yes, the Church declines in many generations, but God more than makes up for it in times of revival.

William Booth pointed to this as the reason why the Salvation Army that he founded was so phenomenally successful. From very humble beginnings in 1865, he started over 2,500 mission stations that gathered over 300,000 people weekly within only twenty-two years. In their services, he taught people to sing in one of his most famous hymns:

Thou Christ of burning, cleansing flame,
Send the fire, send the fire, send the fire!
Thy blood-bought gift today we claim,
Send the fire, send the fire, send the fire!
Look down and see this waiting host,
Give us the promised Holy Ghost;
We want another Pentecost,
Send the fire, send the fire, send the fire!

'Tis fire we want, for fire we plead,
Send the fire, send the fire, send the fire!
The fire will meet our every need,
Send the fire, send the fire, send the fire!
For strength to ever do the right,
For grace to conquer in the fight,
For power to walk the world in white,
Send the fire, send the fire, send the fire![6]

William Booth's massive fruitfulness came from his discovery that the prophet Joel had promised everything would change with the arrival of the Messiah. In the Old Testament, a handful of individuals were filled with the Holy Spirit for short periods of time, but Peter had quoted from these five verses on the Day of Pentecost to proclaim that those days were over. The last days had begun and now everybody was to be a Gideon, a David or an Isaiah. When people barred Booth from their pulpits for giving ordinary people ideas above their station, he decided to plant new churches

---

[6] William Booth in his hymn "Send the Fire" (1894).

in every town. When people laughed at him and asked him where he thought that he would find so many new church leaders, he turned to these verses in Joel and proclaimed that *"We shall get them from the public houses. Men who have felt the fire will be the best men to rescue others, and we shall never fail in getting the right men."* From these verses, he also released thousands of female Gospel preachers, claiming that *"Some of my best men are women."*[7]

So don't fail to spot how radical these five verses are. Joel is promising us that, if the Church repents and turns back to the Lord, he will make it fruitful throughout AD history by pouring out his Holy Spirit on the *"old"*, on the *"young"* and on *"both men and women"*. Nobody will be excluded based on age or gender or nationality. This promise belongs to believers who are as Gentile as the Assyrians as much as it does to those as Jewish as the people of Judah.[8] *"Everyone who calls on the name of the Lord will be saved."*[9]

Joel reminds us in 2:30–31 that AD history will soon come to an end, describing the second coming of Jesus as *"the great and dreadful day of the Lord"*. He wants to instil in us the same urgency that he tried to instil in the people of Judah, to believe the Gospel and, like William Booth, to tell anyone – absolutely anyone – the good news that the Lord wants to forgive them and to recruit them into the ranks of his Spirit-filled army.[10]

---

[7] The Lord promises literally in 2:28 to pour out his Spirit *"on all flesh"*. Our problem is that we tend to judge people's usefulness to God in fleshly terms, whereas his Spirit trumps our fleshly weakness every time.

[8] That's why it is so tragic when any Christian says that being filled with God's Spirit is "not for me". The fulfilment of the Law of Moses in Jesus (Numbers 11:29; Romans 10:4) means that it's for everyone! See Isaiah 32:15; 44:3; Ezekiel 36:26–27; 39:29; Zechariah 12:10.

[9] Joel says two radical things here. First, that Jews cannot be saved by their ethnicity but only by calling on their Messiah. Second, that no Gentile is excluded on the basis of who they are or what they have done. Both inspire Paul to quote this verse in Romans 10:13 as a summary of how to be saved.

[10] Joel ties this back into God's plans for Judah in 2:32. Salvation will come through a Jew being crucified outside the walls of Jerusalem on Mount Zion. Its news will go out to the world through Jewish apostles.

The Last Battle
(Joel 3:1–21)

*Multitudes, multitudes in the valley of decision! For
the day of the Lord is near in the valley of decision!*
(Joel 3:14)

The year 701 BC brought terrible judgment for the people of
Judah. The Annals of Sennacherib, now on display in the British
Museum in London, claim that he brought back 200,150 Jewish
men and women to Assyria as slaves. We do not know how
many more he killed when he captured their fortress cities, but
the slaughter was terrible.

The year 701 BC also brought terrible judgment for the
Assyrians and for the nations allied with them against Judah.
When King Hezekiah finally listened to Isaiah and led the
besieged citizens of Jerusalem in belated prayers of repentance,
the Lord was true to his word. He sent his angel into the valley
beneath the walls of Jerusalem and slaughtered 185,000 soldiers
in a single night.[1] For perspective, bear in mind that fewer
than 20,000 British soldiers were killed on the first day of the
Somme and that fewer than 80,000 Japanese were killed when
the atomic bomb fell on Hiroshima. What happened outside
the walls of Jerusalem in 701 BC was without parallel even in
modern warfare.

It therefore shouldn't surprise us that Joel uses the events
of 701 BC as a picture of the final Day of Judgment when the
Messiah returns. He told us three times in his first two chapters

---

[1] See 2 Kings 19:35–36; Isaiah 37:36–37.

that the plague of locusts was a Day of the Lord that pointed to a greater Day of the Lord that would come in 701 BC.[2] He told us in 2:31 that this second Day of the Lord would itself point to an even greater Day of the Lord at the end of time. The locusts and Assyrians are prophetic pictures of *"the great and dreadful day of the Lord"*.[3]

In 3:1–8, the Lord inspires the prophet Joel to warn the nations that he will destroy them in the Valley of Jehoshaphat unless they repent and become part of the people of God. Understanding that this is a prophecy about the return of Jesus from heaven prevents us from wasting endless hours trying to pinpoint the location of the Valley of Jehoshaphat. There was no such place in the time of Joel. The Lord is likening the destruction of those who resist the Messiah to the destruction of the Assyrian army encamped beneath the walls of Jerusalem in 701 BC.[4] Jehoshaphat means *The Lord Will Judge* and it was the name of a king of Judah who defeated a great coalition of pagan nations in 2 Chronicles 20. God warns the nations that each little Day of the Lord in the past is a prophetic picture of a global Day of the Lord that is coming at the end of time.

The Lord says this final Day of Judgment will take place *"in those days and at that time, when I restore the fortunes of Judah and Jerusalem"* – in other words, at the end of Church history, when the message about the Jewish Messiah and the New Jerusalem that he is building has spread to every corner of the world. God uses the word *my* seven times in 3:2–5 in order to emphasize that the Church will be his people. He uses the word *me* three times in 3:4 to emphasize that any attack on

---

[2] See Joel 1:15; 2:1, 11.

[3] Peter quotes from the Greek Septuagint Old Testament in Acts 2 and so he speaks about *the great and glorious Day of the Lord*. It will be dreadful for those who rebel against God but glorious for those who repent.

[4] Other clues that the name is symbolic are that it is also called *the Valley of Decision* in 3:14 and *the Hill of Megiddo* in Revelation 16:12–16 (*Armageddon* in Greek) – even though Megiddo is 60 miles north of Jerusalem!

the Church is therefore an attack on him.[5] He lists the sins of Assyria and of its pagan allies in 701 BC as a symbol of all the sin he will expose and judge on that final Judgment Day.[6]

In 3:9–11, Joel calls the pagan nations to assemble for a fight. He flips around a famous prophecy from two of his contemporaries in Isaiah 2:4 and Micah 4:3, urging the pagans to turn their ploughshares into swords and their pruning hooks into spears. He calls even the weakest of them to assemble, because the Lord wants to judge everyone. Having lured them into place, he then springs the trap: *"Bring down your warriors, Lord!"*

In 3:12–13, the Lord responds. He promises to harvest the wicked like grapes and to crush them in the winepress of his judgment until his vats overflow. The New Testament picks up on this imagery in Revelation 14:14–20. Make no mistake about it: the Lord is determined to judge all those who reject his offer of salvation through Jesus.

In 3:14–16, Joel celebrates this final Day of the Lord. He renames the Valley of Jehoshaphat the Valley of Decision, not because it is where the pagan nations decide whether or not to surrender to the Messiah, but because it is where he cements the decision that they have already made.[7] If they have chosen to repent and to become part of the people of God, *"the Lord will be a refuge for his people, a stronghold for the people of Israel".* But if they have chosen to persist in their sinful ways, *"the Lord will roar from Zion and thunder from Jerusalem".* This last phrase is a direct quotation from Amos 1:2, which brings us full circle. God has judged his people because he loves them and wants to

---

[5] Jesus does exactly the same thing when talking to Saul of Tarsus in Acts 9:4.

[6] We can tell this is symbolic because the Philistines (who lived in modern-day Gaza) and the Sabeans (the people of Sheba, who lived in modern-day Yemen) ceased to exist as people groups over 2,000 years ago.

[7] Jesus may also have had Joel 3 in mind when he referred to hell as *Gehenna*, which is Greek for *the Valley of Hinnom*. This was the name of the place outside the walls of Jerusalem where rubbish was burned.

bring them to repentance before his judgment falls and decision time is over.

In 3:17–21, God ends the book of Joel by explaining what the Day of the Lord will mean for his people. Again he uses the events of 701 BC as a prophetic picture of his ultimate act of deliverance at the end of time. In the same way that Hezekiah's generation rejoiced that the Lord repelled the Assyrians because he dwelt in the Temple in Jerusalem, the people of God will rejoice throughout eternity that the Lord has rid the earth of all sin and has come down to dwell with them forever. That's why the bumper harvests in the years that followed the events of 701 BC become a prophetic picture of the new heavens and new earth that are described in Isaiah 66 and Revelation 21–22.[8] The abundant water that came from heaven in those years becomes a picture of the river of the Holy Spirit that is described in Revelation 22.[9] Egypt and Edom, both traitors towards Judah in 701 BC, become a picture of those who will be thrown into hell. Jerusalem's survival becomes a picture of the eternal life that belongs to God's people.

Suddenly we begin to see why the Lord is so stern with the people of Israel and Judah in the Minor Prophets. He speaks words of judgment over them and follows through on his threats so that their judgment in this age will spare them from judgment in the age to come. As we end the book of Joel, let's therefore ask the Lord to reveal our own sin to us and let's repent with the tears of a bride who is bereaved on her way to the altar.

Let's prepare to meet the Lord in the Valley of Decision. *Blessing or curse – you decide.*

---

[8] Revelation 21:27 explains that Joel does not mean that no Gentile will be saved out of God's judgment, but that nobody – whether Jew or Gentile – will be saved unless they become part of the true people of God.

[9] We can hear the echo of 3:18 in Psalm 46:4; Ezekiel 47:1–12; Zechariah 14:8; John 4:10–14 and 7:37–39.

What Lies Beneath
(Zephaniah 1:1–6)

"I will sweep away everything from the face of the earth," declares the Lord.

(Zephaniah 1:2)

Captain James Saumarez faced the facts. He was colossally outgunned. The French invasion fleet that was circling the British island of Guernsey carried over twice as many cannon as the few ships that he commanded to defend it. He knew that by the end of the day – Sunday, 8th June 1794 – his ships would lie at the bottom of the English Channel unless he could turn one fact to his advantage: he knew what lay beneath the waves.

Saumarez was a born-and-bred Guernseyman. He knew the underwater rocks around his island better than most people know their own backyards. He was therefore able to fire on the French fleet and withdraw to such rocky waters that the French commanders were too frightened to pursue him and had to give up on their invasion plans. As he piloted his fleet through danger, a fellow Guernseyman encouraged him by pointing to the shore: *"I am quite sure about our position – there is your house and there is mine."*

Zephaniah was a prophet who told the people of Judah what lay beneath the surface of their nation's apparent return to God. His name is Hebrew for *Hidden by God*, so we are meant to see his prophecies as an unveiling of divine truth to a misguided generation. If we want to understand his words, we need to go beneath the surface ourselves and to discover what happened during the century after Micah and Joel prophesied.

King Hezekiah's godly response to the words of Micah, Joel and Isaiah resulted in the Lord delivering Judah in 701 BC from the Assyrian invasion army, just as he had promised he would. Fifteen years later, however, he was succeeded by his son Manasseh, the most ungodly king that ever sat on the throne of Judah. He filled his kingdom with shrines and altars to pagan idols such as the harvest god Baal and the fertility goddess Asherah. He embraced black magic and even sacrificed some of his children in the fire to win the favour of the pagan idol Molech. He executed the prophet Isaiah and tried to purge Jerusalem of anybody else who spoke out against his policy of paganizing Judah. Although he repented of this in his older years and received forgiveness personally, he had set his kingdom on a pathway to destruction. He had created a nation that was more like Israel under King Ahab than Judah under King Hezekiah.[1]

When Manasseh died, his son Amon led the people of Judah into ever-increasing idolatry. Even when he was assassinated two years into his reign and succeeded by his eight-year-old son Josiah, Judah continued its fatal turning away from God. But then something unexpected happened. At the age of sixteen, King Josiah was converted to the Lord. As soon as he was old enough to despatch his regents, he attempted to lead his nation back to God. He summoned everybody to the Temple courtyards so that he could personally read to them the Law of Moses and urge them to choose the path of God's blessing instead of his curse. He led them in a prayer to renew their covenant with God and he demanded that they rid the land of idols.[2] On the surface, it appeared as though the people of Judah had returned to God. That's why the Lord sent the prophet Zephaniah to reveal what lay beneath the surface of their supposed national revival.

[1] 2 Kings 21:1–16; 23:26–27; 24:3–4; 2 Chronicles 33:1–20; Jeremiah 15:4.

[2] 2 Kings 22:1–23:28; 2 Chronicles 33:21–35:19. Josiah began to lead Judah back to the Lord once he was aged 20, from 628 BC, culminating in his summons to listen to the Law of Moses in 622 BC.

The opening verse of Zephaniah introduces him as a great-grandson of King Hezekiah, just like King Josiah, during whose reign it says he prophesied. Although it is tempting to imagine that, as a distant member of the royal family, Zephaniah was instrumental in Josiah's conversion there is actually nothing in this book to indicate that the two men even knew each other on first-name terms. Zephaniah prophesies to the nation of Judah rather than to its king, and he offers several clues in his opening verses which indicate that he is speaking *after* Josiah's national revival, and not before.

For a start, in 1:4 Zephaniah predicts God's judgment on *"every remnant of Baal worship"* in the land of Judah. It would have made no sense to speak of "remnants" of idolatry in the days before Josiah's reforms, since in those days Baal worship was encouraged everywhere. In 1:5, Zephaniah confronts *"those who bow down and swear by the Lord and who also swear by Molech"*, confirming that he is speaking into a context where a nominal commitment to the Lord is masking secret idolatry – something that was not a problem in the openly pagan days when regents ruled for the young Josiah.[3] In 1:6, Zephaniah addresses his warning to *"those who turn back from following the Lord"* – in other words, to those who are reneging on the pledge that they made in the Temple courtyards for the sake of impressing King Josiah.

If this is not clear enough from the words of Zephaniah, his great contemporary Jeremiah explains further. Like Captain Saumarez and his Guernsey crewmate, these two prophets saw what was happening beneath the surface of Judah's national revival. King Josiah had been sincere, but his subjects were motivated more by political expediency than by genuine repentance. Jeremiah warns that *"'Judah did not return to me with all her heart, but only in pretence,' declares the Lord...*

---

[3] *"The starry host"* indicates that the people of Judah worshipped the stars, sun and moon at rooftop shrines (2 Kings 23:4), but it also identifies their idols as demons. The same Hebrew phrase is used in 1 Kings 22:19.

'Faithless Israel is more righteous than unfaithful Judah.'"[4] Shocking though it sounds, the Lord tells Judah that he preferred the barefaced sinfulness of Israel to their spiritual hypocrisy. He sees what lies beneath their superficial repentance. They are exacerbating their idolatry by living out a lie.

In his novel *The Toilers of the Sea*, Victor Hugo describes how vital it was for Guernsey sailors such as Saumarez to know the rocks that lay beneath the waves around their island. *"The true pilot is the sailor who navigates the seabed rather than its surface... You might well think that he carried in his head a map of the sea bottom."*[5] Prophets such as Zephaniah remind us that, in the same way, the Lord wants us to see what lies beneath the spiritual veneer of our own churches and nations too. They will be shipwrecked unless we do.

Zephaniah warns us that the Lord is not impressed by how orthodox we are in our creeds and vision statements. He is not swayed by how loudly we sing about our love for him on a Sunday. He is interested in what is happening beneath the surface of our hearts all week long. As he reverses Genesis 1 at the start of Zephaniah – sweeping away all the people, animals, birds and fish from the earth – he is calling us to be honest with him. *"I will sweep away everything... [to reveal] the idols that cause the wicked to stumble."*

---

[4] Jeremiah 3:6–11. The Lord issues a similar shocking warning to half-hearted Christians in Revelation 3:15. He prefers out-and-out rebellion to a veneer of faith that masks a heart that is still full of idolatry.

[5] Victor Hugo lived in exile in Guernsey from 1855 to 1870 and set his 1866 novel on the island.

Before the Day
(Zephaniah 1:7–2:3)

Gather yourselves together… before the day of the Lord's wrath comes upon you.

(Zephaniah 2:1–2)

Few people saw it coming, but the nation of Judah was about to be shipwrecked on the jagged rocks of its secret sin against the Lord. Zephaniah does not describe what lies beneath the surface of its national revival because he likes complaining, but because God loves his people so much that he always sends prophets and preachers to warn them that he sees beneath the surface of their hearts and that his day of reckoning is near.

Zephaniah reveals the danger gradually, like the tide going out on a beach slowly to reveal reefs that are fatal to shipping at high tide. He chooses his words carefully in order to invite us to repent instead of running away from God. We need to read these verses slowly, because even the best of us still harbour secret sins against God in our hearts. Zephaniah prophesied these words to the people of Judah, but the Lord still wants to use them to speak to you and me. Sin has not become any less fatal over time.

In 1:7, Zephaniah introduces the big theme of his book of prophecies: the Day of the Lord is coming. In his three chapters, he refers to *the Day* a whopping twenty times. Like Amos and Joel, he warns us that the destruction of Israel and the Assyrian invasion of Judah were simply little days that prefigure a far greater Day to come. For Judah, this meant the day of its destruction by the Babylonians in 586 BC, but when Zephaniah says that *"The Lord has prepared a sacrifice; he has consecrated those he has invited"* we are also reminded of the parables in which Jesus describes the final Day of Judgment. He invites us to exchange God's curse for blessing through his death on the cross for our sins, but we need to respond to that invitation.[1] *Blessing or curse – you decide.*

In 1:8–9, the tide recedes further to reveal a terrifying truth. Unless we receive the sacrifice that God has prepared for us in Jesus, we will be sacrificed ourselves. The Lord warned Adam and Eve in Genesis 2:17 that rebellion against his rule will always end in death, so if we fail to say "yes" to the death of Jesus on our behalf, God's justice will be satisfied through our own deaths instead.[2] No wonder Zephaniah tells us in 1:7 to *"be silent before the Sovereign Lord"*, because this is sobering stuff. He says that the Lord sees through the *"foreign clothes"* worn by Josiah's sons and courtiers (speaking of continued pagan influence).[3] He sees *"all who avoid stepping on the threshold"* (speaking of continued pagan superstition, as described in 1 Samuel 5:4–5). He sees all the ways in which the people of Judah are turning his Temple into *"the temple of their gods"* by bringing in idols of *"violence and deceit"*, even as they carry out idols of wood and stone.[4]

I find these verses very challenging. Although I talk about my love for the Lord, I am very aware that sin still lurks in the dark recesses of my heart. I feel challenged that John Calvin was

---

[1] Compare 1:7 with Matthew 22:4 and Luke 14:16–17. The New Testament calls the second coming of Jesus the ultimate *"Day of the Lord"* in 1 Corinthians 5:5; 2 Corinthians 1:14; 1 Thessalonians 5:2 and 2 Peter 3:10. Note therefore the echo of Zephaniah 1:15 in Matthew 24:29.

[2] God's judgment is also likened to the offering of a blood sacrifice in Isaiah 34:5–7 and Jeremiah 46:10.

[3] Josiah's eldest son died prematurely (1 Chronicles 3:15), his second son was left unburied (Jeremiah 22:18–19; 36:30), his third son was blinded (2 Kings 25:7) and his fourth son died in exile (2 Kings 23:31–34).

[4] If the Lord were talking about their pagan temples, the word would be plural. But *temple* is singular.

right to warn Protestants who prided themselves on removing icons from their churches that they must not miss the idols inside their hearts, pointing out that *"The human mind is a perpetual idol factory."*[5] I am reminded of Ezekiel 14:3, which warns that people *"set up idols in their hearts"*, and of Ephesians 5:5, where Paul teaches that greed and sexual immorality are more than simple sins: they are outward symptoms of the fact that we still worship foul idols alongside the Lord in our hearts. As the tide recedes on Zephaniah's beach, I feel uneasy about what God sees beneath the surface of my own heart. If you feel the same conviction of sin, put this book down for a while and confess it to the Lord in prayer. He doesn't want to rub it in. He wants to rub it out.[6]

In 1:10–18, the tide goes out still further to remove any possibility that the Lord might be talking about the pagan nations. Zephaniah makes it clear that he is talking about the secret sins of Judah by referring to the different districts of Jerusalem by name: the Fish Gate, the New Quarter and the Market District.[7] He emphasizes the totality of God's judgment by referring to the merchants, the wealthy and the common people.[8] He prophesies that an army is about to invade their land and succeed where the Assyrian army failed, because this time it will be led by the Mighty Warrior – by the Lord God himself.[9] Zephaniah does not hold

---

[5] John Calvin wrote this in 1536 in his *Institutes of the Christian Religion* (1.11.8).

[6] There is a play on words in 1:7, since the Hebrew word *qādash*, which means *to consecrate* or *to sanctify* can also mean *to set apart* for destruction. Unless we put our sins to death, they will be the death of us.

[7] The *New Quarter* is given as somebody's address in 2 Kings 22:14.

[8] The word for *merchant* in 1:11 is literally *Canaanite*, just as it was in Hosea 12:7. This described traders of any nationality, but in the context it emphasizes that Judah has become like the pagans driven out by Joshua.

[9] The Hebrew text could be saying that *the Day of the Lord will be so terrible that even a mighty warrior will shriek like a baby*, but Isaiah 42:13 suggests a better translation: the Mighty Warrior is the Lord. Zephaniah never identifies the army as that of Babylon, because such detail is secondary. What matters is that it is led by God.

back as he warns his nation that it is about to be shipwrecked by its sin.[10] *"Their blood will be poured out like dust and their entrails like dung. Neither their silver nor their gold will be able to save them on the day of the Lord's wrath."*[11]

In 2:1–3, the tide goes out all the way to reveal the only answer to Judah's predicament. They need to go back to the moment when King Josiah led them in repentance, only this time they need to repent truly instead of pretending to do so. They need to gather together as a nation before the Day of the Lord arrives. They need to humble themselves and to seek the Lord before the Day his anger falls upon them. They need to seek righteousness and to do whatever he commands. Then, and only then, will their nation stand any chance of survival. *"Perhaps you will be sheltered on the day of the Lord's anger."*

If you are a Christian, Zephaniah prophesied these words for you as well as for the people of ancient Judah. He is urging you to look beneath the surface of your own prayers and worship songs to see if there are any secret sins that are about to shipwreck you. He is urging you to gather with the other Christians in your church and to consider how much of your walk with God is real and how much is tainted with hypocrisy. He is warning you that the Day of the Lord is coming, not just for out-and-out unbelievers but also for those who profess to love God's name. He is warning you that the Final Day is very near, but reassuring you that it is the Lord's Day. You can receive his mercy and his forgiveness if you respond to these prophecies before the Day comes.[12]

---

[10] Zephaniah reminds us in 1:12 that God often uses suffering for good in the life of a believer. Like a bottle of wine that is left standing open too long, the faith of a Christian who is never jostled quickly goes sour.

[11] One of Judah's greatest "heart idols" was money, which they believed was the answer to any problem. The people of Judah were not so very different from many Christians and churches today.

[12] The Day of the Lord is *near and fast approaching* (1:7, 14), but the fact that the Lord is in charge of it changes everything (1:14). Those who receive him as Saviour today will be spared him as Judge tomorrow.

When the Sea Gets In (Zephaniah 2:4–3:8)

Of Jerusalem I thought, "Surely you will fear me and accept correction!"… But they were still eager to act corruptly in all they did.

(Zephaniah 3:7)

D. L. Moody was no stranger to the sea. He voyaged back and forth across the Atlantic Ocean more than any other nineteenth-century preacher. He knew what he was talking about when he warned in one of his sermons that *"Christians should live in the world, but not be filled with it. A ship lives in the water; but if the water gets into the ship, she goes to the bottom. So Christians may live in the world; but if the world gets into them, they sink."*[1]

The Lord had intended Judah to be a ship of godliness on the sinful ocean of the world. Like Noah's ark, through which he had saved the human race many centuries before, he wanted Judah to act as a lifeboat for anybody who tired of sin and was willing to be saved. In 2:4–15, Zephaniah therefore reveals God's response to the pagan nations that have refused his Gospel invitation, extended to them through his people.

In 2:4–7, he confronts the Philistines, the long-standing enemies of God's people. He names their four major cities – Gaza, Ashkelon, Ashdod and Ekron – in order to emphasize their total destruction.[2] Like Amos and Isaiah, Zephaniah warns

---

[1] Included by Charles N. Douglas in his compendium of *Forty Thousand Quotations* (1917).

[2] Joshua 13:3; 1 Samuel 6:17. Gath appears to have already been annexed by Judah.

that not a single Philistine will survive the bloodbath that the army of Babylon will unleash upon them.[3] They are Kerethites (the descendants of the Sea Peoples, who came across the water from Crete) and they are about to be shipwrecked on the jagged rocks of their sin. When the people of Judah return from exile, they will possess the fields of Philistia too.

In 2:8–11, he confronts the Moabites and Ammonites, the descendants of Lot's incestuous union with his daughters after the destruction of Sodom and Gomorrah in Genesis 19. The Lord had protected them for the sake of Lot and had invited them to share in his promises to Israel, yet instead of seizing his blessing with both hands they despised him and repeatedly attacked his people.[4] So Zephaniah prophesies that they will reap the same punishment as Sodom and Gomorrah from which their ancestors were saved. But here's the good news: he will do this to humble and save them. When the people of Judah return from exile and rule over them, *the Lord will be awesome to them*. The Moabite and Ammonite survivors will finally surrender their hearts to the God of Israel.

In 2:12–15, the Lord addresses the two fading superpowers of the day. *Cush* refers to Egypt, since the kingdoms of the upper and lower Nile had acted as one nation for over a century. Both will fall to the Babylonians and so will Assyria, destroyed so thoroughly that the ruins of its capital city Nineveh will become a ghost town.[5] Because Assyria had ignored the words of Nahum, they were about to reap the disaster that he prophesied.[6]

In 3:1–8, the Lord addresses one last nation. Although some English translations add the name of its capital city for the

---

[3] Amos 1:6–8; Isaiah 14:28–32. He does not mention Babylon by name because it was still ruled by Assyria.

[4] Deuteronomy 2:8–9, 19–21. The Lord even restored them after they fell to the Assyrians in 715 BC.

[5] Nineveh's boast in 2:15 is very similar to that of Babylon in Isaiah 47:10. One of the easiest ways to spot the jagged rocks of sin in our own hearts is to look out for signs of self-sufficiency and self-promotion.

[6] Nahum prophesied in c. 630 BC, roughly ten years before Zephaniah.

sake of clarity, it isn't in the Hebrew text for a reason. The Lord wants us to make us speculate which city he might mean by *"the city of oppressors, rebellious and defiled"* – surely Babylon?[7] He wants us to make us wonder which city it might be that *"obeys no one"*, *"accepts no correction"* and *"does not trust in the Lord"* – surely Babylon again? He does this so that he can perform a grand reveal. The city that the Lord is describing knows him as *"her God"* (3:2). It has prophets and priests and a temple and it is the custodian of God's Law (3:4).[8] It is the city where the Lord dwells in order to call the nations to salvation (3:5).[9] It is the city that he disciplined through the Assyrian army in 701 BC but which has refused to learn its lesson (3:6). He is describing Jerusalem when, in 3:7, he literally declares: *"I said, 'Surely you will fear me and accept correction!' Then her sanctuary would not be destroyed, nor would all my punishments come upon her. But they got up straightaway and acted corruptly in all they did."*

In this way Zephaniah delivers both a right hook and a left hook to the people of Judah. He begins his book of prophecies with words of judgment for their nation in 1:2–2:3 and, after a brief tour of their pagan neighbours, he returns to pound them again in 3:1–8. He does so out of love for them, because the sea has got into the lifeboat of Judah. They are just like the rest of the world. They may have said the right things when King Josiah called them back to God's plan for them to be like Noah's ark on the sinful ocean of the world, but they didn't activate the bilge

---

[7] God uses two puns in the Hebrew of 3:1. The word *yōnāh* can either mean a beautiful *dove* (God's name for Israel in Hosea 7:11) or a *city of oppressors*. The word *nige'ālāh* can either mean a *redeemed city* or a *defiled city*. Both puns emphasize how far Judah has sunk beneath its calling to be a lifeboat of salvation for the world.

[8] The Hebrew word for *law* in 3:4 is *tōrāh*. To the people of Judah, that meant the Law of Moses.

[9] Note the deliberate contrast in 3:5. *"The Lord within her is righteous"* yet they are *"the unrighteous"*.

pumps. Their superficial response has not succeeded in fooling the Lord. He sees the sin still sloshing around in their hearts.[10]

The reason why the Philistines, the Moabites, the Ammonites, the Egyptians and the Assyrians rejected the Lord was that his own people rejected him first. When the pagan nations looked at Judah, they saw nothing to attract them to the Lord. They saw empty words. They didn't want to step into God's lifeboat of salvation because they could see that it was sinking.

The same is true of many of our churches today. People are not interested in the words we speak because they see the way in which we live our lives. When they look at our marriages and our family lives and our workplace ethics and the way we treat the poor, they lose any interest in the Gospel. When they see Christians promoting their own agenda and church leaders promoting their personal profile, they conclude that the cry of the Church is like that of Nineveh in 2:15: *"I am the one! And there is none besides me."*[11]

Listen to Eugene Peterson, as he reflects on the Church in the Western world:

> *It is useful to listen to people who come into our culture from other cultures, to pay attention to what they hear and what they see. In my experience, they don't see a Christian land... They see something almost the reverse of a Christian land. They see a lot of greed and arrogance. And they see a Christian community that has almost none of the virtues of the biblical Christian community, which have to do with a sacrificial life and conspicuous love.*

---

[10] The word *"Woe!"* that introduces these eight verses was normally the first word of a Hebrew curse (2:5; Amos 5:18; 6:1; Micah 2:1; Nahum 3:1). It says to Judah: *Blessing or curse – you decide.*

[11] This is why the Bible says that judgment always starts with God's people (Romans 2:9; 1 Peter 4:17). The greater our revelation of God, the greater our accountability for how we respond to him (Luke 10:10–16).

> *Rather, they see indulgence in feelings and emotions, and*
> *an avaricious quest for gratification.*[12]

God speaks these words through Zephaniah because he loves us, so let's accept his correction.[13] Let's be honest with ourselves that the sea has got into our ship, both personally and as churches. Let's repent and ask the Lord to help us switch on our spiritual bilge pumps. Let's become the lifeboat of salvation that God intends us to be.

---

[12] He says this in *The Contemplative Pastor: Returning to the Art of Spiritual Direction* (1989).

[13] Zephaniah emphasizes in 3:2 and 7 that it is stubbornness rather than sin that sinks us. In some ways King David sinned far more than King Saul but, unlike Saul, he responded quickly to the Lord's correction.

The Remains of the Day
(Zephaniah 3:9–20)

*On that day you, Jerusalem, will not be put to shame
for all the wrongs you have done to me.*

(Zephaniah 3:11)

A far-fetched story reports a heated exchange between the captain of the USS *Abraham Lincoln* and the Canadian authorities off the coast of Newfoundland in October 1995.

US Captain: Please divert your course 15 degrees north to avoid a collision.

Canadian: Negative. Recommend you divert your course 15 degrees south to avoid collision.

US Captain: This is the captain of a US navy ship. I repeat, please divert your course.

Canadian: Negative again. Please divert your course urgently.

US Captain: This is the aircraft carrier USS *Abraham Lincoln*, accompanied by three destroyers. You must change your course 15 degrees north, that is one-five degrees north, or counter-measures will be undertaken to ensure the safety of this ship.

Canadian: This is a lighthouse. It's your call.

Whether or not such an exchange actually took place, it is helpful to think of it when we read the prophecies of Zephaniah. It is easy to read them as if the Lord has lost his love for the people of Judah. That exchange helps to shift our perspective. The Lord is not being awkward. He speaks so fiercely because he loves the people of Judah and wants to prevent them from making a shipwreck of their souls. We mustn't misunderstand what he is saying at the end of 3:8 when he refers to *"the fire of my jealous anger"*.

We tend to use the word jealousy to mean something entirely negative: you have something I want so I am jealous of you because I wish it were mine. But the word has two meanings, and not just one. It also carries the positive sense of placing proper value on the things we hold most sacred in our lives. I love my daughter, so I am jealous of my time with her and don't want to waste it on other things. I love my wife, so I am jealous of our friendship and want to deal radically with whatever damages it. It is in this second sense that the Lord warns Israel in the Law of Moses to stay away from idols because *"the Lord your God is a consuming fire, a jealous God"*.[1] C. S. Lewis explains:

> When Christianity says that God loves man, it means that God loves man... You asked for a loving God: you have one... Not a senile benevolence that drowsily wishes you to be happy in your own way, not the cold philanthropy of a conscientious magistrate, nor the care of a host who feels responsible for the comfort of his guests, but the consuming fire Himself, the Love that made the world, persistent as the artist's love for his work and despotic as a man's love for a dog, provident and venerable as a father's love for a child, jealous, inexorable, exacting as love between the sexes. How this should be, I do not know: it passes reason to explain why any creatures, not to say creatures such as we, should have a value so prodigious in their Creator's eyes.[2]

---

[1] Exodus 20:5; 34:14; Deuteronomy 4:24; 6:15; 32:21. See Song of Songs 8:6; 2 Corinthians 11:2.

[2] C. S. Lewis writes this in his book *The Problem of Pain* (1940).

The jealous fire that burns throughout the book of Zephaniah is not a mark of God's hatred, but of his fiercely passionate love for his people. The maker of a stained-glass window does not hate the glass he places in the fire. He wants to shape it into something far more beautiful. The farmer who burns the stubble in his field does not hate his farm. He wants to prepare it for a harvest to come. In the same way, the Lord burns with anger in Zephaniah because he wants to restore the holiness of his people. After speaking so much about the Day of his Judgment, he describes in 3:9–13 the glorious remains of that Day. Judah will not repent in time to avert its destruction by the Babylonians, but the Lord will bring forth from that disaster a people who have been humbled enough to repent in truth instead of in pretence.[3] He will relaunch them as his lifeboat of salvation, their hull fixed, their speech purified and their hearts made holy.[4]

We discover in 3:14–17 how much this relaunch costs the Lord. Throughout the book of Zephaniah two sounds have competed for our attention: the cry of divine justice and the song of God's mercy. Now the two sounds come together at the expense of God's Messiah. The one who rode out in judgment as *"the Mighty Warrior"* in 1:14 now pays the price to free us from God's judgment in 3:17 as *"the Mighty Warrior who saves"*. Although Zephaniah does not describe the crucifixion of Jesus in detail, he prophesies about it as he declares that, *"The Lord has taken away your punishment, he has turned back your enemy. The Lord, the King of Israel, is with you; never again will you fear any harm."* Just as two pieces of wood intersected to form the cross of Jesus, so did God's justice and mercy as Jesus died. God's justice was completely satisfied and his

---

[3] God's people will not be sinless, but they will be humble enough to repent quickly when they do sin and to lay hold of God's promise of forgiveness (3:11; Romans 3:21–26). Zephaniah emphasizes that God isn't looking for the strong, but for the *meek* and the *humble* and the *lame* and the *ashamed* (3:12, 19).

[4] The reference to *peoples* in 3:9 and to *Cush* in 3:10 is a promise that many Gentiles will be saved through this new Jewish lifeboat. This reversal of Genesis 11:9 is fulfilled in Revelation 7:9–10.

mercy poured out freely when Jesus bore the judgment for our sin and undid the Devil's work against us.

That's why the book of Zephaniah ends with a very different tune from the one with which it started. The Lord was a Mighty Warrior who shouted a battle cry of judgment over the people of Judah in 1:14, but now he is a Mighty Saviour who sings a love song over them in 3:17. These three chapters have been heavy-going in places, but now we have our reward in one of the most amazing Old Testament expressions of God's love for his people. Zephaniah tells us literally that, *"He rejoices over you with rejoicing. He is left speechless in his love for you. He rejoices over you with loud singing!"* How the Lord can be speechless and sing at the same time is nowhere near as mysterious as how the blood of Jesus can wipe away our sin and cause God the Father to delight in us, declaring that all the merits of Jesus are now counted as if they were our own.

No wonder the Jews returning from their exile in Babylon in 3:18 stop singing funeral dirges and change their tune to match the Lord's. No wonder they respond to his command in 3:14 to *"Sing, Daughter Zion; shout aloud, Israel! Be glad and rejoice with all your heart, Daughter Jerusalem!"* Zephaniah has revealed the sin that lies beneath the surface of our hearts, not because God hates us, but because he loves us and wants to forgive us. We mustn't sing more quietly about this gift of mercy than the Lord!

So put your book down and sing a song of worship to the one who died in your place for your sin, who defeated your enemy the Devil and who now dwells inside you to be a far better King to you than Josiah was to Judah. Josiah tried to change Judah from the outside in and failed, but Jesus changes us from the inside out and he always succeeds.[5]

What a Gospel. What a Saviour. What a reason to sing your own love song back to the One who is singing over you right now.

[5] Josiah couldn't even fully change himself. Although his godliness was genuine, his pride led to his tragic death on the battlefield after siding foolishly with the king of Babylon (2 Chronicles 35:20–25).

Let's Get Personal
(Habakkuk 1:1–11)

*How long, Lord, must I call for help, but you do not
listen?*

(Habakkuk 1:2)

It may sound obvious but be sure that you don't miss it. A
relationship with God isn't first and foremost about the things
you believe about him, but about the conversations you enjoy
with him. When Jesus returns from heaven, he warns that he
will have to say to many people who know a lot about him, *"I
never knew you. Away from me!"*[1]

That's why I love the book of Habakkuk. The eleven other
Minor Prophets received great messages for nations, but this
book is an account of one man's private conversations with the
Lord. Writing just before 605 BC, the prophet speaks with God as
his close friend about what he sees and hears.[2] He made those
conversations public in order to encourage us that the Lord
wants to have similar exchanges with us too. Being a Christian
means walking and talking with God, so if you rarely talk to God
and hear him talking back to you, Habakkuk wants to suggest
that something is very wrong.

In 1:2–4, Habakkuk looks around at the nation of Judah and
vents his frustration in prayer. *"How long, Lord, must I call for*

---

[1] Matthew 7:23. Jesus speaks these words to people who believe they are
Christians.

[2] We know he wrote before 605 BC because the sudden rise of Babylon is still
a surprise in 1:5–6. This took place through their unexpected victory over Egypt
and Assyria at the Battle of Carchemish in 605 BC.

help, but you do not listen?" King Josiah had been killed in battle by the Egyptians in 609 BC and succeeded first by his wicked son Jehoahaz, then three months later by his even wickeder son Jehoiakim, who burned the words of Jeremiah and executed the prophet Uriah.[3] Habakkuk is appalled that the rulers of Judah are now as violent and unjust as their subjects. He longs for God to judge his nation so that it will be quickly humbled and revived, just as the Lord has promised.

This is the first lesson that we learn from Habakkuk. His name is Hebrew for *Hug* or *Cuddle*, but there is nothing soft or sentimental about his friendship with the Lord. With the same honesty as the psalmists, he speaks out exactly how he feels. He is frustrated so he says so. He feels that the Lord is to blame so he says that too. He feels disappointed that God's Law appears weak and powerless in the face of Judah's sin, so he says it. If we want to know God as our close friend, we need to pray with similar honesty ourselves. Tim Hughes points out that *"Questioning God doesn't mean we are disobeying Him... Expressing anger and pain to God is a beautiful and intimate act... In our everyday lives, the people that we are most likely to share our deepest fears and hurts with are those we love and trust the most."[4]* Honesty is the currency of friendship, so God wants us to level with him in prayer. Habakkuk reminds us that it's lying to pray words we don't really mean.

That's why I have kept encouraging you throughout this commentary to put your book down and to talk to God about how the Minor Prophets make you feel. It's not enough to nod at the idea that there are jagged rocks of sin beneath the surface of your heart. God wants you to graduate from nodding to knowing him. He wants you to confess your sins to him so he can set you free from them. It's not enough to agree that the Church today seems very similar to ancient Israel and Judah. God doesn't

[3] Jeremiah 26:20–23; 36:1–32.

[4] Tim Hughes in *Holding Nothing Back: Embracing the Mystery of God* (2007).

want to get you down. He wants to make you look up to him in impassioned prayer. God speaks and we reply. That's the essence of Christianity. It's all about a friendship with the Lord.

In 1:5–11, the Lord responds immediately to Habakkuk's honest prayer. He isn't curt with him, as if annoyed that the prophet is troubling him with personal questions when he prefers to deal with nations. His reply is described as an *oracle* in 1:1, using the same Hebrew word that is used to describe the messages he delivers to the nations elsewhere.[5] In this personal conversation, the Lord reveals more detail about his plans than he has revealed to any of the other Minor Prophets so far, except for Micah.[6] He has only mentioned Babylon once by name, in Micah 4:10, but he is frank with Habakkuk that it is through the Babylonians that he will destroy Judah.[7] Babylon will amass a sudden empire with the speed of a leopard, an eagle or the desert wind. While the priests busy themselves with religious ritual in the Temple and hear nothing from the Lord, he chats freely with his friend about the imminent destruction of Jerusalem.[8]

The second lesson of Habakkuk is therefore this: when we speak to God, he replies. It's easy to forget this because so many of us have lost the art of listening and started to assume that God is far more silent than he is. A Microsoft survey revealed that our attention span fell from twelve seconds in 2000 to eight seconds in 2013. For perspective, a goldfish has an attention span of nine seconds! No wonder the survey concludes that *"The true*

---

[5] The word *massā'* is used in Nahum 1:1; Zechariah 9:1 and 12:1, and Malachi 1:1.

[6] This is a common theme in Scripture. For example, Jesus gives more teaching on worship in a one-to-one conversation with a sinful woman in John 4 than he gives in the rest of the gospels combined!

[7] God refers to them in Hebrew as *Chaldeans* because the rulers of Babylon came from the Chaldean tribe.

[8] God's friendship with Abraham contrasts similarly with complacent Sodom and Gomorrah in Genesis 18:16–33. Babylon would destroy Judah in three stages – first in 605 BC, then in 597 BC, then finally in 586 BC.

scarce commodity is increasingly human attention."[9] Habakkuk reminds us that when we pray, we need to keep our eyes and ears open for God's reply – through a Bible passage that we happen to read, through a seemingly chance conversation with a Christian friend, through a strange turn of events, or through the Holy Spirit speaking to our spirits with the still, small voice of the Lord.[10]

This is the relationship with God that Joel encourages us to expect when he promises that, *"In the last days, God says, I will pour out my Spirit on all people. Your sons and daughters will prophesy, your young men will see visions, your old men will dream dreams. Even on my servants, both men and women, I will pour out my Spirit in those days, and they will prophesy."* It's what Jeremiah means when he prophesies that, *"'They will all know me, from the least of them to the greatest,' declares the Lord."* It's what Jesus tells us to expect when he promises that, *"My sheep listen to my voice"* and that *"the Holy Spirit, whom the Father will send in my name, will teach you all things".*[11] This is basic Christianity. Don't settle for anything less.

So before you move on to whatever else you are doing today, take a moment to have a conversation with the Lord as your closest friend. Ultimately, it doesn't matter how much you understand the message of the Minor Prophets unless you also know God in the way that they did. It doesn't matter how much they can teach you about God's character unless it helps you to deepen your friendship with him. Habakkuk challenges us to get personal with God. Tell God how you really feel and give him your attention until you hear his clear reply.

---

[9] Data taken from a Microsoft Canada survey of "Attention Spans" (2015).

[10] Paul quotes from 1:5 in Acts 13:41 to teach that many of our problems stem from our refusal to be still enough to listen to the words that the Lord is speaking to us and to believe what he says.

[11] Joel 2:28–29 as quoted by Peter in Acts 2:17–18. Also Jeremiah 31:34; John 10:27; 14:26.

Mystery
(Habakkuk 1:12–2:3)

Your eyes are too pure to look on evil; you cannot tolerate wrongdoing. Why then do you tolerate the treacherous?

(Habakkuk 1:13)

Habakkuk heard God reply, but he didn't hear what he expected God to say. That's the third lesson of his book of prophecies. A friendship with God is always full of mystery.

Habakkuk's first complaint, in 1:2–4, was that the Lord appeared unjust in the way he tolerated the wickedness of Judah. The Lord's reply that he is about to destroy Judah at the hands of the Babylonians fails to reassure the prophet, since Babylon is even more sinful than Judah! The Lord admits as much in 1:5–11 when he calls them a *"ruthless and impetuous people"*, who care nothing for God's Law, and a *"guilty people, whose own strength is their god"*. Habakkuk is far from reassured by the Lord's reply. He feels like the old woman who swallowed a fly and tried to deal with it by swallowing a spider. He therefore does what we should all do when God confuses us. He continues his conversation with God in order to understand him better.[1]

In 1:12–17, Habbakuk states the problem in his second prayer. He knows that the Lord is the Eternal One, without beginning or end, who clearly knows what he is doing. He knows that the Lord is the Rock who steadied Moses and David

---

[1] Habakkuk proves that he has listened very carefully to the Lord by using the same pair of Hebrew words for *looking at* and *watching* in 1:13 that God used in 1:5. Friendship is as much about listening as speaking.

whenever they reached the end of their tether.[2] He knows that the Lord is the Holy One, who cannot tolerate the sight of sin, so surely it can't be right for him to work out his purposes through the evil Babylonians? Surely he cannot have turned a blind eye to their treachery towards the kings of Assyria, to their self-promotion, to their brutal lust for conquering lands that are not theirs and to their out-and-out idolatry?[3]

We live in a generation that is uncomfortable with mystery. We like things to be ironed out and buttoned down, even if it means refusing to engage with what really matters in the world. Matthew McConaughey is right when he complains in the movie *Interstellar* that *"We used to look up at the sky and wonder at our place in the stars; now we just look down and worry about our place in the dirt."* But if we want close friendship with the God who made the universe, we had better accept that mystery comes with the territory, so Habakkuk gives us three important pointers in 2:1–3 as to how to handle God's mystery.[4]

In 2:1, he encourages us to enjoy the fact that God is hard to understand. He ends his prayer by promising to wait until the Lord gives him some answers, because close friendship with God is always forged through patient waiting and careful listening. Habakkuk is like the apostle Paul, who delights in mystery, not as impenetrable darkness, but as something that has been *"hidden for long ages past, but now revealed and made known"* to those who are willing to embark on the adventure

---

[2] This is one of their favourite names for God – for example, in Deuteronomy 32:4, 15, 18 and 30–31, and in Psalm 18:2, 31 and 46. Paul reveals the true identity of their Rock in 1 Corinthians 10:4.

[3] Babylon was not a fishing nation, but Habakkuk uses the superstitions of his local fishermen to point out that victory in battle will make the Babylonians worship their weapons of war rather than the Lord (1:11). In the same way, our own scientific discoveries often make people worship creation instead of the Creator.

[4] It always requires faith to believe that God's ways are higher than our own (Isaiah 55:9). Habakkuk could not know that the Lord would use Daniel and his fellow exiles to save many Babylonians.

of knowing God.[5] He is like the eleventh-century theologian Anselm, who told his followers that *"I do not seek to understand in order to believe, but I believe in order to understand."*[6] Faith makes us linger before the Lord in prayer until we understand the hidden depths to his character.

As a relatively young believer, I was faced with a major crossroads in my life. When I went to see a Christian mentor for advice, he gave me a Bible passage and sent me packing. Refusing to answer my questions, he instructed me to sit under a tree in the garden with my list of questions until I heard God reply to each one of them in turn. I still remember that hour and a half as one of my earliest encounters with the Holy Spirit. By the time I got up from the tree I knew that many of the questions I was asking were wrong, and I had clear answers to all of the right ones. Looking back, it makes me wonder why I expect anything less of God each day. Maybe I've got too busy. Maybe I have fallen for the idea that Christianity isn't meant to be quite so up close and personal with God. Maybe I need Habakkuk to remind me that it's all about waiting and listening.

In 2:2, he informs us that the task of Christian leaders is to grapple with God's mysteries for the sake of those they lead. He says that the Lord instructed him, as a prophet of Judah, to *"Write down the revelation and make it plain on tablets so that whoever reads it can run with it."*[7] In the same way, a Christian leader is somebody who can say to people, "This is what Jesus has revealed to me, so follow me as I follow him." It's why Jesus taught his disciples that their primary role as church leaders was, *"What I tell you in the dark, speak in the daylight; what is whispered in your ear, proclaim from the roofs"*, and it's why

---

[5] Romans 16:25–26. Paul clearly believes in Romans 11:25 and 1 Timothy 3:16 that God's mystery is knowable.

[6] Anselm says this in the first chapter of his great work, the *Proslogion*.

[7] The Hebrew word *hāzōn* in 2:2 does not mean *vision* in the sense of writing down a man-made vision statement, but in the sense of writing down God-given *revelation* for his people.

they were determined to *"give our attention to prayer and the ministry of the word"*.[8] It's why church leaders today need to spend more time in prayer than they do in meetings and on email. Unless we preach and write down what God says to us, the busy and distracted people that we lead will never work it all out for themselves.[9]

In 2:3, Habakkuk informs us that hearing God is one thing and that seeing his words fulfilled is quite another. He says that the Lord warned him that *"the revelation awaits an appointed time; it speaks of the end and will not prove false. Though it linger, wait for it; it will certainly come and will not delay."* Jerusalem would survive its first defeat by Babylon in 605 BC. It would also survive its second defeat in 597 BC. It would only be destroyed utterly in 586 BC. Friendship with God does not just require waiting in faith for an answer. It also requires waiting for quite some time for that answer to be fulfilled.

We will look at the Lord's answer to Habakkuk's second prayer in the next chapter, but for now take some time to watch and wait, like the prophet, for God's word to you. Do what I did when I wrote down a list of questions for God and talked to him about each one of them as I sat under a tree. Begin to learn the art of two-way conversation with the Lord. Believe the promise Jesus makes you in John 16:13–14:

> *When he, the Spirit of truth, comes, he will guide you into all the truth. He will not speak on his own; he will speak only what he hears, and he will tell you what is yet to come. He will glorify me because it is from me that he will receive what he will make known to you.*

---

[8] Matthew 10:27; Acts 6:4.

[9] Even in this personal conversation, Habakkuk is aware that he is getting answers for the people of Judah who have similar questions. He says in 2:1, *"I will look to see… what answer I am to give to this complaint."*

Faith and Force
(Habakkuk 2:4–20)

See, the enemy is puffed up; his desires are not upright – but the righteous person will live by his faithfulness.

(Habakkuk 2:4)

The Lord was not offended that Habakkuk should dare to question his plan. His response to the prophet's second prayer is so full of revelation that it is quoted three times in the New Testament as a pithy summary of the Gospel. These verses are meant to encourage us that God delights to reveal his secrets to anybody who is willing to invest the time it takes to get to know him as our friend.

The Lord assures Habakkuk that he isn't blind to the sins of Babylon. He knows that *"The enemy is puffed up; his desires are not upright"* and he lists for the prophet the sins he sees among the Babylonians.[1] They are arrogant.[2] They are insatiably greedy.[3] They stockpile stolen goods from all the people they have murdered in their lust for an empire that is

---

[1] The five *woes* that the Lord speaks over Babylon in 2:6–20 are similar in format to the six *woes* that he speaks over Jerusalem in Isaiah 5:8–30 and the six *woes* that he speaks over the Jewish leaders in Luke 11:39–52.

[2] The proof of this is that they are *"never at rest"* (2:5). When we refuse to down tools each evening and to take a day off each week, it often reveals sinful egotism within our hearts. See Psalm 46:10.

[3] Proverbs 27:20 and 30:15–16 also liken human greed to *she'ōl – the grave or hell –* which never stops demanding new souls each day. To escape it, learn the mystery of contentment in God (Philippians 4:12).

built on the corpses of the innocent.[4] They are immoral, they are violent and they are heading for disaster.[5] The Lord has seen the foolish way in which they worship mute idols of wood and stone, instead of the God who converses with his followers as friends, so he reassures Habakkuk that after he has used Babylon to destroy sinful nations such as Judah, he will then destroy Babylon in its turn.[6] The prophet can trust him to know what he is doing: *"The Lord is in his holy temple; let all the earth be silent before him."*

The Lord also assures Habakkuk that he cares more about his glory in the world than the prophet does. He wasn't wrong to question God's wisdom in granting military successes to a nation that will attribute them to its own strength and to its idols, but he needs to get a bigger view of God. The Lord's plans to glorify his name will not be thwarted by a few self-promoting humans. *"Has not the Lord Almighty determined that the people's labour is only fuel for the fire, that the nations exhaust themselves for nothing? For the earth will be filled with knowledge of the glory of the Lord as the waters cover the sea."* The waters don't just cover the sea. They are the sea! The Lord assures us that his mysterious plans will glorify his name throughout the world far better than any plans of our own.[7]

The Lord also reassures Habakkuk that he hasn't forgotten to save his people. While proud unbelievers rush around to build

---

[4] The Babylonians used the rubble of their enemies' houses to build their own. Therefore the Lord warns in 2:11 that the very fabric of their houses cries out that he should judge them for their sin.

[5] Drinking *the cup* of God's judgment in 2:16 is a common metaphor in Scripture. See Psalm 75:8; Isaiah 51:17; Jeremiah 25:15–16; Lamentations 4:21; Ezekiel 23:32–34; Zechariah 12:2; Mark 14:36; John 18:11.

[6] Babylon was captured unexpectedly by the Medes and Persians in 539 BC and, after several failed uprisings, completely demolished in the decades that followed.

[7] This repeats a promise in Isaiah 11:9. The Lord's glory is already visible in every corner of the earth (Psalm 8:1; Romans 1:20), but he is determined to use the events of history to reveal that glory to all people.

empires that will quickly pass away, he is busy saving anyone who is humble enough to stop and put their faith in him instead. There is deliberate ambiguity in the Hebrew text of 2:4, since the Hebrew word *'emūnāh* can either mean *faith* or *faithfulness*. Romans 1:17, Galatians 3:11 and Hebrews 10:38 all quote this verse to mean both – the Lord saves anybody who puts their faith in him by bestowing on them his own faithfulness to his Law.[8] Martin Luther sparked the Reformation at the beginning of the sixteenth century by following Habakkuk's lead and spending long hours grappling with the Lord about what this verse truly means.

> *Despite the irreproachable character of my life as a monk, I felt I was a sinner before God and my conscience was extremely disturbed... Finally God took pity on me. While I was meditating, day and night, and examining the implications of the words... "the righteous shall live by faith," I perceived that the justice of God must be understood as the righteousness which God imparts and by which the righteous man lives if he has faith. So the meaning of the phrase is that the Gospel reveals to us the righteousness of God, and this is the passive righteousness by which God in his mercy justifies us by means of faith... Immediately I felt born again.*[9]

Never underestimate the power of your one-on-one conversations with the Lord. Habakkuk's private exchanges pointed the way for many people in Judah to be saved, they helped the early apostles to understand the Gospel fully and they helped Martin Luther to restore the Gospel to a Church that

---

[8] Paul quotes from this verse to emphasize that people are saved through faith. He quotes from 1:5 in Acts 13:41 to emphasize the flipside of this: people therefore perish through unbelief.

[9] He recalls his conversation with God about Habakkuk 2:4 in the preface to his *Commentary on the Psalms*.

had forgotten it over the years. These verses ought to encourage you that time spent chatting with the Lord is never wasted. They also ought to make you want to check that you are living by this Gospel every day.

The big contrast in these verses is not between Babylonians and Jews, but between those who trust in force and those who trust in faith. There were plenty of people in Judah who relied on human muscle and, as we discover in the book of Daniel, there were many Babylonians who laid hold of the offer of divine mercy. When the Lord promises literally in 2:16 that on the Day of Judgment people will *"be seen as uncircumcised"*, it is meant to make us question whether we ourselves are living each day by force or by faith.

Do you truly know that you have been forgiven by faith in the righteousness of Jesus? It's very easy to tell. People who rely on their own actions for forgiveness are *"never at rest"* and *"never satisfied"* because nothing they can do is ever enough. People who rely on the actions of Jesus for their forgiveness are very different. They are *"silent before him"* because they know that their salvation is all about his work, not their own.[10]

In your struggles with sin, are you aware that freedom is as much a gift of God as forgiveness? Are you seeking to sanctify yourself by human willpower and resolve? If you are, you will become like all the other uptight religious people who are *"never at rest"*. Paul explains in Romans 6 that we are freed from sin by believing that we have died and been raised to new life with Jesus – not by adding further efforts of our own.

In your desire to be fruitful as a Christian, are you aware that any lasting fruit you bear can only be a gift of God through that same faith in him? Have you grasped that God has deliberately arranged Christian ministry so that people who admit their weakness and partner with his Holy Spirit bear much fruit,

---

[10] Compare 2:20 with Isaiah 30:15. We are saved by resting by faith in what Jesus has done for us, not by seeking to add to it efforts of our own.

while people who believe that they can serve God in their own strength find *"that the people's labour is only fuel for the fire, that the nations exhaust themselves for nothing"*? Have you come to a realization that Christian fruitfulness is as much a gift of grace as forgiveness and holiness? Have you surrendered to the words of Jesus in John 15: *"Apart from me you can do nothing… You did not choose me, but I chose you and appointed you so that you might go and bear fruit – fruit that will last"*?

Have you grasped that friendship with God is all about faith and not force? Have you learned to be still and know that he is God – all your forgiveness, all your freedom and all your fruitfulness?

Music Lesson
(Habakkuk 3:1–19)

For the director of music. On my stringed instruments.
(Habakkuk 3:19)

Habakkuk is so excited by his conversations with God that he does what Christians always long to do when they come to know the Lord as their close friend. He begins to sing a worship song. It's important that we spot this. His final chapter of prophecy isn't simply a prayer. It is a song that he sings to the sound of a marching beat,[1] that he marks *"for the director of music"* like fifty-five of the Psalms, and that he evidently wrote *"on my stringed instruments"* during one of his private conversations with God.[2]

Those who know God best have always sung him worship songs. The apostle Paul frequently bursts into song throughout his letters.[3] Many of the Early Church Fathers were better known for their hymns than for their books of theology. When Martin Luther rediscovered the Gospel in Habakkuk 2:4, he wrote many hymns and taught his converts to make such worship songs part of their time alone with God. He taught that *"Music is a gift and grace of God, not an invention of men... I would*

---

[1] *Shigionoth* in 3:1 is the plural of the Hebrew noun *shiggaion* in the title of Psalm 7. We do not know what type of musical instrument it refers to, but both songs call for God to march out with the armies of heaven.

[2] He also uses the word *selāh* in 3:3, 9 and 13, a Hebrew musical term that is used 71 times in the book of Psalms and that means *silence* or *instrumental solo*.

[3] For example, in Romans 11:33–36; Ephesians 5:14; Philippians 2:6–11; 1 Timothy 3:16; 2 Timothy 2:11–13.

allow no man to preach or teach God's people without a proper knowledge of the use and power of sacred song."[4]

Great hymns and choruses also marked the Baptists in the seventeenth century, the Methodists in the eighteenth century, the Salvation Army in the nineteenth century and the Pentecostals in the twentieth century. Habakkuk therefore remains intensely personal as he ends his book by teaching us to worship. Such songs have always been a key feature of any movement in which people truly come to know God as their friend.

In 3:2, Habakkuk begins his worship song by confessing that he trusts God, even though he does not fully understand him. He looks back over history and sings out that he trusts God to know the best way to balance his angry judgment and his tender mercy towards the people of Judah. *"Lord, I have heard of your fame; I stand in awe of your deeds, Lord. Repeat them in our day, in our time make them known; in wrath remember mercy."*[5]

In 3:3–15, Habakkuk sings about what the Lord did for the Exodus generation. Some of his words require a little explanation, but they reward our careful attention. By praising God for his work in the past, he does more than express his faith in God. He also increases his faith that God will still work everything for the good of his people today.[6]

Teman refers to the nation of Edom to the south of Judah, and *Mount Paran* refers to the desert between Edom and Egypt, so Habakkuk is celebrating what he has read about in Deuteronomy 33:1–3 – that God brought Israel out of Egypt to Mount Sinai and then through hostile territory into the

---

[4] Quoted by Kenneth W. Osbeck in *101 Hymn Stories* (1982).

[5] *"Repeat them in our day"* is the only request in the whole of Habakkuk's song. He understands that prayer is more about seeking to discover God's will than it is about seeking to alter God's will.

[6] He says literally at the end of 3:6 that *"the goings of eternity belong to him"*. If the Lord has been in charge of all the comings and goings of history, we can trust him with all of our comings and goings today.

Promised Land.[7] *Cushan* is another name for Midian, so he is celebrating the way God routed Israel's enemies before them.[8] The reference to the Lord striking seas and rivers celebrates the way that he parted the Red Sea and the River Jordan for them. The reference to the sun and moon standing still in the sky celebrates their victory over the Canaanites in Joshua 10, and *"the leader of the land of wickedness"* who was destroyed in the sea by his own weapons of war is Pharaoh.[9] But you don't have to be familiar with all the ins and outs of Israel's history to see what Habakkuk is doing here. By singing about God's faithfulness towards his people in the past, he is increasing his faith that God will work in the present.[10]

In 3:16, Habakkuk translates into the present day what he knows about the Lord from history. He is appalled that God has told him in their private conversations that he is about to destroy Judah at the hands of the Babylonians – *"I heard and my heart pounded, my lips quivered at the sound; decay crept into my bones, and my legs trembled"* – but he is convinced that the Lord knows what he is doing and that he will make good on his promise to destroy Babylon – *"I will wait patiently for the day of calamity to come on the nation invading us."* He trusts that the God who rode the chariots of heaven to victory against Egypt in 3:8 will ride them again to victory over Babylon. He believes that the God who delivered Israel from slavery through the Exodus in the past will deliver Judah from captivity through a second Exodus in the future. Although he dreads his nation's impending humiliation, he trusts the Lord to turn it into Judah's

---

[7] Genesis 36:10–11; Amos 1:11–12; Obadiah 9. *Plague* and *pestilence* in 3:5 refer to the Ten Plagues that God inflicted on Egypt in Exodus 7–12.

[8] Numbers 25:16–18; 31:1–10.

[9] The Hebrew word for *anointed one* in 3:13 is *messiah*. Habakkuk may not have realized what he was prophesying, but he presents the Red Sea as a picture of the Messiah's future victory over the Devil.

[10] This is why the book of Psalms contains so many history songs. Ignorance of God's faithfulness towards his people in the past leads to panic in the present. Church history and Christian faith are intertwined.

salvation.In 3:17–19, Habakkuk ends his very personal book of prophecies with his personal reaction to the disaster that is coming on Judah. It is easy to trust God when we understand what he is doing, but the prophet accepts that faith means living with a large dose of mystery. It is easy to trust the Lord when he promises us peace and prosperity, but the prophet accepts God's promise that he may never see either again. He sings out that the Lord is enough for him. If he can know God as his friend, that will make him rich enough to endure any kind of poverty. *"Though the fig-tree does not bud and there are no grapes on the vines, though the olive crop fails and the fields produce no food, though there are no sheep in the sheepfold and no cattle in the stalls, yet I will rejoice in the Lord, I will be joyful in God my Saviour."* So long as he can carry on his private conversations with God, he feels strong enough to walk whatever path lies before him. *"The Sovereign Lord is my strength; he makes my feet like the feet of a deer, he enables me to tread on the heights."*

Habakkuk's worship song is as personal as his prayers, but note that he ends his book by encouraging one of the Jewish worship leaders to teach it to anybody else who wants deep friendship with God. Frankly, we need the lessons that it teaches us. At a time when many Christians are giving up on God because he hasn't given them all they wanted, and when many church leaders are quitting their posts because the number of sheep in their sheepfolds is falling fast, we need to sing along with Habakkuk.

We need him to teach us afresh that Christianity is an invitation to know God as our friend, speaking out and singing out how we feel and waiting to hear a reply. We need him to teach us afresh what it means for each one of us to walk each day with God.

The Final Word
(Obadiah 1–21)

The vision of Obadiah. This is what the Sovereign Lord says about Edom.

(Obadiah 1)

In 586 BC, it finally happened. The Babylonians destroyed Jerusalem. They burned its Temple, reduced its walls to rubble and slaughtered almost everyone who lived there. Fewer than 20,000 Jewish men and women survived the bloodbath of that Day to be taken into exile in Babylon.[1] The once great nation of Judah was wiped off the map and its few survivors wept over the tragic consequences of a nation ignoring God's prophets and choosing to invoke his Plan "B" for his people.

That's why the short book of Obadiah became essential reading for the Jewish survivors when the first copies of it arrived on their doorsteps in Babylon. Although it addressed the nation of Edom, it contained a crucial message for the people of Judah. It reassured them that the Lord had not finished with their nation, despite the fact that it had disappeared from the map of the world and that the Edomites were gloating that they had spoken the final word over their enemy of old. The Lord sent Obadiah to make it clear to them that he alone speaks the final word over the nations of the world. The message of this shortest book in the Old Testament is that the Lord still loves

---

[1] Actually, the vast majority of the Jewish captives in Babylon were taken there after earlier raids in 605 and 597 BC. The Day of the Lord in 586 BC was an almost unmitigated scene of slaughter.

the nation of Judah and that he still has a glorious future for them as his people.

In verse 1, the prophet Obadiah introduces himself. He is frustratingly short on detail. His name means *Servant of the Lord* and it was one of the commonest names in Israel. There are a dozen other Obadiahs in the Old Testament, and the prophet does not name his father or date his vision to inform us which one of them he was, if any at all. We have to work out the date of his vision from its contents. It came after the fall of Jerusalem in 586 BC (verses 14–16) but before the destruction of Edom by the Babylonians in 553 BC (verse 15).[2] It therefore dates from early on in the Jewish exile in Babylon and it declares that God never gives up on his people. He is still prophesying about them.

In verses 2–4, Obadiah tells the Edomites that the Lord has had enough of their pride. They had good reason to be confident. Their capital city Sela (known later to the Greeks as Petra) was built on a high mountain and protected by towering rocks on every side.[3] It was surrounded by desert but watered by a perennial stream, giving them such an advantage over any would-be besieger that even the mighty King Nebuchadnezzar of Babylon decided not to turn south-east after destroying Jerusalem and attempt a similar conquest of Edom. Nevertheless, the Lord warns the Edomites that all their confidence is in vain. No mountaintop refuge can ever protect a proud nation from his judgment.

In verses 5–14, Obadiah points out that the Edomites ought to have placed their confidence in the Lord. He calls the people of Judah *"your brother Jacob"* because the Edomites were descended from Isaac's son Esau, the twin brother of Israel and

---

[2] Linking the book of Obadiah to the prophet mentioned in 1 Kings 18:1–16 makes no sense in the context of what he prophesied. It also ignores how much the book echoes Jeremiah 49:7–22, also prophesied in c. 586 BC.

[3] The Hebrew name *Sela* in verse 3 and the Greek name *Petra* both mean very simply *Big Rock*.

the grandson of Abraham. They of all nations ought to have responded to the Law of Moses that was preached to them by Judah, since the whole of Genesis 36 declared that God cared for Edom as well as for Israel. The Lord even stated in Deuteronomy 2:5 that *"I have given Esau the hill country of Seir as his own."* Although God's lifeboat of salvation was in a sorry state, the fact that they were the descendants of Abraham ought to have been enough to make them see past Judah's problems to place their own faith in him.[4]

Instead, the Edomites had been inveterate enemies of God's people. They had attacked the Israelites after the Exodus and throughout the reigns of Saul, David and Solomon. When the northern kingdom succumbed to the Assyrians, they had taken advantage of its weakness to sell Israel's undefended communities wholesale into slavery.[5] As a result, "Edom" had become shorthand for any nation that hated the Lord, and now they had gone one step further.[6] When the Babylonians destroyed Jerusalem, they gloated and rejoiced that they had spoken the final word over their enemy.[7] They supported Nebuchadnezzar, carrying off Jewish treasures, slaughtering Jewish fugitives and handing over Jewish survivors to slavery in Babylon, so Obadiah prophesies that they are about to reap what they have sown.[8] They will be betrayed and destroyed by their Babylonian allies in 553 BC. Their nation will be destroyed, without any survivors.

In verses 15–21, Obadiah uses the nation of Edom as a picture of every sinful person that refuses to surrender their

---

[4] In this, they had repeated Esau's sin by despising God's promises to Abraham (Genesis 25:29–34).

[5] Numbers 20:18; 1 Samuel 14:47; 22:18; 1 Kings 11:14; 2 Chronicles 28:17; Psalm 60:1; Amos 1:11–12.

[6] For example, in Isaiah 34:1–17; 63:1–6; Malachi 1:2–5.

[7] See Proverbs 24:17–18. Their treaty alliances would no more save them than their mountaintop home.

[8] They are also condemned for this in Psalm 137:7 and Lamentations 4:21–22.

heart to the Lord. *"The day of the Lord is near for **all nations**,"* he warns, because the destruction of Edom was a prophetic picture of the Final Judgment Day at the end of time, when not a single sinner will escape God's justice. *"The Lord has spoken"*, in verse 18, is a guarantee that all he threatens will come true.

Now for the good news. Even as he speaks about the destruction of Edom, the Lord pledges to restore the fortunes of the little band of Jewish survivors in Babylon. He prophesies that he will not only bring them back to the land that they have lost, restoring Mount Zion to the holiness of its heyday, but that he will also give them the fields of Edom and Philistia and Lebanon and the northern tribes of Israel too.[9] He has ravaged their region and has humbled the people of Judah alongside the pagan nations for a reason. He will relaunch them as his lifeboat of salvation for the world.[10]

Imagine how it must have felt as a Jewish captive in Babylon to read this little book of prophecy for the first time. The Edomites are gloating over you and the Babylonians are boasting that their empire will last forever, but the Lord has the final word. He has not forgotten you and he still loves you. He still pledges that *"The kingdom will be the Lord's."*

Judah chose God's Plan "B" for their nation and they paid a terrible price. But now God promises to restore them to his Plan "A" and to turn their nation into an army of Gospel preachers who will preach his message of salvation to the entire world.[11]

---

[9] *Zarephath* was a city between Tyre and Sidon in Lebanon. The exact location of *Sepharad* is unknown. The Lord had promised in Amos 1:6–8 to destroy every last Philistine, so their fields had been vacated too.

[10] The Negev of Judah was closest to Edom, its foothills were closest to Philistia, Benjamin was closest to Gilead and Israel was closest to Zarephath. In other words, everyone has a role to play in reaching the world.

[11] Jesus is the ultimate *mōshiya'*
, or *Deliverer*, who declares that *"The kingdom of God has come"* (Mark 1:15). However, the Hebrew noun is plural in verse 21 because he would send out Jewish apostles from Jerusalem as *deliverers* that preached the arrival of his Kingdom to the nations of the world (Luke 9:1–2; Acts 1:8).

Part Four:

A Better Israel

Underdog Story
(Haggai 1:1–15)

They came and began to work on the house of the Lord Almighty, their God.

(Haggai 1:14)

Everybody loves a good underdog story, and they don't come any better than what happened to the survivors of Judah in 539 BC. Nations that went into exile in Babylon were not expected to come back. Think about it: have you ever met a Russian Edomite, a British Moabite or an American Ammonite? Of course you haven't, so never lose your sense of wonder that there are so many Russian, British and American Jews today. They only exist because the Lord suddenly performed an astonishing rescue of his people.

In October 539 BC, the Day of the Lord that Habakkuk had prophesied fell on Babylon. It was so unexpected that the king was partying with his friends when his city fell. Even the Persian general who surprised him had confessed that, *"I cannot see how anyone could take by storm walls so massive and so high."*[1] Cyrus did not know it, but God had chosen him to play a key role in an amazing underdog story. It suddenly dawned on him that the River Euphrates passed under the city's impregnable walls, so if he commanded his men to build makeshift dams to divert the flow of the river he could lead his army along the empty river bed and through the breaches in the wall. Babylon was the most

---

[1] Daniel 5 describes Belshazzar's party. Xenophon records the words of Cyrus in his *Cyropaedia* (7.5.7).

populous, most powerful and most secure city in the world, yet it fell in a single day.

Cyrus then did something that nobody expected except for the prophets of the Lord. He issued the decree that is recorded at the beginning of the book of Ezra, which sent the Jewish survivors back to their homeland with instructions to rebuild the Temple in Jerusalem. The Lord made good on his promises. Out of nowhere, he began to create the new and better Israel that he had prophesied, one that would always choose his Plan "A" for their nation and that would become an ark of salvation for the nations of the world.

The immediate excitement was palpable. Fewer than 20,000 Jews had gone into exile but they had been busy in Babylon. Over 42,000 of them returned. Very quickly, however, they grew discouraged. It didn't feel much like a new and better Israel when they were ruled by a governor, instead of a king, when the Ark of the Covenant had been destroyed by the Babylonians and when their building work hit some major challenges. They therefore stopped work in 535 BC and slowly gave up on the idea of a new and better Israel. They began to fall back into their old sinful ways.

Haggai started prophesying on 29th August 520 BC. We don't know much about him, other than the fact that his name is Hebrew for *My Festival* and that he was probably in his eighties, but we cannot fault the way he dates his prophecies with meticulous precision.[2] He appears to be aware that he is making history and that the Lord is using him to get his plans for a new and better Israel back on the road without delay.[3]

Haggai prophesies to Governor Zerubbabel, the great-

---

[2] He reveals his age by boasting in 2:3 that he is one of the few people who can remember the Temple that fell in 586 BC. Having waited so long to begin his public ministry, Haggai was a bit of an underdog himself.

[3] One sign of his confidence that the Lord will surely use him to fulfil his great promises to his people is the fact that he refers to him as *Yahweh Tsebā'ōth*, or *the Lord Almighty*, 14 times in just 2 chapters.

grandson of King Josiah and heir to the throne of David, and to Joshua, heir to the high priesthood of Aaron.[4] Both of them are pretty miserable, since Zerubbabel doesn't feel like much of a king while under Persian rule and Joshua doesn't feel like much of a priest while he has no temple. They accept the majority view within Judah that *"The time has not yet come to rebuild the Lord's house"* and so they are pouring their energies into building fancy homes and farms for themselves instead of into building the new and better Israel that the Lord has promised.

Haggai issues a strong rebuke to these two leaders and the rest of the Jewish survivors. He asks, *"Is it a time for you yourselves to be living in your panelled houses, while this house remains a ruin?"* He then points out all the ways in which Judah is reaping the curses of God's Plan "B" for his people instead of the blessings of his Plan "A".[5] Their harvests have failed them and their savings are never enough. Their lives are full of drought and thirst and hunger and shivering cold because they have not returned with all their hearts to the Lord, so Haggai commands them to get rebuilding the Temple in order to exchange God's curses for his blessing. When they respond to his words, Haggai is overjoyed and reassures them: *"'I am with you," declares the Lord."*[6]

He is overjoyed because he is already witnessing a new and better Israel. Not once in the books of the first nine Minor Prophets are we ever told that God's people *"obeyed the voice of the Lord their God and the message of the prophet"*. Not once are we ever told that *"the people feared the Lord"* or that he stirred up the spirits of his people to obey him willingly and to embrace his Plan "A" for their nation. Haggai is therefore overjoyed

---

[4] Matthew 1:11–12. Zerubbabel means *Born in Babylon* and Joshua means *The Lord Saves*.

[5] He even says in 1:2 that they have caused the Lord to view them as *"these people"* instead of as *"my people"*.

[6] This prophecy is only two words long in Hebrew. Prophecies don't have to be long to change people's lives.

because he sees that the Lord's plan to humble his people into repentance and faith in him is actually working. The decades of exile in Babylon and the fifteen years of discouragement back in Judah have finally created a people who are obedient to the Lord. Within three weeks, by 21st September 520 BC, they are busy rebuilding the Temple.

This first chapter of Haggai ought to challenge us as individuals. It is never easy to devote ourselves to the work of building a house for the Lord. There is always a good reason for us to prioritize our work, our friends and family, our hobbies and our own houses above the church that we are part of, but it is deeply displeasing to God. He created us as worshippers, so if we fail to give him all our devotion, those other things will quickly become our gods.[7] That's why he exhorts us twice, in 1:5 and 7, to *"Give careful thought to your ways."* The Devil doesn't have to persuade us to say "no" to God in order to disobey him. He simply has to trick us into saying "yes – but not now".

This first chapter of Haggai also ought to challenge us as churches. It is easy to fool ourselves that our small number of converts and our high dropout rate is due to the difficult spiritual climate in our nation, instead of facing up to the fact that this is one of the primary curses listed in Deuteronomy 28 whenever God's people grow lax in their devotion to him. It is easy to assume that very little active Gospel-sharing is a normal state of affairs, without recognizing it as a sign that God's Spirit is not as much at work in our midst as he was in Jerusalem in 1:14, long before the Day of Pentecost.

It is easy to assume that the words of this chapter are for someone other than us, but they are not. The Lord still offers us the same choice today: *Blessing or curse – you decide.*

---

[7] They already had enough timber to rebuild the Temple (Ezra 3:7), so 1:8 informs us that they had stolen timber for their own houses from the Temple stockpile. That's tragic, because if we seek God's Kingdom first, he will provide all we need for the other aspects of our lives (Malachi 3:8–12; Matthew 6:33).

The Greatest Temple
(Haggai 2:1–9)

Who of you is left who saw this house in its former glory? How does it look to you now? Does it not seem to you like nothing?

(Haggai 2:3)

Zerubbabel and Joshua knew that they were not exactly building the greatest Temple. Cyrus had been generous towards them, but they couldn't match the vast supply of gold, silver and bronze that King Solomon had used to build the Temple that was destroyed in 586 BC. They were building something smaller and shabbier, and in many ways its architecture was the least of their problems. The whole point of the Temple in Jerusalem was that its sanctuary housed the Ark of the Covenant, above which the Lord's presence had dwelt at the heart of Israel for almost a thousand years. But the Babylonians had destroyed the Ark, so this new Temple was just a shell. No wonder we are told in Ezra 3:12 that those who were old enough to remember Solomon's Temple wept bitterly when they saw the poor state of what was being built to replace its former glory.

That's why the Lord sent the prophet Haggai to encourage Zerubbabel, Joshua and the other survivors of Judah that their efforts were not in vain. He did more than simply warn them that spiritual nostalgia is foolish (since things are rarely as good as we remember) and fatal to our active partnership with God today (since we can't serve him in the past, but only in the present).[1] Haggai went much further by telling them that, though many people saw their new Temple as a disappointment, it was actually far better than Solomon's Temple in a fundamental way. If they could only grasp what the Lord had planned for his people, they would regard it as the greatest Temple of all time.

In 2:1–3, Haggai faces up squarely to the problem. It is now 17th October 520 BC, so a month of building work since he last prophesied has made it plain to everyone that their new Temple is going to be several sizes smaller than Solomon's. Haggai points out in 2:3 that he knows this better than most people, since he is old enough to have visited the former Temple as a young boy. *"Who of you is left who saw this house in its former glory?"* he asks them. *"How does it look to you now? Does it not seem to you like nothing?"* Haggai knows that there is no point in pretending. He freely admits that, when it comes down to the Ark and architecture, it isn't a patch on its predecessor.

In 2:4–5, Haggai insists that the new Temple's external shortcomings do not matter. They don't need a golden box to conjure up the presence of God, nor do they need silver and gold, like the pagans, to attract people to God. What made Solomon's Temple the greatest building on the earth was not the way it looked, but the person who lived there, and Haggai prophesies that God's presence will be felt in this shabby Temple just as powerfully as in the heyday of King Solomon. The Lord still reassures them, *"I am with you."*[2] He still promises to do *"what I covenanted with you when you came out of Egypt"*. It doesn't matter that they have lost the spiritual trappings of yesteryear. They haven't lost the essence of God's Temple: *"My Spirit remains among you. Do not fear."*

---

[1] Ecclesiastes 7:10 is particularly scathing about the harm that nostalgia often does to us today. These moaners had forgotten that the old Temple courtyards were usually jam-packed full of idols and hypocrisy.

[2] This simple prophecy in 2:4 echoes the one in 1:13. Prophecies don't have to be complicated to lift our gaze.

We need to remember this, because harking back to the way that God has moved in the past often spoils our response to what he is doing among us in the present. When I hear Christians speaking longingly about the Early Church, the medieval monastics or the early days of Pentecostalism, it reminds me of the Woody Allen movie *Midnight in Paris*. Owen Wilson plays a writer who views 1920s' Paris as the great golden age of culture. He is so overcome by nostalgia that he finds a way to travel back in time to be there – only to discover that many people in the 1920s are bored and view the 1890s as a golden age! He decides to return to the present and to enjoy it, because he finally sees his nostalgia for what it really is: a fear of making the most of today. Whatever great things God has done in the past, you and I don't live there. All we can do is respond to what he is doing today and to his charge in 2:4 to *"Be strong, all you people of the land, and work."*[3]

In 2:6–9, Haggai prophesies that something will happen in the courtyards of this Temple that will make it the greatest building of all time. Its significance won't be found in its size and its finery, but in one of its worshippers. Solomon's Temple looked far better, but it never saw *"what is desired by all nations"*.[4] The Messiah will come to this small and shabby Temple, not to Solomon's. As a baby he will be brought into its courtyards, as a twelve-year-old he will return to discuss Scripture with its rabbis and as an adult he will turn its courtyards into a mighty centre for preaching and healing.[5]

The Jews, then, must not be fooled by external appearances when their Temple looks increasingly irrelevant in a world that is being shaken by the rise and fall of mighty empires – first the Persians, then the Macedonians, then the Seleucids, then

---

[3] This is a deliberate repeat of David's charge to his son Solomon in 1 Chronicles 28:20 to build the Temple.

[4] The Hebrew can also be translated *One Desired by All Nations*. Malachi 3:1 is clear it refers to the Messiah.

[5] Luke 2:27, 46; 20:1; 22:53.

the Romans.[6] The Lord does not lack gold or silver, but he has chosen to make his Temple nondescript in order to turn all eyes on his Messiah. *"'The glory of this present house will be greater than the glory of the former house,' says the Lord Almighty. 'And in this place I will grant peace.'"*

We need to remember this in a world where the Church is often sidelined and treated as the irrelevant relic of a bygone age. It was in the courtyards of this small and shabby Temple that the Early Church gathered to proclaim that *"Silver or gold I do not have, but what I do have I give you."*[7] It was in this place that the Lord used a ragtag band of former fishermen and tax collectors to establish the new and better Temple that was prophesied in the final chapters of Ezekiel – a Temple built, not with gold and silver and stone, but with the bodies of men and women who are filled with the Spirit of God.[8]

There will be times when you look at the Church and feel like weeping. There will be times when you feel nostalgic for its former glories and want to give up on today. But Haggai warns you not to judge by external appearances. The Lord has not forgotten his promise to build a new and better Temple. He still says to us, *"Be strong and work!"*

---

[6] Hebrews 12:26 quotes from 2:6 – the only New Testament quotation from Haggai – and explains that this verse also prophesies about the turmoil leading up to the Messiah's Second Coming. See 2:21.

[7] Acts 2:46; 3:1–10; 5:12, 20–25, 42.

[8] Jesus began this New Temple (John 2:19–21) and he is still building it today (1 Corinthians 3:16–17; 6:19; 2 Corinthians 6:16; Ephesians 2:14–22; 1 Peter 2:4–5). He is the true and better Zerubbabel.

"I will make you like my signet ring, for I have chosen you," declares the Lord Almighty.

(Haggai 2:23)

Don't get me wrong. I'm a big fan of the royal family. I have taken my children to Buckingham Palace and I made them stand out in the rain to watch the Queen's Diamond Jubilee Pageant on the River Thames. But let's be honest with one another. Monarchs don't exactly have a lot of power nowadays. They can't throw you in the Tower of London for insulting them. They can't pass laws or dictate policy. They are a pale shadow of the royal families of long ago. They are a figurehead, and very little more.

In the same way, it was pretty obvious to everyone that Zerubbabel was a pale shadow of the former kings of Judah. He was the great-grandson of King Josiah and the heir to David's throne, but he was merely a governor. The land of Judah was nothing more than a province in the Persian Empire and its governor was nothing more than a puppet ruler, easily appointed and just as easily fired. Given all the prophecies before the exile that the Lord would raise up a new and better King to rule his people, this was a colossal disappointment. Zerubbabel wasn't the Messiah. He wasn't even a monarch.

Haggai therefore ends his book with two separate prophecies, delivered on the same day to address the same problem. The first of them, in 2:10–19, confronts the fact that Zerubbabel has had even less success in leading the people of

Judah back to God than King Josiah before the exile.[1] Haggai speaks to the priests, not to Zerubbabel, and asks them questions that will lead them to confess that, for all the governor's efforts, the Jews have continued to choose God's Plan "B" for their nation.[2] They have continued to reap the curses that are listed in Deuteronomy 28 because they have not truly returned to God with all their hearts. Haggai repeats the date and turns it into a line in the sand for Israel.[3] Up until 18th December 520 BC, they have reaped God's Plan "B" for their nation – famine, blight, mildew, hail and curses on their land – but from 18th December 520 BC they will start to reap God's Plan "A". They will receive the blessings that always accompany obedience to God, instead of the curses that accompany our rebellion.

God could hardly have been clearer in this call to decision throughout the Minor Prophets. Again and again he has challenged us: *Blessing or curse – you decide.* Now Haggai says that it is high time for us to respond. We must not be like the Jewish survivors, who assumed that because they were back in the Holy Land they must therefore be holy. We must not assume that because we are active members of a church we must therefore be obedient believers. We must not assume that because our churches are full of crosses they must therefore be walking the death-and-resurrection road with Jesus. *"Give careful thought to this from this day on,"* the prophet Haggai

---

[1] 2:15 recalls the fact that Zerubbabel started to lay the foundation of the Temple in 536 BC. For 16 years he had been unable to persuade the people consistently to choose God's Plan "A" for their nation.

[2] Clothing became holy by touching meat on the altar but did not make what it touched holy (Leviticus 6:27), whereas anything defiled by touching the dead meat of a corpse also defiled whatever it touched (Numbers 19:11–13). In the same way, the sins of Judah had contaminated everything that was good about their nation.

[3] The Lord is modelling for us here how we are to preach the Gospel. Calling for people to make an active response at the end of a sermon isn't just a good idea. It is biblical.

warns us.[4] Don't wait any longer to repent fully and to exchange God's curses for his blessing.[5]

In 2:20–23, Haggai prophesies to Zerubbabel on the same day that he challenged the unruly people he was trying so hard to lead. He reassures him that, even though he is a lowly governor of a Persian province rather than a king, the Lord is about to shake the empires of the earth to show that earthly thrones and sceptres carry only an illusion of real power. The Persian kings will fall to Alexander the Great. He will die young and be succeeded by the Seleucids and the Ptolemies. Those kings will in turn fall to the Romans, and even the might of Rome will fall before the true King of kings. A day is coming, the Lord declares, when he will invest the true and better Zerubbabel with all authority and power to rule the universe. Note that Haggai is doing more in 2:23 than simply encouraging Zerubbabel that he has authority, despite feeling like the lapdog of the king of Persia. He is prophesying that the shabbiness of his rule is like the shabbiness of the Temple. It is intentional, in order to focus all eyes on the Messiah.[6]

We live at a time like Zerubbabel. Looking at the state of the Church and at the way in which the name of Jesus is despised, it is very easy to get discouraged and to give up on the work of building a house for the Lord. Some of this failure is the result of our own secret sin, reaping God's Plan "B" for the Church instead of the Plan "A" that is described in the book of Acts. But some of it is also that we have forgotten how much the Lord loves to display his power by using the weak and despised things of the world to shame the strong. We have forgotten that the Church's

---

[4] Three times in 2:15 and 2:18 Haggai repeats his charge of 1:5 and 7: *"Give careful thought to your ways."*

[5] Haggai presents these blessings in financial terms, but the New Testament gives us a broader view of what God's blessing may mean for us. It may involve his making us content in our poverty, like Jesus, Paul and many of the early Christians (Matthew 8:20; Philippians 4:11–13; 1 Timothy 6:17; Hebrews 10:34).

[6] There would never be another king of Judah in the sense Zerubbabel expected. All the prophecies about a new and better King of Judah would be fulfilled 550 years later through his heir Jesus (Matthew 1:6–17).

many weaknesses are part of God's deliberate plan to direct all the glory for its successes towards Jesus, not to us. We have forgotten that our own faints and failures are a daily invitation from God to die to our own strength and to start living by his resurrection power. The apostle Paul explains:

> *God chose the lowly things of this world and the despised things – and the things that are not – to nullify the things that are, so that no one may boast before him... We have this treasure in jars of clay to show that this all-surpassing power is from God and not from us. We are hard pressed on every side, but not crushed; perplexed, but not in despair; persecuted, but not abandoned; struck down, but not destroyed. We always carry around in our body the death of Jesus, so that the life of Jesus may also be revealed in our body.*[7]

So don't grow discouraged, like Zerubbabel, when you feel weak and feeble. Don't throw in the towel as a leader because people refuse to follow you, and don't give up on the Church when it looks so much worse than the Bride of Christ you see in Revelation. Hear what the Lord says to Governor Zerubbabel about the true source of his authority, conveyed in the ancient world by the seal made by a signet ring on a letter of command: *"'I will make you like my signet ring, for I have chosen you,' declares the Lord Almighty."*[8]

Recognize that Jesus is the true King of Israel and that he has complete authority over the world. Believe that he has turned his weak and unimpressive servants into his living, breathing signet rings. Go in the authority that he has given you. *"Be strong and build."*

---

[7] 1 Corinthians 1:28–29; 2 Corinthians 4:7–10. See also 2 Corinthians 12:8–10.

[8] God doesn't merely promise to give Zerubbabel his signet ring. He promises to make him like it! Contrast this with the curse about a signet ring spoken over his grandfather Jehoiachin in Jeremiah 22:24–30.

The Future for Jerusalem
(Zechariah 1:1–2:13)

I will return to Jerusalem with mercy, and there my house will be rebuilt.

(Zechariah 1:16)

If you find the Minor Prophets difficult to understand, spare a thought for Martin Luther. He had to translate them from the Hebrew in order to produce his German Bible. He complained that *"They have a strange way of talking, like people who, instead of proceeding in an orderly manner, ramble off from one thing to the next, so that you cannot make head or tail of them or see what they are getting at."*[1]

Nowhere is this truer than in the book of Zechariah. He isn't just hard to understand. He actually wants to be. He writes in a style that we have not yet encountered in the Minor Prophets, a style known as "apocalyptic writing". This comes from the Greek word for *revelation*, which is why the final book of the Bible is often referred to as the Apocalypse, but that is only half the story. It specifically describes revelation that is given in a context where the prophet doesn't want eavesdroppers to understand. Apocalyptic writing only appears in the Bible in contexts where God's people are living under foreign rule – in Daniel, Ezekiel, Zechariah and Revelation – and Daniel 12:10 explains that it is used to ensure that *"none of the wicked will understand, but those who are wise will understand"*. If you take the time to study Zechariah, you will not be surprised that he

---

[1] Martin Luther in his *Works* (volume 19) – *Lectures on the Minor Prophets*.

prophesies using guarded code. If he had shouted openly that the Lord was going to destroy Persia, free Jerusalem and elevate its King, he would have been carried away by the executioners.

In 1:1–6, Zechariah begins to prophesy in late October or early November 520 BC. This is when Haggai was also active, and his ancestry reveals that he was among the priests rebuked by Haggai in the December of that year.[2] Nevertheless, he is clearly equally passionate about the rebuilding of Judah. His name means *Remembering the Lord* or *Remembered by the Lord*, and these introductory verses show us that he was very aptly named.[3] He points out to the Jewish survivors that their ancestors went into exile because they refused to listen to God's prophets and to lay hold of his Plan "A" blessings for their nation. God was not unfaithful to his covenant when he judged them, but was simply doing what he had promised in Deuteronomy 28. *"The Lord Almighty has done to us what our ways and practices deserve, just as he determined to do."*[4] Zechariah prophesies that God will surely bless his people if they follow through on their prayers of repentance. *"'Return to me,' declares the Lord Almighty, 'and I will return to you.'"*[5]

This launches Zechariah into an account of eight apocalyptic visions in 1:7–6:8, all of which he received during the single night of 15th February 519 BC. If they seem baffling, bizarre and frankly more than a little weird, remember that what he says here to the Jewish survivors would have been

---

[2] Jeremiah and Ezekiel were also priests (Jeremiah 1:1 and Ezekiel 1:3), and so were roughly 10% of all the Jews who returned from Babylon (Ezra 2:1–64).

[3] This was a very common name in Israel, especially among the priests. There are 30 Zechariahs in the Bible.

[4] Like Haggai, who refers to God as *Yahweh Tsebā'ōth*, or *the Lord Almighty*, 14 times in just two chapters, Zechariah refers to God as *Yahweh Tsebā'ōth* 53 times in his book of prophecy.

[5] We are saved entirely by God's grace, but how we respond to his grace affects how he responds to us. See 7:13; Malachi 3:7; 2 Chronicles 7:14; Isaiah 1:15. Blessing or curse – we get to decide.

viewed as incredibly subversive by the Persians had the Lord not spoken cryptically in order to shield his message from their understanding.

In 1:8–17, the Lord gives Zechariah a vision of a horseman among some myrtle trees in a ravine, with different coloured horses behind him. Although the prophet knows nothing of television, he experiences something like a God-given movie in his mind.[6] An angel acts as his guide throughout these visions, and he explains that the horseman is the Angel of the Lord and that the horses represent all of the angels at work throughout the nations of the world.[7] They have reported back on the sinfulness and complacency that is prevalent everywhere and that indicates that God's Plan "B" for Judah has been widely misunderstood. Instead of sensing that the Lord has disciplined his rebellious people, the nations have mistaken the weakness of God's people for the weakness of God himself.[8] This calls for a change of plan: *"I am very jealous for Jerusalem and Zion... I will return to Jerusalem with mercy, and there my house will be rebuilt... My towns will again overflow with prosperity, and the Lord will again comfort Zion and choose Jerusalem."* For the beleaguered Jews, disappointed both by their Temple and by their governor, this heralded amazing news. It meant that God had relaunched his Plan "A" for their nation.

In 1:18–21, the Lord gives Zechariah a second vision that would be even more seditious, were the Persians able to

---

[6] It is described as a *vision* rather than a dream because Zechariah was awake. When he nodded off after four visions, the angel woke him up in 4:1 to give him four more. Joel 2:28–29 encourages us to expect similar visions ourselves. Zechariah's experience of God before the Day of Pentecost now belongs to every believer.

[7] He acts as Zechariah's guide in 1:9; 1:19; 2:2–3; 3:1; 4:1; 4:4–7; 4:11–14; 5:2–3; 5:5–6; 5:10–11 and 6:4–6. He is distinct from *the Angel of the Lord*, who also appears in the visions and who is the pre-incarnate Jesus.

[8] The angel does not explain the significance of the *myrtle trees*, but in Jewish thought they represented immortality, never-ending vigour, success and prosperity.

understand his Jewish code. This time the prophet sees four horns, which the angel explains represent the four nations that have ravaged Israel and Judah – probably Assyria, Egypt, Babylon and Persia.[9] The Lord promises to bring four craftsmen against them in order to pay them back for what they did to Judah and to break their power forever. He fulfilled this prophecy through the four lieutenants of Alexander the Great, between whom his empire was divided after his premature death.

In 2:1–13, the Lord gives Zechariah a third vision.[10] This time he sees the angel that serves as his guide going out with a measuring line to measure the walls of Jerusalem.[11] He is intercepted by the same Angel of the Lord that appeared as a horseman in his first vision, and who this time tells the angel to inform Zechariah that Jerusalem will become far too populous ever to be enclosed by man-made walls.[12] *"'I myself will be a wall of fire around it,' declares the Lord, 'and I will be its glory within.'"* The prophet gains an early insight into the relationship between God the Father and God the Son, as the Angel of the Lord speaks both as the Lord Almighty and as the one who is sent into the world by *"the Glorious One... the Lord Almighty"*. This vision therefore speaks about the Jewish nation, calling those who have not yet returned from Babylon to do so straightaway,[13] and it also speaks about the Church that will be grafted into the Jewish nation through its Messiah.[14] Zechariah hears the pre-

---

[9] Any Jew familiar with Scriptures such as Psalm 18:2 would know that *horns* represented strength.

[10] Whereas Haggai was in his 80s, Zechariah was in his 20s or 30s since the angel refers to him in 2:4 as a *lad*.

[11] This follows on from a promise in Zechariah's first vision, in 1:16.

[12] Following the logic of Matthew 22:41–46, this angel has to be the pre-incarnate Jesus, since he says in 2:8–11 that he is both the Lord and the one sent by the Lord.

[13] The only other place in the Bible where Israel is referred to as *the Holy Land* is Psalm 78:54. Babylon is also described as *the land of the north* in Jeremiah 1:14–15; 4:6; 6:1; 6:22; 10:22; 16:15; 23:8; 25:9; 31:8; 46:10 and 46:24.

[14] This should already have been obvious from the fact that Nehemiah did build walls for Jerusalem!

incarnate Jesus promise that *"'I am coming, and I will live among you,' declares the Lord. 'Many nations will be joined with the Lord in that day and will become my people. I will live among you and you will know that the Lord Almighty has sent me to you.'"*

I hope you feel as excited about this as Zechariah. These three visions were exactly what the Jewish survivors needed to hear. They meant that God had not yet finished with the nation of Judah. In fact, he had only just begun.

Whiter Than White
(Zechariah 3:1–10)

"Take off his filthy clothes... See, I have taken away your sin, and I will put fine garments on you."

(Zechariah 3:4)

It's a horrible feeling to know that you are failing at your job. The high priest Joshua felt it every bit as acutely as Zerubbabel. Not only had he failed for sixteen years to persuade the Jewish survivors to keep on rebuilding the Temple, but Haggai had also needed to rebuke his team of priests for what had happened to the people of Judah on the watch over which he had presided. Joshua felt pretty miserable, so the Lord gave Zechariah a fourth vision that preached the Gospel to the high priest in his darkest hour.

Zechariah sees Satan standing by Joshua's side to accuse him of being a failure. The Greek name *Devil* means *Liar* or *Deceiver*, reminding us that we have a spiritual enemy who makes up stories against us, but the Hebrew name *Satan* means *Adversary* or *Accuser* or *Prosecution Attorney*, reminding us that he is highly skilled at using the truth against us too.[1] You don't have to have been a Christian very long to know that Satan is both very real and very good at his job.[2] He is the one who whispers in your ear that "You are useless" and that "God won't forgive you" and that "You might as well give up trying to follow

---

[1] In order to demonstrate this, the Hebrew verb for *accusing* in 3:1 is in fact *sātan*.

[2] Even the Angel of the Lord is careful how he challenges the Devil in 3:2. The fact that Satan has been defeated doesn't stop him being good at his job. If you fail to take him seriously, he will devour you (Jude 9).

Jesus at all." He is the one who tries to discourage you about the state of the Church, about the sinfulness of your own heart and about the spiritual stubbornness of your unbelieving friends. He was working overtime on Joshua.

In 3:2, the vision teaches us how to respond to Satan's accusations. We need to let the Word of God do the talking. We have already noted that the Angel of the Lord in these visions is in fact the pre-incarnate Son of God, who was only given the name Jesus when he was born as human baby, so we are watching the Trinity in action when Zechariah tells us that, *"The Lord said to Satan, 'The Lord rebuke you, Satan!'"*[3] Jesus reminds the Devil that God's Word says that the friends he seeks are not the sleek and the strong, but the weak and the weary. Satan can accuse the high priest Joshua as much as he likes of being nothing more than *"a burning stick snatched from the fire"*, because that's what the Lord loves about him.[4] He explains in Matthew 9:13. *"Go and learn what this means: 'I desire mercy, not sacrifice.' For I have not come to call the righteous, but sinners."*[5]

In 3:3–4, the vision unpacks this further. It warns us not to attempt to resist Satan's accusations by denying the truth about ourselves. Freedom only comes when we admit that we are even worse than what people say about us.[6] The Angel of the Lord does not pretend that Joshua's high priestly clothing (which represents his character and his usefulness to the Jewish nation) has not been soiled. He admits the full scale of

---

[3] Jesus explains to us in Matthew 22:41–46 that, although such Trinitarian passages may have confused the Jews before his birth, we need to understand them as pre-incarnate interactions between him and his Father.

[4] We are also described as burning sticks snatched from the fire in Amos 4:11 and Jude 23.

[5] Jesus quotes from Hosea 6:6 to emphasize that he is not looking for people who are strong enough to make their own sacrifices for him, but for people who are so weak that they need his merciful sacrifice for them.

[6] Satan stands next to Joshua to accuse him, but he never actually speaks a single word in the vision. He is utterly silenced by the Lord's frank confession that he knows the worst about Joshua but loves him anyway.

the problem when he commands the angels to *"Take off his filthy clothes."* Isaiah 64:6 says our best actions are like *menstrual rags* next to God's holiness, so Zechariah follows up this graphic imagery in 3:3 and 4 by using the Hebrew word *tsō'*, which means literally *excrement*.[7] Never try to argue that you are sinless. Simply remind the Devil that you have a Saviour.[8]

In 3:4–5, we discover what happens whenever we respond to Satan's accusations with a frank admission of our shortcomings and by throwing ourselves on God's mercy. The Angel of the Lord tells Joshua that he has dealt with all his sin and failure. *"See, I have taken away your sin, and I will put fine garments on you."* These are the *"garments of salvation"* that are mentioned in Isaiah 61:10, and Zechariah is so excited about them that he cannot hold himself back from the action. He shouts out for the angels to complete the job and *"Put a clean turban on his head."*[9] Suddenly Joshua finds himself whiter than white. Galatians 3:27 explains that he has been clothed with the righteousness of Jesus, and Mark 9:3 describes what this means: *"His clothes became dazzling white, whiter than anyone in the world could bleach them."*

Imagine how the high priest Joshua must have felt when Zechariah dealt with his despondency by relating this vision to him. How much must he have felt like worshipping the Lord? If you are familiar with Satan's accusations yourself, this vision is for you too. Learn to worship in those moments by singing the old hymn:

> *When Satan tempts me to despair and tells me of the*
> *guilt within,*

---

[7] *Tsō'* means literally *that which exits*, and is therefore much more likely to refer to faeces than to filth. It is clear from what *"the angel"* says that this is the Angel of the Lord rather than Zechariah's angel guide.

[8] The Angel of the Lord *stands by* in 3:5 to counter Satan standing by in 3:1. We must not forget that we now have a Defence Attorney (Romans 8:1; 1 John 2:1). The Hebrew verb *'ūd* in 3:6 means literally *to testify*.

[9] A *turban* was an important part of the high priest's clothing. See Exodus 28:36–39.

Upward I look and see him there who made an end to
    all my sin.
Because the sinless Saviour died, my sinful soul is
    counted free,
For God, the Just, is satisfied to look on him and pardon me.[10]

In 3:6–10, the vision now ends by teaching us how to respond to God's mercy. It ought not to make us treat sin more lightly, but pick our side more firmly.[11] It ought to make us even more determined to choose the path of God's blessing by recommitting ourselves to following Jesus and to partnering with his Holy Spirit every day.[12] It ought to make us more determined than ever to choose the blessings of his Plan "A" for us.[13]

It ought also to make us eager to tell others about this message of God's salvation. We are surrounded by people like the high priest Joshua – people who feel guilty about their sin, people who feel weighed down by their character flaws and people who feel that they are useless – so this vision ought to excite us to go out and tell them the good news of 3:9. Jesus dealt with Satan's accusations *"in a single day"* when he died in our place on the cross. He offers us his clean clothes because at Calvary he wore our own.

What a Saviour. What an offer. What a reason to put this book down and worship.

---

[10] This is the second verse of "Before the Throne of God Above" by Charity L. Bancroft (1863).

[11] It should make us share Zechariah's passion in 3:5 for God's work to be fully completed in our lives. Though we are saved by grace and not by works, being saved makes us want to work (Ephesians 2:8–10).

[12] When 3:8 says that Joshua and his fellow priests *"are men symbolic of things to come"*, it is a clue that the *Branch* and the *Stone* are both pictures of the coming Messiah (6:12; Psalm 118:22; Isaiah 4:2; Jeremiah 23:5; 33:15; 1 Peter 2:4–8). The *Seven Eyes* refer to his Holy Spirit (4:10; Revelation 5:6).

[13] Sitting peacefully under one's own vine and fig-tree was Jewish shorthand for enjoying all the Plan "A" blessings promised to those who obey God's Law (1 Kings 4:25; Isaiah 36:16; Micah 4:4).

Power Supply
(Zechariah 4:1–14)

"Not by might nor by power, but by my Spirit," says the Lord Almighty.

(Zechariah 4:6)

Power tools. You've got to love them. Last summer I spent an entire day attempting to remove an old tree stump with an axe and spade, and I got nowhere. I came back to it the following day having hired an expensive power tool, and within minutes all that was left of the stump was a pile of sawdust. It was worth every penny.

Governor Zerubbabel and the high priest Joshua were trying to build a Temple without power tools. I don't just mean literally. They were relying on human strength to achieve spiritual goals, and they were getting about as far as I did in removing my stump with an axe and spade. Jesus really means it when he warns us in John 3:6 that, when we try to achieve spiritual goals by human effort, we are always doomed to fail.

That's why the Lord woke Zechariah a little later on that same night of 15th February 519 BC to give him a fifth apocalyptic vision. He saw a golden lampstand with seven branches, just like the one that he and the other priests were meant to tend in the Temple, but this lamp's seven branches were kept burning by seven pipes that kept feeding them fuel from a large vat of olive oil. He also saw an olive tree on either side of the vat to ensure that the supply of oil to the branches would never run dry.

The angel that the Lord sent to guide Zechariah through these visions fails to answer his question in 4:4. He assumes that it is obvious who is represented by these two olive trees. Hasn't he seen the way that Zerubbabel and Joshua are labouring hard in their own strength and feeling crushed by the impossible demands of their service to God?

The angel tries to make it clearer by using two different Hebrew words in 4:6 to describe their reliance on human strength. *Hayil* means *the might of a team*, which is why the word is often used in the Old Testament to refer to an army. The governor and the high priest had hoped to build the Temple by organizing the Jewish survivors into an effective workforce, but they had failed. Their team had become so discouraged by the difficulties that they had downed tools completely for sixteen years. They had returned to work a few months ago when Haggai prophesied to them, but anyone could see that the strength of their team was entirely insufficient for the task that God had given them.

Kōah means *the power of an individual*, which is why the word is used in Proverbs 5:10 to describe a person's disposable income. When the governor and high priest had seen that the people of Judah were unreliable, they had attempted to complete the work by working even harder on their own, a bit like the busy pastor who ends up doing everything in the church because he feels that those around him are too slow, or like the new believer who believes the Church is bound to see revival now that they are in the picture. But Zerubbabel and Joshua were dog-tired and the Temple was a dog's dinner.

The angel therefore prophesies to these two well-meaning but self-reliant leaders. His words in 4:6 are both a strong rebuke and a very precious promise. *"This is the word of the Lord to Zerubbabel: 'Not by might nor by power, but by my Spirit,' says the Lord Almighty."* The Lord calls the governor and high priest to repent of their idolatrous faith in the might of a team and the strength of an individual to achieve the things of God. He wants them to repent so that he can teach them real faith in the power of his Spirit. He wants to turn them into olive trees – two ordinary men filled with his extraordinary Spirit – whose example will cascade down to the entire nation of Judah.

This vision is just as relevant to us as it was in the days of Zerubbabel and Joshua.[1] The world is full of hard-working Christians attempting great things for God in their own strength and getting nowhere. It is also full of church leaders whose stressed-out faces betray the fact that they are trying to carry the world on their own worn-out shoulders. This vision rebukes us for such well-meaning self-reliance and it proclaims good news. We don't have to try hard to be messiahs. God has already got a Messiah for us.

In 4:7–10, the vision promises what will happen if we exchange our reliance on human muscle and on church teams for reliance on being filled with the Holy Spirit instead. The governor felt as though a mountain of obstacles lay before him in the Temple building project, so the Lord exclaims, *"What are you, mighty mountain? Before Zerubbabel you will become level ground."* The governor was so weary of the building project that he had started to lose faith that it would ever be completed, so the Lord reassures him, *"He will bring out the capstone... The hands of Zerubbabel have laid the foundation of this temple; his hands will also complete it."*[2] The governor had placed his leadership credibility on the line and he felt terribly exposed and alone, so Zechariah prophesies that, if the governor is willing to switch his human hand tools for God's power tools, he is happy to place his own credibility on the line with him. These things will happen so that *"you will know that the Lord Almighty has sent me to you".*

---

[1] Revelation 1:20 suggests that this vision is as much about churches today as it was about Judah. Revelation 11:3–4 suggests that it is as much about church leaders today as it was about Zerubbabel and Joshua.

[2] The *Stone* and the *Seven Eyes* in 4:7 and 10 are meant to echo 3:9. A capstone is the final stone laid in a building. We can tell from 2 Chronicles 16:9 and Revelation 5:6 that the *Seven Eyes* refer to the Holy Spirit.

The governor felt the pain acutely when people wept at the building site of his small and shabby Temple. The mocking voices of his critics had driven him to work hard in his own strength to prove them wrong. Zechariah prophesies that this is never a good reason for us to build the house of the Lord. We need to stop reacting to our human critics and to start focusing on the Holy Spirit's reaction to our saying "yes" to partnering with him. *"Who dares despise the day of small things, since the seven eyes of the Lord that range throughout the earth will rejoice when they see the chosen capstone in the hand of Zerubbabel?"*[3]

In 4:11–14, we discover that Zechariah has still failed to grasp the identity of these two olive trees. I feel a lot of sympathy towards him, because I have learned the hard way that self-reliance is one of the hardest sins to spot in ourselves. Zechariah asks the angel for a second time in 4:11 who these two olive trees might be. When he fails to get an answer, he asks a third time in 4:12. The angel therefore ends this fifth vision in 4:14 with a grand reveal. *"These are the two who are anointed to serve the Lord of all the earth."* It's Zerubbabel and Joshua. It's you and it's me.[4]

God doesn't just want to save us and sanctify us by his grace. He also wants to empower us by his grace too. We can only bear spiritual fruit if we convert to his spiritual power supply.

---

[3] The Hebrew text of 4:10 refers literally to *a tin stone*, either meaning a capstone or a builder's plumb line.

[4] See Revelation 11:3–4. Zechariah reminds us in 4:12 what the vision taught us in 4:2–3. Whether or not church leaders change their power supply cascades down to those they lead. Self-reliant church leaders produce self-reliant churches, while Spirit-filled church leaders produce Spirit-filled churches.

Homeland
(Zechariah 5:1–6:8)

"Where are they taking the basket?"… "To the
country of Babylonia to build a house for it."

(Zechariah 5:10–11)

The Lord still had three more apocalyptic visions to give to Zechariah before he could go to sleep on the night of 15th February 519 BC. They all explore what it means for the Jewish survivors to be back from exile in their homeland. The God who had brought them out of Babylon pledges that he will also bring Babylon out of them.

In 5:1–4, the prophet sees his sixth vision. It is of a giant flying scroll. It represents all the curses that the people of Judah are earning for themselves by persisting in sin, as they continue to choose God's Plan "B" of being glorified by judging his people instead of his Plan "A" of being glorified by blessing them. The imagery here is by no means subtle. The scroll is almost ten metres long and five metres wide, representing the sheer scale of their sins against the Lord, written out in extensive detail. It wasn't normal practice in the ancient world to write on both sides of a scroll but, despite its colossal size, it has required both sides of this scroll to list the persistent wickedness of Judah. The angel explains to Zechariah that this vision speaks of their certain destruction to come.

In 5:5–11, the seventh vision acts a follow-up to the sixth. The prophet sees a basket large enough to hold a fully grown woman.[1] When he asks the angel what she represents, he is told that *"This is wickedness"* and *"the iniquity of the people throughout the land"*.[2] The basket is sealed with a heavy lid made of lead to signify that the Jews are unable to backtrack on any of this sin. The seventh vision seems like a rerun of the sixth, but there is a twist. God promises to remove every remnant of Babylon from the remnant of Judah.

First, the Jewish survivors need to recognize that they had to spend so many years in exile because they chose to disobey the Lord. They did not act like a people called to live in the Jewish homeland and to demonstrate God's glory to the pagan nations, so he carried them off to Babylon, a city so wicked that its very name is still proverbial for sin. The survivors also need to confess that when the Lord showed his compassion on them by bringing them back to the Jewish homeland, they ought to have left their sinful disobedience behind. It isn't right that they have come home from Babylon but are still so full of the city's ways that their sins can fill a giant scroll or a man-sized measuring basket. They need to confess that they actually deserve to go back into exile again.

But they also need to believe that they have a Saviour who is greater than their sin. Zechariah sees two winged women, representing angels, pick up Judah's basketful of wickedness and fly away with it to Babylon. It's a picture of God graciously forgiving his people, as he removes all the evidence for a guilty verdict against them. It's a picture of the Lord freeing his people, as he removes sin through the inner work of his Holy Spirit that none of King Josiah's external cajoling had been able to remove.[3]

---

[1] The Hebrew word *ephah* in this vision means literally a *measuring basket*. Like the sixth vision, the seventh proclaims that God knows the full extent of Judah's sin – but that he has decided to forgive them.

[2] Zechariah is not making a statement against women here, as can clearly be seen from the fact that two angels are also represented as women in 5:9. *Wickedness* simply happens to be a feminine noun in Hebrew.

[3] The Hebrew word for the *wind* in the wings of the women is *rūach*, the word normally used for God's *Spirit*.

Most of all, it is a picture of the God who brought the remnant of Judah out of Babylon bringing the remnants of Babylon out of Judah. The angel announces in 5:11 that Judah will no longer be a fertile homeland for sin. The homeland for sin will be back in Babylon.

The eighth vision, in 6:1–8, carries on from the sixth and the seventh. If you read it carefully, you will also notice that it echoes the first and second visions too. Zechariah sees two great mountains made of bronze. The angel does not explain to him what they mean, but when the Lord brought the Israelites into the Promised Land he commanded six tribes to climb Mount Gerizim to proclaim his Plan "A" blessings for their nation if it obeyed him and six tribes to climb Mount Ebal to proclaim his Plan "B" curses for their nation if it refused.[4] These mountains therefore appear to signify the great choice that the Lord has laid out before all nations: *Blessing or curse – you decide.*

The war chariots pulled by different coloured horses appear to represent the same thing as the different coloured horses in Zechariah's first vision.[5] They are the angels that are at work among the nations, seeing who has chosen the path of obedience and blessing, and who has chosen the path of disobedience and destruction. They bring God's judgment down on every sinful nation in the world, but the Lord particularly focuses in 6:8 on the way that he is going to judge Babylon. *"Look, those going towards the north country have given my Spirit rest in the land of the north."*[6] The Lord promises to deal fully with sin, once and for all, so that his people can enjoy the fullness of their salvation.

---

[4] Deuteronomy 11:26–32; 27:11–26; Joshua 8:32–34. Perhaps these bronze mountains formed the *ravine* that is mentioned in 1:8, since the angel failed to explain its significance in that first vision.

[5] The word *rūach* in 6:5 can either be translated *wind* or *spirit*. The first vision indicates the latter.

[6] We saw in 2:6–7 that *the land of the north* is an Old Testament codename for Babylon.

These three final visions, then, go together as a single declaration that the Lord will forgive Judah for its sin and destroy the pagan nations that rebel against him. It comes as fantastic news to his beleaguered people, but it poses an obvious question: how can the Lord be just in forgiving Judah? How can he treat a nation that is manifestly guilty differently from its equally guilty neighbours? We were given the answer to that question in Zechariah's fourth vision, but we also find another clue here. When Psalm 16:10 prophesies the death and resurrection of the Messiah, it refers to him as the *hāsīd*, meaning *the Holy One*. When Zechariah attempts to explain how the sins of Judah can be carried away from them to Babylon in 5:9, he likens their flight to that of the *hāsīdāh*, meaning *the stork*, which was given that name because it is fiercely loyal to its mate and to its nesting place. It's pretty subtle, but it points to the saving work of the Messiah.

Zechariah has reached the end of his eight apocalyptic visions on the night of 15th February 519 BC. He can finally get himself some sleep. But we know that these eight visions brought fresh faith to the discouraged builders of the Temple in Jerusalem, and so they also ought to bring fresh faith to us as we carry on their work today.

We ought to expect the truths revealed in these eight visions to make us as fruitful as the people of Judah in Ezra 5:1–2.

Haggai the prophet and Zechariah the prophet, a descendant of Iddo, prophesied to the Jews in Judah and Jerusalem in the name of the God of Israel, who was over them. Then Zerubbabel son of Shealtiel and Joshua son of Jozadak set to work to rebuild the house of God in Jerusalem. And the prophets of God were with them, supporting them.

Priest and King
(Zechariah 6:9–15)

"He will be a priest on his throne. And there will be harmony between the two."

(Zechariah 6:13)

There was an overriding principle behind the government of ancient Israel and Judah. Kings could never be priests, and priests could never be kings. This ancient separation of powers was meant to act as a safety net for their rulers. If a king went bad, his priests could challenge him, and if the priests went bad, their king could return the favour.

This was such a fundamental principle of government for God's people that the Lord reacted swiftly and unequivocally whenever it was ignored. When King Saul offered sacrifices, it cost him his kingdom. When King Uzziah did the same, he was struck down with leprosy.[1] Everybody knew that God chose his kings from the tribe of Judah and his priests from the tribe of Levi. Zerubbabel and Joshua knew that, and so did Zechariah.

They also knew that history had exposed a gaping flaw in this supposed safety net for Israel. There had been many occasions when the kings and priests had been as bad as one another. Instead of balancing each other out, they had goaded one another on to lead the Israelites into even greater acts of disobedience to the Lord. As a result, what the survivors of Judah really needed was not a renewal of this separation of powers, but the renewal of something that had not been seen in

---

[1] 1 Samuel 13:8–14; 2 Chronicles 26:16–23.

Jerusalem since the days of Abraham. In Genesis 14:18–20 we are told that Melchizedek, who ruled the city in around 2100 BC, served the Lord as both his priest and his king. Instead of reinstating a failed system of government, what the Jewish survivors really needed was a single ruler who could be trusted to wield complete power and authority for the Lord.[2]

Instead, they had Zerubbabel and Joshua. They had a lowly provincial governor who proved incapable of persuading them to carry on rebuilding the Temple, let alone to live in complete obedience to the Lord. They had a high priest on whose watch the priests had needed to receive a sharp rebuke from the prophet Haggai and whose influence on his nation was depicted in chapter 3 by filthy excrement all over his high priestly clothes.

This was the problem facing Zechariah when a new influx of exiles arrived back from Babylon, possibly as a result of his prophetic exhortation in 2:6–7.[3] They came bearing gifts of gold and silver, items that Zerubbabel might have liked to use to make his Temple look a little more impressive or to forge a make-believe crown for his head to make him feel a little better about being merely a provincial governor for the Persians. The Lord has a better idea, however. He tells Zechariah to take the gold and silver to a metalworker in the city and ask him to forge a kingly crown for the high priest Joshua. It was time for him to prophesy the end of Israel's separation of powers.[4] The reason why Zerubbabel and Joshua were such pale imitations of their predecessors was that the Lord had decided to unite both elements of Israel's government in a single person. The Messiah would be both the King of kings and the Great High Priest.

---

[2] Melchizedek is mentioned Psalm 110 and in Hebrews 5:1–10 and 6:20–10:22 as a prophetic picture of the Messiah. For Jesus as the Great High Priest, see Hebrews 2:17; 3:1; 4:14; 5:5–6; 6:20; 8:1.

[3] This undated revelation came sometime between 15th February 519 BC (1:7) and 7th December 518 BC (7:1).

[4] The Hebrew 'atārōth is actually a plural noun in 6:11 and 14, meaning crowns. Although the metalworker made one crown, its design must have communicated that it represented more than one crown combined.

Imagine how Joshua must have felt when Zechariah suddenly arrived on his doorstep to place this new crown on his head. He must have felt uncomfortable that it appeared to transgress Israel's ancient separation of powers. He must have been concerned about what Zerubbabel would think, let alone the king of Persia. But he must also have been excited when the prophet reassured him that by wearing it he was prophesying that Israel's separation of powers was coming to an end.[5] A better high priest was coming, who would also be the better king hailed by the prophets as a new *Branch* of David's fallen dynasty.[6] Joshua's crown prophesied that a day was coming when the priesthood and kingdom of Israel would come together in a Saviour faithful enough to be entrusted with unrestricted power and authority. *"Here is the man whose name is the Branch, and he will branch out... He will be a priest on his throne. And there will be harmony between the two."*

Of course, Joshua could not keep on wearing his double crown. If word got out to the king of Persia that the Jewish high priest had been inspired by apocalyptic visions to sport a royal crown, he would have been deposed and executed without delay. Accordingly, Zechariah prophesies that the crown should be given to the exiles who had provided its silver and gold, and that they should display it at the Temple as an ongoing encouragement that, because of Joshua and Zerubbabel's personal shortcomings, a better Priest and King was on his way.

We discover in the New Testament that when Joshua entrusted this double crown to them, he became a further prophetic picture of what the Messiah was going to do. Zechariah emphasizes that *"It is he who will build the temple*

---

[5] Haggai had made Zerubbabel a prophetic picture of the Messiah but, as a member of the high priest's team, Zechariah makes Joshua a prophetic picture instead. Zechariah did not know it, but the high priest's name – *Yehoshua* or *Yeshua* in Hebrew – would be the name that we translate as Jesus.

[6] Isaiah 4:2; 11:1; Jeremiah 23:5; 33:15; Ezekiel 17:22; Zechariah 3:8.

of the Lord" because the Messiah would do more than be a brilliant Priest and King. He would also build a new Temple out of ordinary believers who were so full of God's extraordinary Spirit that they could be said to have become a living, breathing Temple – an entire nation of kings and priests too.[7] Joshua's action prophesied that the Messiah would create a Church in which every single Christian could experience God's presence as tangibly as one of Israel's priests and wield God's Kingdom authority in the world like one of Israel's kings.

This is the prophecy that Revelation 5:10 has in mind when it worships Jesus after his death and resurrection because, *"You have made them to be kings and priests to serve our God, and they will reign on the earth."*[8] This is what it means for us to be Christians today. We are those who are called to stand before God in prayer for the world and to go out to proclaim the Gospel, reconciling sinful men and women to their holy God.[9]

So worship Jesus for the double crown he wears, but don't forget that one of the best ways you can worship him is to remember that he has given you a double crown of your own. Accept his call on your life to be one of his priests and kings in the world. Pray, preach, teach, proclaim, bless, curse, fight and protect. Be everything that Zechariah saw.

---

[7] Joshua and Zerubbabel had refused to trust foreigners to build with them (Ezra 4:1–3), but the Messiah would be such a great Saviour that he could gather even *"those who are far away"* to build.

[8] Most modern English translations follow the Nestle-Aland Greek text which reads *"a kingdom and priests"*, but older translations follow alternative Greek texts that read *basileis kai hiereis* – meaning *"kings and priests"*. The New Testament also describes Christians as *royal priests* in 1 Peter 2:9 and Revelation 1:6.

[9] This is what Paul means when he says he has been given *"the priestly duty of proclaiming the gospel of God, so that the Gentiles might become an offering acceptable to God"* (Romans 15:16). See also 2 Corinthians 5:18–21.

Shortcut to Revival
(Zechariah 7:1–8:23)

SHORTCUT TO REVIVAL (ZECHARIAH 7:1–8:23)

*Ten people from all languages and nations will take
firm hold of one Jew by the hem of his robe and say,
"Let us go with you, because we have heard that
God is with you."*

(Zechariah 8:23)

Christian bookshops are full of handy shortcuts to revival. We
are used to finding life hacks that quickly solve the problems in
our work and private lives, so we assume that there must be life
hacks that will quickly solve the problems in our churches too.
An endless list of titles promise readers that they will see revival
if only they pray in a particular fashion, fast with a particular
intensity, rearrange their small groups according to a particular
model or learn to share the Gospel in a particular way.

On 7th December 518 BC, the prophet Zechariah was
appalled to discover that this was also the case in Israel. Things
were going well in the construction of the Temple and they had
pencilled a date in the diary for its completion sometime in 516
BC. Things were also going well in persuading the survivors
of the ten northern tribes to return to the God of Israel. Even
Bethel, the centre of the northern kingdom's idolatry before
the exile, had now become a centre for worshipping the Lord.[1]
That's why Zechariah was so disappointed to hear that a group
of Israelites from Bethel had arrived in town to ask the priests
and prophets about a handy shortcut to revival. They had come

---

[1] 1 Kings 12:26–33; Hosea 10:15; Amos 3:14; 4:4; 5:5–6; 7:10–13.

to ask whether or not they ought to keep on scheduling special months of fasting over the destruction of the Temple now that the new Temple was nearing its completion.[2]

In 7:4–14, the Lord inspires Zechariah to prophesy that there are no shortcuts to revival.[3] There is one way, and one way only, for a church or nation to be revived and that is by surrendering wholeheartedly to the Lord. Israel's fasting for the past seventy years had done nothing to offset the fact that they were still only selectively obedient to God. Instead of living for him, they were living for themselves and continuing to reap his Plan "B" of being glorified by judging his rebellious people. If Israel truly wanted to see revival then, instead of relying on spiritual life hacks, it needed to accept the message of the prophets and devote itself to following God's Law. The only way that we can start to reap God's Plan "A" of being glorified by blessing his obedient people is to become obedient! The Lord's message hasn't changed: *Blessing or curse – you decide.*

That's why Zechariah spells out here for the Israelites what obedience to God's Law really means. It is about committing to live out God's justice, mercy and compassion, even when those things are far costlier than the shortcuts we are offered to revival. It is about loving the lost and the least and the lonely in the name of Lord. It is about becoming his lifeboat of salvation, uncontaminated by the salt water of the sinful world. That's what Israel had refused to do, which is why the Lord destroyed the northern kingdom and scattered its ten tribes among the nations. It is also what the new generation of Israelites needed to rectify if they wanted their national fortunes to change.

[2] In 7:3, they merely ask if they should *nāzar*, or *separate themselves*, in the fifth month. English translations extrapolate from 7:5 that this meant *"mourn and fast"* over the destruction of the Temple in the fifth month of 586 BC (2 Kings 25:8). The traditional Jewish fast of Yom Kippur took place in the seventh month (Leviticus 16:29).

[3] 7:12 gives us a great definition of prophecy. *The Lord* sends words to *his prophets* through *his Holy Spirit* so that they can partner with the Triune God in reaching out to the world. See also 2 Peter 1:20–21.

Frankly, I find this message very challenging. I like shortcuts and life hacks. Part of me hates the idea of having to go deeper to find spiritual solutions to spiritual problems. I find it easier to pick up a paperback that tells me to try fasting a little more than accept the message of the prophets that our fasting has no power unless it is accompanied by genuine turning away from our sins.[4] I find it easier to attend a conference that reassures me that my church's problems are organizational than face up to God's warning that its problems are relational – people who claim to love one another but truly love themselves, and people who talk about unity while looking down on one another.[5] I find it easier to persuade myself that all it requires is a little more concerted prayer than to face up to the Bible's frequent warning that how we act affects how much our prayers are answered.[6] I find it easier to do just about anything than trace my problems back to disobedience, yet Scripture is very clear: *Blessing or curse – you decide.*[7]

In 8:1–23, the Lord makes several promises that are meant to persuade us that it is worth the effort of abandoning our shortcuts and digging deeper. He reassures us that nobody is more passionate about reviving his people than he is. Nobody is more committed to turning them back into his *Faithful City* and his *Holy Mountain* than he is. He commands us to go deeper in repentance because he truly wants his holy presence to dwell among us so that he can be glorified by blessing us.[8] *"It may*

---

[4] Isaiah states this even more clearly in Isaiah 1:11–17 and 58:1–14.

[5] The Hebrew words translated as *"Do not plot evil against each other"* in 7:10 and 8:17 can just as easily be translated as *"Do not think evil of each other."* 1 John 3:18 warns us that God sees our hearts.

[6] Proverbs 15:8, 29; 21:13; 28:9; Isaiah 1:15; 1 Timothy 2:8; Hebrews 5:7; James 5:16; 1 Peter 3:7.

[7] 7:13 states the flipside of 1:3. If we return to God, he will return to us, but if we chase shortcuts to revival instead of listening to his call to repentance he will not listen to our prayers.

[8] In 8:4–5, people growing old and children playing safely are classic Hebrew pictures of God's blessing.

seem marvellous to the remnant of this people at that time, but will it seem marvellous to me?"

He also reassures us that nobody is more committed to seeing his people grow than he is. In 8:7–8, he promises to convert scores of unbelievers on the left and the right, just as soon as believers take him seriously. In 8:20–23, he promises to spark such a Gospel chain reaction among unbelievers that they will even start to preach the Good News to one another. I like books on evangelism. I've even written a few. But you won't find anything in those paperbacks to unleash the scale of revival that God promises to bestow on obedient communities of believers here: *"This is what the Lord Almighty says: 'In those days ten people from all languages and nations will take firm hold of one Jew by the hem of his robe and say, "Let us go with you, because we have heard that God is with you."'"*[9]

The Lord ends by reminding us that actions speak louder than words. He is less interested in how much time we spend praying and fasting than he is in what we do when we get up off our knees at the end of our prayers.[10] For Zechariah's generation that meant obeying his repeated command to *"Let your hands be strong so that the temple may be built."* For our generation, it means getting radical with sin in our own lives and churches.[11] It means rediscovering the path of God's blessing by offering him total obedience, instead of placing our faith in spiritual life hacks. It means confessing that many of our failures are self-inflicted, part of the curse that falls on the disobedient.

---

[9] Zechariah refers to God 53 times in his book as *the Lord Almighty* to emphasize that none of the spiritual shortcuts that we take in our own strength are ever as fruitful as lining up our lives with the power of God.

[10] Compare 8:19 with 7:5. The Lord loves prayer and fasting so much that he wants us to increase our practice of it – but he wants what we say to be matched by what we do.

[11] 8:23 prophesies that, while the Lord will restore the fortunes of the Jewish nation, Jews will quickly be outnumbered ten-to-one by Gentiles in the Church that their Messiah will build.

It means taking the Lord seriously when he says there are no shortcuts to revival and dares us to go deeper in repentance: *"Do not be afraid, but let your hands be strong."*

SHORTCUT TO REVIVAL (ZECHARIAH 7:1-8:23)

Building Instructions
(Zechariah 9:1–11:17)

> *See, your king comes to you, righteous and*
> *victorious, lowly and riding on a donkey, on a colt,*
> *the foal of a donkey.*
>
> (Zechariah 9:9)

Last Christmas I bought my daughter a beautiful IKEA cabin bed. The problem was that I didn't actually buy it from IKEA. I bought it second-hand to save money and when I came to assemble it I discovered that it didn't have any building instructions. It took me hours to make head or tail of the unlabelled collection of nuts, bolts, screws and dowels scattered on my daughter's bedroom floor. That's how most people feel when they come to the two long prophecies that form the final six chapters of Zechariah. It's like trying to assemble an IKEA cabin bed without any building instructions.

Their problem stems from the fact these two prophecies are undated. The first eight chapters were all labelled as belonging to the years in which Zerubbabel and Joshua were struggling to rebuild the Temple, which acts as a key to unlock their meaning. These final six chapters, on the other hand, no longer talk about the Temple because the Temple was completed on 12th March 516 BC, after which the Jewish survivors faced a different set of challenges.[1] These last two prophecies are considerably longer than Zechariah's earlier visions, and much of it is written in poetry rather than in prose. All of this makes

---

[1] Ezra 6:15. This was 70 years after its destruction, as promised in 1:12 and in Jeremiah 25:11–14 and 29:10.

them harder to follow, but we mustn't succumb to skim-reading here. These final six chapters are arguably even more important than the first eight, since the New Testament never quotes from Zechariah 1–8 but it quotes six times from Zechariah 9–14.

To unlock the meaning of these final two prophecies, we simply need to use a different type of key. The key word in Zechariah 1–8 was Temple, since all those visions focus on the task of building a house for God, but the key word in Zechariah 9–14 is *Messiah*, since the focus now shifts to God's plan to build a new and better Israel. Understanding this change of key unlocks the meaning of what Zechariah prophesied in his older years.[2]

In 9:1–17, Zechariah prophesies that the Messiah is going to come soon and that he will lead the people of Israel to victory over all their enemies, saving all those who receive him as King and destroying all those who refuse.[3] He will do this by riding into Jerusalem on the foal of a donkey, exemplifying what we learned in 4:6, that in order to access God's strength we need to revel in our weakness without him.[4] Matthew 21:5 and John 12:15 both quote from 9:9 when they describe the triumphal entry of Jesus into Jerusalem on a donkey in order to be crucified. That's why 9:11 talks about *"the blood of my covenant"* and it's why salvation suddenly breaks out from Jerusalem to all the nations of the world.[5]

[2] Zechariah may have continued prophesying as late as 470 BC, since he was still a young man in 2:4. The last book of the Hebrew Old Testament is 2 Chronicles, so Matthew 23:35 probably refers to the death of a different Zechariah mentioned in 2 Chronicles 24:20–22, who also had an ancestor named Berekiah.

[3] Damascus, Hadrak and Hamath were cities in Syria. Tyre and Sidon were port cities in Lebanon. Ashkelon, Gaza, Ekron and Ashdod were cities in Philistia. 9:7 explains that this is about conversion, not just conquest.

[4] Kings had ridden on donkeys before (1 Kings 1:33), but never on the mere foal of a donkey.

[5] The Hebrew text of 9:1 is deliberately ambiguous. It either promises that Israel and all nations will see the Lord, or declares that God's eyes of salvation are on the nations as well as on Israel.

In 10:1–11:3, Zechariah explains what the Lord meant in 9:13 when he promised to turn his Jewish followers into his bows and arrows and his Gentile followers into a warrior's sword. He meant that the Messiah would teach all his followers how to access God's strength by confessing their weakness and walking in his footsteps down the death-and-resurrection road. He will transform *sheep* into *warriors* and *warhorses*, because he is the *cornerstone*, the *tent peg* and the *battle-bow* of his people.[6] He will not only save many of the survivors from the northern and southern kingdoms, but he will transform them into an army of missionaries who preach salvation to the world.[7] Lebanon, Assyria and Egypt symbolize the most unreachable nations, yet even they will surrender to the Lord.

We ought to find these verses as encouraging as the Jewish survivors did in the days of Zechariah. They ought to make us cry out in prayer for the Lord to bless his people by reviving them and causing them to see a Gospel harvest everywhere. *"Ask the Lord for rain in the springtime; it is the Lord who sends the thunderstorms. He gives showers of rain to all people, and plants of the field to everyone."* They ought to make us fearless in attempting to plant churches and in opening up new people groups for the Gospel.[8] *"They will fight because the Lord is with them, and they will put the enemy horsemen to shame."* These verses ought to make us view church decline as something unusual and entirely reversible. *"Surely I will redeem them; they will be as numerous as before... and there will not be room enough for them."*[9] They ought to make us take our eyes off our

---

[6] The Messiah is called these things in 3:9 and 4:7, in Psalm 118:22–23 and in Isaiah 8:14–15 and 22:23.

[7] In 10:6, the two divided kingdoms of *Judah* and *Joseph* are reunited under one King.

[8] When church leaders are too fearful to do this (10:2), ordinary church members are to do it instead (10:3).

[9] Lebanon, Gilead and Bashan were the far extremities of Israel that had long since been lost to other nations. The Lord is promising that, however great Israel becomes, it will not be able to contain all that the Messiah wants to do.

own shortcomings and all the obstacles that lie before us. *"I will strengthen them in the Lord."*[10]

In 11:4–17, Zechariah is honest with us that it will not all be plain sailing.[11] Although the one who enters Jerusalem on a donkey is far more powerful than those who ride on warhorses, many Jews will refuse to hail him as their Messiah. They will reject the Lord who reunited their divided kingdom and will ask worthless rabbis to shepherd them instead.[12] Matthew 27 explains that 11:12–13 are a prophecy about the Messiah's betrayal by Judas Iscariot and the flippant way in which the leaders of Israel rejected him.[13] These three chapters are brimful of amazing promises, and yet they end in national tragedy. Zechariah warns that this revival will involve many Jews being slaughtered, scattered, divided and handed over to be ruled by the kind of leaders they deserve.[14]

This long prophecy is not easy to follow, but our efforts are rewarded when we understand that the building instructions have shifted their focus and that the key word to unlock them is *Messiah*. Although there will be setbacks, the Lord promises that Jesus will be everything we hope for and more. Armed with

---

In the same way, our plans as churches must always include breaking open new territories.

[10] Lebanon and Bashan were famous for their dense forests. In 11:1–3, their juniper, cedar and oak trees therefore represent the obstacles that stand against us. The might of hell can no more stop us than the Red Sea stopped Israel (10:11) or the Roman Empire stopped the early Christians (Colossians 1:29).

[11] Zechariah may have actually taken a job as a shepherd to deliver this prophecy that echoes Ezekiel 37:15–22.

[12] Far from shepherding people in the Law of Moses, we are told in 11:16 that any rabbi who teaches people to reject Jesus as the Messiah is like a shepherd who rips off the sheep's hooves. The curse in 11:17 ought to be sobering for church leaders as well. It isn't only rabbis who can do this (James 3:1).

[13] Matthew also observes how much this prophecy echoes the words of Jeremiah 19:1–13.

[14] The breaking of the two staffs and the revoking of the covenant is a picture of the destruction of Jerusalem by the Romans in 70 AD. In his mercy, the Lord would give the Jews 40 years in which to change their mind.

these promises, he encourages us to put our faith in Jesus and to take our own place in his Gospel army that traverses the entire world.[15]

---

[15] 9:12 calls us *"prisoners of hope"*. Having caught this great glimpse of who the Messiah is, we can no longer escape the implications of what it means for us to have faith in him. We are bound to make a decision. Archbishop Desmond Tutu was quoting from this verse when he famously corrected David Frost in a TV interview, insisting that *"I'm not an optimist. I'm a prisoner of hope."*

The Future for Israel (Zechariah 12:1–14:21)

"They will look on me, the one they have pierced, and they will mourn for him."

(Zechariah 12:10)

How you felt about the prophecy in Zechariah 9–11 largely depends on whether you are a Gentile or a Jew. If you are not Jewish, you were probably excited by the promise of salvation for all nations, but if you are Jewish, you were probably as appalled by the way it concluded with Israel's rejection of the Messiah. Zechariah understands how the Jewish survivors must feel so he brings a second prophecy about the future of Israel.[1]

In 12:1, he tells us that these three final chapters of prophecy are about what will happen to Israel. Although the New Testament sometimes uses "Israel" to mean the Church, the simplest way of understanding the word here is that the prophet is going to tell us what will happen to the Jewish nation after it rejects its Messiah. The Church has not replaced Israel in God's mind, even though he spoke about revoking his covenant in 11:10. The Church is Israel because the Lord founded it through twelve Jewish apostles to extend the Israel of old to include all those who share the faith of Abraham and confess the Jewish Messiah as their Saviour.[2] Zechariah seeks to reassure his

---

[1] 9:1 and 12:1 indicate that these are two distinct prophecies that follow on from one another.

[2] Galatians 6:16; Matthew 19:28; Acts 28:20. This is why the apostles take God's prophecies to Israel and apply them to the Church without any hesitation throughout the New Testament.

horrified Jewish readers in these three chapters that God has not forgotten their nation. He still has a glorious future for Israel.

In 12:1–9, Zechariah prophesies that there will be a large Jewish revival in the end. The God who created the earth and every human spirit will not have his plans for Israel thwarted by anyone – not even by the Jews themselves. The fact that he still loves Israel is obvious from the way its people have been persecuted throughout AD history. There are two groups of people that have been consistently threatened and besieged by unbelievers for the past 2,000 years: the Christians and the Jews. Despite the ugliness of anti-Semitism, it therefore reveals something glorious. The Devil still knows that the best way to try to get at God is to play on his undying love for the Jews. Zechariah promises that the Lord will thwart every attack against them. He will turn the Jewish nation into his *cup* of judgment, into an *immoveable rock* on which he dashes his foes and into a *flaming torch* through which he consumes unbelievers. He will destroy any nation that attacks them, turning even the feeblest Jew into a giant-slayer like David. We can still say, *"The people of Jerusalem are strong, because the Lord Almighty is their God."*[3]

In 12:10–14, Zechariah explains how this is just and fair. Although the Jews have largely rejected Jesus as their Messiah, they will not do so forever. A day is coming when the Lord will pour out his Spirit on the Jewish nation in such a powerful way that they will cry out in prayers of repentance for their sin and for having crucified God's Messiah. *"They will look on me, the one they have pierced, and they will mourn for him as one mourns for an only child, and grieve bitterly for him as one grieves for a firstborn son."*[4] This verse is quoted during the account of Jesus' crucifixion in John 19:37 and it teaches us that Calvary was not

---

[3] Note that this promise is given to the Jewish nation, not the modern state of Israel. Christians drift into error when they forget that they are not quite the same thing.

[4] 12:11 refers to the wave of mourning that followed King Josiah's death in battle (2 Chronicles 35:22–25).

the end of the Jewish story.[5] One day all the great families of Israel will regret what they did and turn back to the Lord.

One of the big refrains in Zechariah's final prophecy is the phrase *"on that day"*, which occurs sixteen times in these three chapters. In chapter 14 it refers to the Messiah's second coming, but in chapters 12–13 it refers to the moment in history when the Jewish nation finally wakes up to the fact that it has missed the Messiah's first coming. In 13:1–6, Zechariah prophesies about the instant effects of their repentance. *"On that day a fountain will be opened to the house of David and the inhabitants of Jerusalem, to cleanse them from sin and impurity."* The blood that dripped down a cross outside the city walls of Jerusalem in 30 AD will flow freely to forgive the Jews as soon as they return to faith in the Lord. Once forgiven, they will reject the rabbis who led them astray (symbolized here by the false prophets of Zechariah's day[6]) and they will renounce the demon-idols and the spirit of impurity that blinded them for so many years to Jesus as their Messiah.[7]

In 13:7–9, the prose turns back into poetry, as the Lord gets so excited about the success of his plan that he calls for it to be enacted quickly. He tells the Jewish nation to be swift in rejecting his Messiah. *"Awake, sword, against my shepherd, against the man who is close to me!... Strike the shepherd, and the sheep will be scattered."* Jesus quotes this verse without any resentment in Matthew 26:31 and Mark 14:27 because he is just as committed to this plan of salvation as God the Father. It is going to work. Although a majority of Jews will reject Jesus, the Lord will rescue many of them from the crucible of his judgment

---

[5] Note the Trinity at work in 12:10: *"They will look on me... and they will mourn for him."*

[6] These false prophets dressed up like Elijah in order to masquerade as servants of God (2 Kings 1:8), but under their clothes their scars showed that they were far more like the prophets of Baal (1 Kings 18:28).

[7] The Hebrew word *rūach*, meaning *spirit*, in 13:2 suggests demonic blindness. The Hebrew word *dāqar* that is used in 13:3 for parents *stabbing* their children was used in 12:10 for God allowing his Son to be *pierced*.

and make their precious souls like refined silver and gold.[8] *"They will call on my name and I will answer them; I will say, 'They are my people,' and they will say, 'The Lord is our God.'"*

The grand finale to this prophecy comes in 14:1–21. The Devil will not take this end-time Jewish revival lying down. We do not know exactly what is signified by the coalition of nations that attacks Jerusalem, but it sounds horrible. The Jewish Christians will need to stand strong because, if they do, in the nick of time they will witness the second coming of Jesus. He will descend to the Mount of Olives, the same mountain from which he ascended to heaven in Acts 1:9–12, and his Kingdom will finally come on earth as it is in heaven.[9] Zechariah uses an avalanche of Hebrew imagery to convey this – the riverless city of Jerusalem becoming the source of a river that fills even the Dead Sea with fresh water,[10] its walls being lifted up high out of reach of its enemies while a plague rots away their faces, and the Temple being purified while the Lord reinforces the blessings and curses of his Law to all nations. All of the imagery amounts to the same thing: *"The Lord my God will come, and all the holy ones with him... The Lord will be king over the whole earth. On that day there will be one Lord, and his name the only name."*

Zechariah has come to the end of his book of prophecy. He has explained to us that there is still a future for Israel. He has assured us that, before the Messiah returns, the Lord will bring the Jewish nation back to himself. That's what Paul celebrates in Romans 11:25–26:

[8] *Two thirds*, *one third* and a *half* in 13:8–9 and 14:2 are symbolic fractions here.

[9] The Mount of Olives is split in two in 14:4–5 to signify that Judgment Day will split the world into two camps. *Azel* means *separate*. Those who choose badly will find hell as awful as it sounds in 14:12–15.

[10] Ezekiel 47 suggests that 14:8 describes the new earth being completely filled with the Holy Spirit.

Israel has experienced a hardening in part until the full number of the Gentiles has come in, and in this way all Israel will be saved.[11]

---

[11] *All* does not mean 100% any more than a *third* and *half* mean precisely 33% and 50% in 13:8 and 14:2. It simply conveys the scale of God's promise in 12:12–14. Jews from every tribe, clan and family will be saved.

Yeah, Right
(Malachi 1:1–2:9)

> *"I have loved you,"* says the Lord. But you ask, *"How have you loved us?"*
>
> (Malachi 1:2)

Philip Yancey believes that many of us are disappointed with God. He suggests that

> *For many people there is a large gap between what they* ***expect*** *from their Christian faith and what they actually experience. From a steady diet of books, sermons, and personal testimonies, all promising triumph and success, they learn to expect dramatic evidence of God working in their lives. If they do not see such evidence, they feel disappointment, betrayal, and often guilt. As one woman said: I kept hearing the phrase, "personal relationship with Jesus Christ." But I found to my dismay that it is unlike any other personal relationship. I never saw God, or heard him, or felt him, or experienced the most basic ingredients of a relationship. Either there's something wrong with what I was told, or there's something wrong with me.*[1]

Maybe you can identify with what Philip Yancey means. The Jewish survivors did, in boatloads. They had completed the Lord's Temple in 516 BC. They had rebuilt the walls of Jerusalem in only fifty-two days under Nehemiah in 445 BC. They had listened to

---

[1] Philip Yancey in his book *Disappointment with God* (1988).

Ezra read the Law of Moses to them and had rededicated their nation to the Lord, but twelve years later they felt that they had not seen any of the blessings they expected. No bumper harvests, no independence from Persia and no sudden spiritual revival. They had grown so cynical and resentful towards God that when he spoke to them about his blessings and curses, their instinctive reply was: *Yeah, right.*

That's why the Lord sent Malachi to help them. We know little about this prophet other than that his name in Hebrew means *My Messenger*, but we can date his ministry from the book of Nehemiah.[2] The issues he addresses are so similar to those addressed and eliminated in Nehemiah 13 that he must have prophesied a few months before, during the year when Nehemiah was absent from Jerusalem, between the end of his first term as governor (445–433 BC) and the start of his second term (432 BC).[3] This dates Malachi to 433 BC, making his the last book of the Old Testament chronologically as well as the last on the contents page. He tried to help the Jews to grapple with the crushing disappointment that they felt towards God.

In 1:2–5, Malachi prophesies to the Jews that the Lord loves them. They are so disappointed that they reply: *Yeah, right.* How can the Lord love them when their Temple is shabby and their land is a province of Persia? How can he love them when he hasn't sent his Messiah or done any of the things that he prophesied he would? Maybe you feel a bit like they did. Maybe you feel that God has not delivered on much of what he promised you. If that's the case, you need to listen carefully to the Lord's reply.

These verses are the first of six prophetic dialogues between the Lord and the people of Judah. In this initial dialogue, he seeks to show them that the problem is all at their

---

[2] The prophet's name comes from the same Hebrew word used three times in 2:7 and 3:1 for *messenger*.

[3] Nehemiah 5:14–18 says that he never demanded offerings like his replacement in Malachi 1:8.

end.[4] Like many of us, they have failed to appreciate all that he has done for Judah. Since the prophets often use the nation of Edom as shorthand for all the enemies of God, he tells them to compare their situation with that of the nation founded by Jacob's twin brother. It should be fairly obvious to them that *"I have loved Jacob, but Esau I have hated."*[5]

Are the Edomites back in their land? No, it is still in ruins. Are they planning to return? It makes no difference, because whatever they rebuild the Lord will demolish. The Edomites are doomed to die out, just as he promised in the book of Obadiah. There is an important lesson for us here. Much of the disappointment that the Jews felt towards God was caused by their losing sight of where they would now be without him. Their eyes were so fixed on their problems that they had failed to spot all the blessings that he had given to them and withheld from their neighbours. They needed to take a broader perspective and to see the truth: *"Great is the Lord – even beyond the borders of Israel!"*[6]

In 1:6–2:9, Malachi senses that the people of Judah are still saying: *Yeah, right.* He therefore gives a second reason why the problem is all at their end. Their actions demonstrate that they have learned nothing from their exile in Babylon. They are no more obedient to God's Law than their ancestors, so it really shouldn't surprise them that they are reaping the curses listed in Deuteronomy 28 instead of the blessings. Although they feel disappointed with the way the Lord has been a Father to their

---

[4] Like Haggai and Zechariah, who refer to God as *Yahweh Tsebā'ōth*, or *the Lord Almighty*, 14 and 53 times, Malachi emphasizes that he is no disappointment by calling him *Yahweh Tsebā'ōth* 24 times in just 4 chapters.

[5] Paul quotes from 1:2–3 in Romans 9:13 to point out that God chose to bless Jacob while he was in his mother's womb, before he had done anything good or bad (Genesis 25:23). This is proof enough of his love.

[6] In the same way, Christians need to look beyond the walls of their churches. See Psalm 24:1.

nation, they have not honoured him as they do their natural fathers or their Persian overlords.[7]

The people of Judah instinctively resist this rebuke. We need to learn from this, because disappointment always makes us say *yeah, right* to God's Word.[8] He responds patiently but firmly to their request for some concrete examples. He points out that they palm off on to him their sickly animals as sacrifices, while they would never dream of trying to do so with their Persian governor.[9] It makes him want to close their new Temple down.[10] Add to that the fact that they treat any blood sacrifice for their sin as a burden, and it is a wonder that the Lord has given them any of the blessings in his Law at all.

As for the priests, they are nothing like the ones described in the Law of Moses.[11] Instead of stopping the people from sinning by instructing them in God's Word, they have tolerated and participated in their sin themselves. When Joshua's priestly garments were covered in faeces in Zechariah 3, listening to God's Word made his garments clean, but the Lord promises that any priest who preaches his Word selectively will have their garments smeared with the faeces of the sickly animals they sacrifice to him.[12] Again this is vital. Many of our disappointments with God are our own fault. We have left his

---

[7] The Lord says in 1:5, 11 and 14 that he is a greater King than any Persian ruler and that, if the Jews will not admit it, he will take his Kingdom to the pagan nations instead. Time was running out for Judah.

[8] For example, it is easy for us to point to Job and Joseph as examples of people who obeyed the Lord and yet reaped misery. However, their misery was short-term and the Lord is stating a general principle here.

[9] This not only insulted God the Father. It also insulted Jesus the Son, to whom those sacrifices pointed.

[10] This is important. A sacrifice offered to God reluctantly is worse than no offering at all (2 Corinthians 9:7).

[11] We find a simple job description in 2:5–9 for our work as God's priests and kings in the world. We are to fear God's name, preach God's Word, walk God's way and follow God's Law.

[12] The Lord condemns *partiality* over his Word in 2:9. Church leaders must preach it all.

path of blessing and have provoked him to say to us, *"I will send a curse on you, and I will curse your blessings. Yes, I have already cursed them, because you have not resolved to honour me."*

So the next time you feel disappointed with God, take a sheet of paper and draw a line down the middle. On one side list the blessings he has given you and on the other side list the sins which mean he ought not to have blessed you at all. Then pray with this new perspective. Tell him that you are no longer disappointed with his mercy towards you.

What About You?
(Malachi 2:10–3:5)

Do we not all have one Father? Did not one God create us?

(Malachi 2:10)

In their first two prophetic dialogues with the Lord, in 1:2–2:9, the people of Judah doubted that he had been faithful towards them. Now in these third and fourth prophetic dialogues they doubt that he has been fair to them. Instead of confessing humbly that they have indeed dishonoured him, their disappointment makes them very stubborn. When the Lord points out their shortcomings, they reply: *What about you?*

In 2:10, they try to pin the blame on God. Since he is their Father and Creator, their shortcomings are surely his fault because they are just the way he made them. Besides, it isn't fair that so much of his Law deals with their private lives. Why should he care who they sleep with and whether or not they are faithful to their husbands and wives?

The Lord has to explain to them that their private lives aren't private. He has covenanted to be their God, so they defile that covenant whenever they take their sexual ethics and their marriage guidance from the unbelieving world. This third dialogue is hugely relevant to us, since we live in an age that tolerates just about anything – premarital sex, gay sex, adulterous sex, group sex and divorce to have sex with someone new. It tolerates anything at all, it seems, except for following God's path and pursuing sexual purity. Christians who are as influenced by the world as these Jewish survivors try to deny the Bible's prohibitions and to blame God for making them a certain way.

The Lord points out to the people of Judah that the way they are living isn't how he created them. It is how the Devil spoiled them. What were they thinking of when they married good-looking foreigners instead of Jewish girls, even though they knew that many of those women were worshippers of idols? What were they thinking of when they divorced the godly Jewish wives that he had given them in order to shack up with unbelievers?[1] In his anger, God calls the curses of his Law down upon them. May their Temple sacrifices go unheeded and may they be cut off from Israel! It's very simple: *Blessing or curse – you decide.*[2]

The Lord gives the men of Judah some of the clearest teaching in the Old Testament about the importance of our sex lives and of our marriages.[3] The New Testament unpacks these verses in more detail, but here we have the basic headlines.[4] What we do with our bodies matters as much as what we do with our spirits. The way we observe the vows of our marriage covenant has a direct impact on how much we can enjoy the blessings of the covenant that God has made with us. The Lord will judge us for the way in which our lifestyles shape the next generation, as the children he has entrusted to us look and learn from what we do. The Lord reveals himself as a divorce victim in Isaiah 50:1 and Jeremiah 3:8, so he knows its pain from personal experience and he tells us here that he hates divorce

---

[1] We can read more about this in Ezra 10:1–17 and Nehemiah 13:23–29. It is sobering that the Lord declares in 2:11 that such actions desecrate his Temple. It means that such actions also desecrate our churches too.

[2] 2:12–13 warns us not to use God's grace as an excuse to ignore these commands. The Lord warns us twice that, if our actions show a lack of repentance for our sin, we forfeit any share in his grace at all.

[3] The Hebrew text of 2:12 warns literally that God will judge *both the one who initiates and the one who responds.*

[4] See for example Matthew 5:31–32; Mark 10:2–12; Luke 16:18; 1 Corinthians 6:9–7:40; 1 Peter 3:7.

with a passion.[5] If we are unfaithful to our marriage vows, we can't blame him when our lives start to unravel. *"'The man who hates and divorces his wife,' says the Lord, the God of Israel, 'does violence to the one he should protect.'"*[6]

The men of Judah show no signs of repentance. They simply move on, in 2:17, to state a second reason why they believe that the Lord has been unfair to them. There is only one thing worse than bad things happening to good people, and that is good things happening to bad people, yet when they look around it appears that *"all who do evil are good in the eyes of the Lord, and he is pleased with them... Where is the God of justice?"*[7]

The Lord is patient but very firm with the people of Judah. They will get the judgment they are asking for, but it will fall on them! The Day of the Lord will soon be upon them. Malachi will be the last prophet of the Old Testament, and the very next prophet God sends will be the final warm-up act for his Messiah. *"I will send my messenger, who will prepare the way before* **me.**" Three times the New Testament quotes these words from 3:1 to refer to the ministry of John the Baptist.[8] Just one more prophet, then the Messiah will finally come to the courtyards of their small and shabby Temple. *"Suddenly the Lord you are seeking will come to his temple; the messenger of the covenant, whom you desire, will come."*

In 3:2–5, the Lord therefore turns their self-justifying question back on them: *What about you?* Will the Messiah find

---

[5] This means that there is clearly such a thing as an innocent party in divorce – someone who has been cheated on (Matthew 19:9), abandoned (1 Corinthians 7:12–16) or abused (Exodus 21:10–11). Note that even then, however, God seeks reconciliation with unfaithful Israel rather than abandoning her to look elsewhere.

[6] The Lord is warning us that not all divorces recognized by the state are recognized by him.

[7] This is still a common complaint today, although Job 40:8 warns us starkly that it is blasphemy.

[8] Matthew 11:10; Mark 1:2; Luke 7:27. The Hebrew word used twice in 3:1 for *messenger* is the root of the name Malachi, which means *My Messenger*. In other words, after *My Messenger* will come *my messenger*.

them ready on that Day or will they get a whole lot more than they have bargained for?[9] They complain that God is slow at enforcing his justice. Very well then, the Messiah's arrival will bring his judgment crashing down upon them. Their reaction to him will reveal the true state of their hearts. He will become to them like a refiner's fire that removes dross from gold and silver, or like a harsh laundry detergent that removes the filth from people's clothes.[10] He will grant them the justice that they complain is too slow in coming, but many of them will wish he hadn't. Their disobedience to the Law will be exposed when he declares that their Jewish ancestry is not enough to save them or to make them fit to enjoy God's covenant. They will be exposed as the rebels that they are when the Messiah offends their Jewish sensibilities by commanding them to follow him and to be baptized like a filthy bunch of Gentiles.

So be careful what you ask for. God might just say "yes". Be careful also what you say about the Lord in your moments of disappointment in him. God is not being unfair to you and, even if he were, your true need has never been his justice. It has only ever been his mercy. Praise the Lord that his Messiah has come to bear away the curse of your sin by dying on the cross for you. Now respond by loving your spouse, if you have one, as much as Jesus has loved you. Above all, stop pointing the finger at God and become as passionate about his holiness as you used to be about fighting your own corner.

Don't look at other people and take your standards from them. Even if the whole world disobeys him, the Lord still asks with eyes of fire: *What about you?*

---

[9] The Lord hints at this in 3:1 by referring to the Messiah as *the one whom you desire*. The people of Judah had put their false expectations of what the Messiah would be like ahead of their obedience to God's Law.

[10] There is a play on words here in Hebrew, since the word for *covenant* is *berith* and the word for laundry *soap* is *bōrīth*.

The Test (Malachi 3:6–12)

"Bring the whole tithe into the storehouse, that there may be food in my house. Test me in this," says the Lord Almighty.

(Malachi 3:10)

One of my favourite classic movies is *The Sting*, starring Paul Newman and Robert Redford, who play a pair of conmen with a brilliant idea for making money. They set up a betting shop in which the results of horse races appear to be announced live, but are actually announced a few minutes after they are wired through. Since they know the winner of each race before it even begins, they are able to gamble everything, knowing that they cannot lose. The true test of how sure we are isn't what we say, but what we do.

That's the Lord's point in his fifth prophetic dialogue with the people of Judah. He points out that the way they spend their money proves that they don't really believe in him. They claim to have faith in what the Law of Moses says about him, but their actions prove that they are very uncertain about his character. They refuse to gamble everything on him. They have no more confidence in his Word than their ancestors did. The true test of their faith isn't what they claim to believe, but what they do with the money he has entrusted to them.

To help the people of Judah to believe in him, the Lord says three things. First, he points out that he never changes. To demonstrate this, he commands them to *"Return to me, and I will return to you"* – the same command he gave to their great-grandparents eighty-seven years ago in Zechariah 1:3. Second, he reminds them that this means he is still *Yahweh Tsebā'ōth*, or *the Lord Almighty* – a name which speaks of his invincibility and that is used fourteen times in Haggai, fifty-three times in Zechariah and twenty-four times in Malachi. Third, he points out that they can know both of these things for certain from the fact that their nation has not been destroyed like Edom and Philistia. They are like Paul Newman and Robert Redford in *The Sting*. They know the outcome of God's promises before the race is run.

The disappointed people of Judah respond in the same way as before: *Yeah, right.* They believe that they have returned to the Lord already, yet their nation is still in tatters. They have gambled everything on God and lost. The Lord responds by asking them to take a look at their recent financial transactions, since there is no statement of faith quite as accurate as a bank statement. He points out that they are not bringing a tenth of their income to the Temple, as commanded by the Law of Moses.[1] They cannot plead ignorance, because on 30th October 445 BC, when Ezra read the Law to them in Nehemiah 10, they pledged specifically that *"We will not neglect the house of our God."* They have failed to put their money where their mouth is. The way that they have hoarded their money proves that they do not truly believe they can trust the Lord enough to gamble everything on him. Transactions speak louder than words.

That's why their personal finances are in such a mess. *"You are under a curse – your whole nation – because you are robbing me."*[2] Their withheld tithes and offerings prove that they have no more turned back to God's Law than their ancestors in the days of King Josiah, so he has brought on them the curses listed in Deuteronomy 28. The crops in their fields have been devoured by pests and the grapes have fallen off their vines

---

[1] Leviticus 27:30–31; Numbers 18:21–32; Deuteronomy 12:6; 14:22–29; 16:17.

[2] As elsewhere in Scripture, theft is not just taking what isn't ours but also hoarding what isn't ours to keep.

prematurely. They are caught in a vicious circle of unbelief, refusing to believe that they can trust the Lord to prosper them and therefore finding as a result that he doesn't. This is often the case for us too, whenever we fail to gamble everything on God.

Now I'm not teaching you that you should tithe. Luke 11:42 and 21:1–4 make it clear that that old benchmark for Israel is a poor guide for Christians today, since we have received far greater revelation of God's grace than they had. Nor am I acting like a prosperity preacher, promising you guaranteed health and wealth just so long as you fill in a few credit card details. I despise all that spiritual razzmatazz as much as you do. But what I am saying is that Malachi is teaching us a principle here, and that if we ignore what he has to say, we will find ourselves just as impoverished as the people of Judah. If we refuse to give generously to God – to his Church, to the work of spreading his Gospel and to helping the poor – we will not reap his Plan "A" of being glorified through blessing us. We will reap the curses of his Plan "B" of being glorified by disciplining his disobedient people in front of the unbelievers who have lost out as a result of their thievery from God.

"Test me in this," the Lord urges the people of Judah, *"and see if I will not throw open the floodgates of heaven and pour out so much blessing that there will not be room enough to store it... Then all the nations will call you blessed, for yours will be a delightful land."*[3] I am deeply grateful for the people who mentored me when I became a Christian by teaching me that the essence of faith is to gamble everything on God. Although they pointed out areas of sin across my whole life, they particularly warned me that how I spent my money would be the litmus test of my newfound faith in God. Since I could set up a monthly bank transfer and then sit back, simply increasing the size of it every

259

---

[3] The Lord hates it when we test him in the sense of demanding proof before believing what he says (Deuteronomy 6:16; Matthew 4:7), but he loves it when we test him in the sense of proving his character by gambling everything on his promises (Hebrews 11:1–2).

time I got a pay rise, it was one of the easiest acts of Christian obedience. Furthermore, they told me that if I got my money straight with God, lots of other areas would automatically straighten out too. When you have demolished the great kingpin idol Money, a whole army of other little idols tumble down like skittles behind it.[4]

I have learned to gamble everything on God, just like Paul Newman and Robert Redford gambled everything on their dead-cert horses in *The Sting*. I know that I have given enough when I feel like vomiting, knowing that unless the Lord steps in I am in serious trouble. I wouldn't claim to be loaded as a result of this, but I can truly say that God has passed the test. I have never lacked anything. I bought into the housing market at just the right time and saw the value of my house treble in five years. Just before I made a bad investment that would have lost me thousands, I felt a sense of unease in my spirit and pulled out in the nick of time. I have found repeatedly that, as we prove our faith in God by giving away large amounts of money, he throws open the floodgates of heaven to us, just as he said he would through the prophet Malachi.[5]

What do your recent financial transactions show that you believe about God? Are you stealing from him or are you gambling everything on him? These verses were prophesied for your sake and for mine. "*'Test me in this,' says the Lord Almighty.*"

---

[4] Hebrews 13:5–6 indicates that giving away money undermines it as a rival source of security to God.

[5] 3:10 says literally, "*Test me in this: see if I will not throw open heaven's windows to you.*"

When God Is Silent
(Malachi 3:13–4:6)

*"See, I will send the prophet Elijah to you before that
great and dreadful day of the Lord comes."*

(Malachi 4:5)

These are the last verses of the Old Testament. After this comes
425 years of silence, only broken when John the Baptist finally
appears. It makes sense, therefore, that this sixth and final dialogue
addresses how we are to respond when our disappointment in
God has been caused by his appearing to go silent on us.

In the previous five dialogues, the people of Judah have
complained that God is unfaithful and unfair. In this one, they
complain that he is inaudible. If he sees what is happening in the
world, he seems to hide it very well. Sinners prosper and Jewish
survivors seem no better off as a result of their obedience to
him.[1] They have had enough. *"It is futile to serve God. What do
we gain by carrying out his requirements and going about like
mourners before the Lord Almighty?"*[2]

Of all the things that can make us feel disappointed in
God, his going silent on us has to be among the worst. One of
my friends walked away from the Lord because she found it
too hard to hear him speak to her. Another friend gave up on
fighting his same-sex attraction in confused silence and became

---

[1] The Hebrew word *bāhan*, or *to test*, in 3:15 is the same word that is used
in 3:10. This hints that the Jews were not as righteous as they liked to believe.
They weren't putting God to the test enough!

[2] They betray their continued sinfulness by their self-focus. They care little for
his gain and *his* glory.

a promiscuous user of Grindr instead. Many Christians are less honest about how they feel than this, continuing to go to church and continuing to go through the motions. But they are just as backslidden on the inside. They may not admit it, but God's silence has made them give up on him. If you can identify with any of this, these final words of Malachi were written for you.

The Lord responds to this final complaint from the people of Judah by keeping silent. Don't miss the irony. Instead of giving them an answer, he listens to their discussion of the matter among themselves. After hearing what each person has to say, he instructs an angel to record in the annals of heaven the names of all those who have shown that they still trust him.[3] This seems to suggest that God finds these times of silence as precious as we find them frustrating. We will only discover on the Final Day how much he has valued our faithfulness towards him in the silent times of testing. There will be some surprises when his book of remembrance is read aloud. *"'On the day when I act,' says the Lord Almighty, 'they will be my treasured possession... And you will again see the distinction between the righteous and the wicked, between those who serve God and those who do not.'"*[4]

The Lord does not explain in these verses why he often appears to go silent on us. He simply presents it as a trial that reveals how much we truly love and trust him. In 4:1–3, he reassures us that such times never last forever. In fact, the people of Judah were about to witness a momentous step change in their nation's experience of God.[5]

---

[3] The people of Judah knew that the kings of Persia kept such records (Esther 2:23; 6:1–2). We can be encouraged that so does the Lord (Exodus 32:32–33; Psalm 56:8; Daniel 12:1; Revelation 20:12).

[4] Elsewhere in the Old Testament the Hebrew word *segullāh*, that is used in 3:17, refers to the *private treasure collection* of an ancient king (1 Chronicles 29:3; Ecclesiastes 2:8). The Lord has a collection of his own (Exodus 19:5; Deuteronomy 7:6; 14:2; 26:18; Psalm 135:4; Ephesians 1:14).

[5] Don't let the chapter divisions blind you to the fact that 4:1–3 is still part of this sixth dialogue. There isn't even a chapter 4 in the Hebrew text. Malachi 4:1–6 appears as Malachi 3:19–24.

The Day of the Lord is coming. Not his Final Judgment, but the moment when the Messiah will appear in order to bear God's judgment away. That Day will reveal the true state of people's hearts, destroying root and branch those who are disobedient to the Lord.[6] Then at last those who follow him will receive the full reward for their devotion. The Messiah will be like the sun to them and his righteousness like sun-rays. Although he will be crucified, as Zechariah prophesied, he will rise again like the sun at dawn, beaming sun-rays of healing and salvation down on all who have faith in him.[7] He will make them as joyful as cooped-up calves that are finally let out of the cow-shed to play freely in the fields. He will give them power and authority over demons and over every other enemy. The Lord promises that *"on the day when I act"* no one who has been devoted to him will weep any more over the moments he appeared to go silent on them.

The final three verses of Malachi serve as a conclusion to the book, to the Minor Prophets and to the Old Testament as a whole. In 4:4, the Lord commands the people of Judah to remember the Law of Moses.[8] If they respond to God's forgiveness by surrendering their lives to him in full obedience, they will be blessed with his Plan "A" of being glorified in the eyes of all nations by granting them the blessings that are listed in Deuteronomy 28. If they despise his forgiveness by persisting in living their own way, they will be cursed with his Plan "B" of being glorified in the eyes of all nations by bringing down on them the curses that are listed in Deuteronomy 27–28.

In 4:5, the Lord commands the people of Judah to remember the message of the Prophets. All of them are personified by one

---

[6] The Hebrew words in 4:1 for *arrogant* and *evildoer* are the same words used in the complaint of 3:15 – but the Lord warns the people of Judah that the Final Day will reveal that many of them are among them.

[7] John the Baptist's father echoes Malachi 4:6 in Luke 1:17 and Malachi 4:2 in Luke 1:78.

[8] *Horeb* is the other name for Mount Sinai (Deuteronomy 5:2).

of the first and greatest prophets, Elijah, and the New Testament treats this verse as a promise that an even greater prophet will come. John the Baptist would call Israel to repent in preparation for the arrival of the Messiah.[9]

In 4:6, the Lord prophesies that John the Baptist will succeed in his mission. *"He will turn the hearts of the parents to their children, and the hearts of the children to their parents."* This is meant to remind us that our obedience or disobedience to God's Law is best seen by the way in which we handle our relationships with one another. This final verse, and therefore the entire Old Testament, ends with the Hebrew word *hêrem*, which means curse of destruction. It's a very odd note to end on, unless we remember that this has been the choice that God has laid before us on almost every page of the Minor Prophets.[10]

Now God goes silent. He does not inspire any more books of the Bible for another 500 years. He has told us how much he loves us and how much he wants to bless us, but he has also told us that it is up to us how much we want to get on board. We are saved entirely by grace, but how we respond to the grace that has saved us makes a monumental difference. The choice God offers us is simple: *Blessing or curse – you decide.*

---

[9] Matthew 11:10–14; Mark 9:11–13; Luke 1:17. The meaning of *Moses* and *Elijah* in Malachi 4:5–6 is the same as why Jesus met with both men on the Mount of Transfiguration in Luke 9:28–33.

[10] The New Testament also ends on a very similar note of blessing and cursing. See Revelation 22:7–21.

Conclusion: Blessing or Curse – You Decide

"Remember the law of my servant Moses… or else I will come and strike the land with a curse."

(Malachi 4:4, 6)

As they emerged from several painful decades of communism, the leaders of modern China looked curiously to the West to find a better path to prosperity. They asked themselves a simple question: how had a cold and rainy backwater continent like Europe become so wealthy and dominant over world affairs? A senior scholar from China's Academy of the Social Sciences describes the delegation's surprising conclusion:

> *We were asked to look into what accounted for the… pre-eminence of the West all over the world… At first, we thought it was because you had more powerful guns than we had. Then we thought it was because you had the best political system. Next we focused on your economic system. But in the past twenty years, we have realised that the heart of your culture is your religion: Christianity. That is why the West has been so powerful. The Christian moral foundation of social and cultural life was what made possible… the successful transition to democratic politics. We don't have any doubt about this.*[1]

---

[1] Quoted by the historian Niall Ferguson in *Civilization: The Six Killer Apps of Western Power* (2011).

Although surprising, the conclusion of the Chinese delegation is rather less surprising to us now that we have read through the twelve Minor Prophets together. Their major theme has been that God really means it when he says in Psalm 144:15, *"Blessed is the people of whom this is true; blessed is the people whose God is the Lord."*

They have repeatedly taken us back to the Law of Moses. They have been clear with us that our obedience cannot save us, teaching us repeatedly that even our best actions are insufficient and that only the Messiah's actions can grant us forgiveness. At the same time, they have been equally clear that how we respond to that merciful gift of forgiveness makes a world of difference. If it makes us surrender our lives completely to the God who saved us, we will reap his Plan "A" for our lives – to bless us so much in the sight of unbelievers that they see God's glory at work within us and decide to surrender their own lives to him too. If we refuse to surrender our lives to God, or if we merely pretend to, we will incur the pain of his Plan "B" for our lives – to curse us so thoroughly that unbelievers sit up and take God seriously as a result of our being an object lesson of misery. The prophets have insisted that God really means it when he says in Psalm 76:10, *"Surely your wrath against mankind brings you praise, and the survivors of your wrath are restrained."*

They have repeatedly brought us back to the long list of blessings and curses in Deuteronomy 27–28. The Lord promised King Solomon that:

> *If you walk before me faithfully with integrity of heart and uprightness, as David your father did, and do all I command and observe my decrees and laws, I will establish your royal throne... But if you or your descendants turn away from me and do not observe the commands and decrees I have given you and go off to serve other gods and worship them, then I will cut off*

Israel from the land I have given them and will reject this temple.[2]

The prophets have therefore shown us how Israel and Judah repeatedly reaped God's judgment through the poor choices that they made. They have also shown us how swift the Lord was to bless them whenever they made good choices. He was even quick to save pagan cities that repented, like Nineveh.

Having journeyed through these twelve Minor Prophets together, we are therefore less surprised by the conclusions of the Chinese delegation than many other observers are. Nor are we surprised that Europe's decline in pre-eminence comes on the heels of its firm rejection of its Christian heritage. Even the atheist president of Poland, Aleksander Kwasniewski, when bringing his nation into the European Union, complained about its constitution, pointing out that, *"There is no excuse for making references to ancient Greece and Rome, and to the Enlightenment, without making reference to the Christian values which are so important to the development of Europe."*[3] The predictions of the prophets are as relevant as ever. Nations rise and nations fall as they acknowledge the authority of God's Word.

We noted in the introduction of this commentary, however, that the purest application of these prophecies in our own day is not to secular nation states, but to the Church. Looking back on history, it is easy to see that those congregations that have remained obedient to God's Word have tended to grow and to expand, while those that show the same selective commitment to Scripture as ancient Israel and Judah have tended to be cursed with a famine of converts, dwindling congregations and eventually closure. We need to look around in our own day and take the radical steps that the prophets tell us are required for

---

[2] 1 Kings 9:1–9. For other examples, see Joshua 1:7–8; 1 Chronicles 22:13; 2 Chronicles 31:21.

[3] Quoted by the historian Michael Burleigh in *Sacred Causes: Religion and Politics from the European Dictators to Al Qaeda* (2006).

our backslidden churches. In June 2015, the British magazine *The Spectator* ran a feature on the Western Church which echoed them:

> *It's often said that Britain's church congregations are shrinking, but that doesn't come close to expressing the scale of the disaster now facing Christianity in this country. Every ten years the census spells out the situation in detail: between 2001 and 2011 the number of Christians in Britain fell by 5.3 million – about 10,000 a week. If that rate of decline continues, the mission of St Augustine to the English, together with that of the Irish saints to the Scots, will come to an end in 2067. That is the year in which the Christians who have inherited the faith of their British ancestors will become statistically invisible... [They are] one generation away from extinction.*[4]

Like the Chinese delegation, *The Spectator* magazine simply corroborates the ancient predictions of the twelve Minor Prophets. Although by no means a Christian publication, it calls on church leaders to have the courage to bring their congregations back to radical obedience to God's Word before it is too late for them: *"They're led by middle-managers who are frightened of their own shadows. They run up the white flag long before the enemy comes down from the hills... It can't be stressed too often that the secularisation that happens inside churches is as important as the sort that happens outside them."*

So if you are a Christian, don't imagine that these twelve prophets wrote for somebody other than you. They are still the Lord's warning to his people that the manner in which they respond to his Word is a matter of life or death, both for them and for the world.

[4] The article was entitled "2067: The End of British Christianity" (13th June 2015).

As you end this commentary, get down on your knees and make a personal choice to surrender your life totally to God. Repent of your selective obedience and tell the Lord that you choose his Plan "A" of blessing, not his Plan "B" of disaster. Then gather some people from your church and pray the same prayer of commitment as a congregation. Tell the Lord that you have made up your mind once and for all to obey.

God's message to his people through the Minor Prophets is very simple: *Blessing or curse – you decide.*

OTHER TITLES FROM PHIL MOORE:

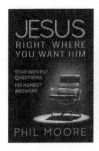

ISBN 978 0 85721 677 9

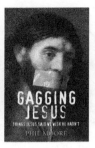

ISBN 978 0 85721 453 9

ISBN 978 0 85721 551 2

ISBN 978 0 85721 801 8

STRAIGHT TO THE HEART SERIES

TITLES AVAILABLE: OLD TESTAMENT

ISBN 978 0 85721 001 2

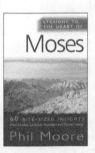

ISBN 978 0 85721 056 2

ISBN 978 0 85721 252 8

ISBN 978 0 85721 428 7

ISBN 978 0 85721 426 3

ISBN 978 0 85721 754 7

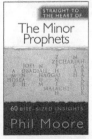

ISBN 978 0 85721 837 7

STRAIGHT TO THE HEART SERIES

TITLES AVAILABLE: NEW TESTAMENT

ISBN 978 1 85424 988 3

ISBN 978 0 85721 642 7

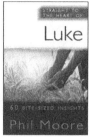

ISBN 978 0 85721 799 8

ISBN 978 0 85721 253 5

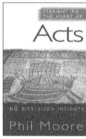

ISBN 978 1 85424 989 0

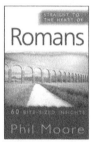

ISBN 978 0 85721 057 9

ISBN 978 0 85721 002 9

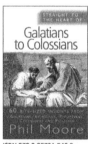

ISBN 978 0 85721 546 8

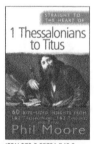

ISBN 978 0 85721 548 2

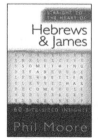

ISBN 978 0 85721 668 7

ISBN 978 0 85721 756 1

ISBN 978 1 85424 990 6

Printed and bound by CPI Group (UK) Ltd, Croydon, CR0 4YY

25/03/2025

14647347-0003